New Expand

M000210971

Become The *New*

A Better Managing

Manager God's

Of God's Money

Resources — The Basics

Michel A. Bell

Managing
GOD's Money

Milton, Ontario, Canada

The *New* Managing God's Money — The Basics
Copyright © 2007, Michel A. Bell

Library and Archives Canada Cataloguing in Publication
Bell, Michel A.
   The New Managing God's Money-The Basics: Become a Good Manager of God's Resources / Michel A. Bell. — 3rd ed.

ISBN 978-0-9735902-2-7

   1. Christians—Finance, Personal. 2. Finance, Personal—Biblical teaching.
I. Title.

BR115.E3B42 2007   332.0240088'27   C2007-901739-8

1st Printing February 2000
2nd Printing, November 2001
3rd Printing May 2007
4th Printing February 2011

Other Books by Michel A. Bell

The new managing God's Money: Mes finances, ses ressources (2008)
Managing God's Money: 7 Branches Workbook (2006)
Managing God's Time: Improving Personal Effectiveness (2004)
Managing God's Money: The Basics (2001)
Managing God's Money: The Basics WORKBOOK (2001)

**For more information or
To order copies, please contact:**

 *Managing
GOD's Money*

info@managingodsmoney.com,
www.managinggodsmoney.com

Managing God's Money is a Christ-centred teaching organization helping folks to manage God's money, time, talents,
and other belongings, for His glory
and to further His Kingdom.

Essential Concepts

The Money Triangle (3M's of Money)

Merchant – Designs, produces, markets goods and services and often uses coercive, seductive approaches to get ...
>   Me – To buy what I don't need and can't afford because I couldn't resist the Merchant's bait ...
>>   Money – The bridge the Merchant accepts to part with his goods and services.

GAS Principle: Three Key Truths in the Bible about money:

- **Key Truth #1: God Owns Everything** (Psalm 24:1-2, Colossians 1:16)
- **Key Truth #2: Accept What You Have** (1 Timothy 6:7-8, Hebrews 13:5)
- **Key Truth #3: Seek First His Kingdom And Submit Your Requests To Him** (Matthew 6:33, Proverbs 19:21)

PEACE Budgetary Control: A closed looped planning and doing procedure that allows you to reach **goals** methodically:

- **P**lan for a specific period to do precise **goals**.
- **E**stimate and record the expenses needed to do those **goals**.
- **A**ct on the plan and record results as you do those **goals**.
- **C**ompare results **with plan** and with **estimated expenses** needed to do the **goals**.
- **EXECUTE** needed changes to do the **goals**.

PLANE Spending Analysis: Five questions to answer before you commit to a major expense:

P Did I Plan and include this expense in my budget?

L Will the expense raise my Loans?

A Are there realistic Alternatives to fulfill the identified need?

N Is the expense Necessary to fulfill the identified need?

E Is this the most Effective use of funds compared with my life, budget and other goals?

A **goal** is the **destination** — where God wants you to be, or what God wants you to do.

    A **plan** is the **journey** — how to get there, or how to do a job, your road map.

        An **estimate** is the **likely cost** of the plan: the cost of the steps in the plan.

            A **budget** is the **record** of the results of the plan and estimate, your money map.

Contents

Introduction

In 1995, shortly after returning home to Montreal from living in Japan, still a relatively young Christian, I started to learn about church folks' personal debt. The high and growing level disturbed me. Five years later while working at a challenging and demanding job, by God's grace, I published my first book, *Managing God's Money-The Basics.* Three more books, over 50 TV appearances, and more than 50 seminars later, I am writing this introduction for the third edition of *Managing God's Money-The Basics,* with the same concern.

Much changed since the first edition, chiefly my knowledge and me. Though I saw several negatives, the positives I experienced since 2000 outweigh them. The most significant positive change came in 2002. Then, I believed I would work another 10 years as an executive in industry, but God had other plans. He led me out of *Alcan Inc.* where I worked in a job I would have paid to do—that's correct, I loved working at Alcan—to His full-time unpaid Managing God's Money ministry. As His Word promises, He put everything in place for me to do this ministry, which I am doing today.

I continue to see great joy in many families who embrace God's ownership and their stewardship of everything; the resulting freedom from financial stress that follows is infectious and lasting. Since 2000, I saw a few churches and Christian ministries turn to God to provide funding for their work, rather than follow the slick, seductive, or other marketing path. They got more than they needed! As well, I saw families in need call out to God and He fulfilled their needs. What a blessing to see God supply needs in His time, in His way, and not always with money!

Still, today, more church folks accept as normal and unavoidable the pervasive personal debt among Christians. *Tithing* seems more entrenched as many appear unwilling to learn Bible teachings that show clearly early believers never practised or taught tithing. Rather, they "presented" 100% to God (Acts 2; 2 Corinthians 8).

Perhaps the greatest negative change, and most disturbing, is the pressure and manipulation some churches and Christian ministries exert to raise funds. They exploit the tithing attitude of giving to get; they exploit the sick, promising healing; and they exploit the ignorant. Growing numbers of churches and ministries encourage credit card giving while appealing to selfishness and greed. Sadly, many believers respond and give, hoping to get healing, get money or other emotional and, or material benefit. They forget they have direct access to Jesus and His love, mercy and grace, and so do not need to *give to get* Jesus' healing, love, and everything they need.

Today, I am even more convinced than when I wrote the first edition that our Sunday Schools, churches and Christian schools need to teach biblical attitudes to money. Even more important, I realize one main reason for the lack of knowledge of good *attitudes* to money among Christian families is husbands and wives, especially dads, do not accept their God ordained roles. Dads do not accept primary responsibility to teach their families to love the Lord their God with all their hearts, minds and souls, and to model and practice biblical truths. As Mother Teresa said in her book, *A Simple Path:*

> When you know how much God is in love with you then you can only live your life radiating that love. I always say that starts at home: family first, and then your own town or city. It is easy to love people who are far away but it is not so easy to love those who live next to us.[1]

In this third edition, I continue custom-fitting to household finances, good business practices and solid bible teachings. Though I rewrote many and added four chapters, the basic message of God's ownership of everything remains. Topics added include:

1. Money and happiness (chapter 1)
2. Quick Start Action Plan—Learning your ABCs (new chapter 3)
3. Debt: its costs, effects and the way out (new chapter 5)
4. Investing (chapter 6)
5. Quick start budget kit (chapter 8)
6. Family Finances (new chapter 12)
7. Retirement planning (chapter 18)
8. Writing a financial plan (new chapter 19)
9. Annual financial check-up (chapter 20)
10. Sixty five money saving ideas (chapter 20)

Except for *investing*, this edition deals with the *basics*. I included the investment section as a reference guide to fill a need I saw. Many folks asked for help to oversee their pensions, education savings plans, and other investments. They do not want to be experts, just to know enough to ask right questions. Folks complained about their investments' performance and about their *investment advisors'*; they don't realize that these days, they can't tell what a financial professional does from his title.

Some folks lost pensions by reacting to reports about over hyped companies like *Enron, WorldCom, Nortel, and "Yahoo!"*. Sadly, with some awareness, these folks could have seen these companies' earnings forecasts (and so stock prices) were not sustainable.

Then again, I decided to go a bit deeper than the basics in the investing chapter when I saw Statistic Canada's research showing that in 2005, 89% of Canadian families held financial assets (stocks, bonds, mutual funds, and income trusts). I pray this section will help you place God's funds where He directs.

My goal in this edition is to present again, *Three Key Biblical Truths* as the foundation to develop right attitudes toward money so your giving, spending, and saving will honour God. I do not claim the skills and tools I offer will allow you to become rich in material terms; I do not have the ability to do this.

Contrary to prosperity teachings, the Bible does not promise material riches for our efforts. I disagree with Christians who say if we are good stewards of God's property, He will bless us always with wealth; He might! His will for each of us is different. The Bible shows examples of people blessed with material wealth and some blessed with *spiritual wealth* only. Read about the lives of David and Job. In 1 and 2 Samuel, and in the book of Job, both in the Old Testament of the Bible, we see two individuals who had hearts for God and who sought always to do His will. He blessed them with wealth.

But it was different with the twelve apostles whom Jesus chose; He did not bless them with material stuff. Their blessing, *spiritual wealth,* came from walking with Jesus Christ. The richness that results from *seeking first His Kingdom and His righteousness*, and honouring our Lord with our finances is not necessarily material. There may be other blessings, such as grandchildren!

God asks us to *come* in a relationship with Him, and then He asks us to *come* and be His disciple. After, He tells us to *go* make disciples. Meanwhile, He tells us the world will persecute us, but He will be with us. To do His will, He gives us everything we need. And those to whom He gives much, He expects much. To be sure, He will not give you more than you can manage. So, be content with what you have and do your best with it.

In Matthew 19:24, referring to the wealthy unbeliever whose heart condition was to get more wealth for his own purposes, Jesus said "... it is easier for a camel to go through the eye of a needle than a rich man to enter the kingdom of God." Jesus wants our hearts, all, not just parts. He has promised to provide for our needs, do you believe He will?

That's a key question you need to answer as you go through this book. To be sure, you might have committed your life to Christ, but when the car breaks down at 7:00 PM on Sunday, and you *have to go to work at 7:00 AM* on Monday, do you believe He will supply your needs in time? I address similar issues you face daily—giving, spending, saving, investing—I suggest some helpful tools, and point you to the Author and Creator of everything, Jesus Christ, who has all the answers; even when we don't know the questions!

Reading this book won't change you; that will happen when God convicts you of truth and reveals needed changes. So, stay close to Him, listen for His call, and do as He asks. Then you will become a better manager of His possessions and experience His richest blessings.

I pray you will get to know in a special way, the God of peace, love, joy, hope, long suffering, who loves you so much He died for you! I give Him all the glory!

Throughout, I used *feminine* and *masculine* references interchangeably.

---

1. Mother Teresa, *A Simple Faith* (New York: Random House, Inc., 1995) p. 87.

Tables and Figures

Tables

Figures

Section I

Money and Three Key Truths

To depend on Jesus to satisfy our needs
means more than crying out to Him
when we need help.
It means accepting Him as Lord and Saviour
and obeying everything He commands.

1

Money and Three Key Truths

M oney management means *lifestyle* management, a challenging *journey* that uncovers our values. It is part of working out each believer's personal relationship with Jesus Christ—it is not a *destination*. We will get it right only when we reach heaven. Still, it is exciting, intriguing, and fulfilling when we use right *attitudes*—a key word to keep in mind along the way.

In Luke 14:28 (RSV), speaking about the cost of becoming His disciple, Jesus said, "for which of you, desiring to build a tower, does not first sit down and count the cost, whether he has enough to complete it?" We must evaluate the implications of our decisions before committing to a path. So, *before* starting this tour to learn to manage God's money (see Appendix 1, for a quick look at the *Money Management Journey's* outline) "count the cost"!

As you start the journey, know that everything is possible for God:[1]

- You might be in debt!
- You might think you botched your finances—maybe you did, everybody does!

- Learn to apply to the future, principles discussed in this book.
- Do not look back and be hard on yourself!
- Learn from your experiences and move ahead!
- Most important, be patient; keep your eyes riveted on Jesus, and keep in mind His words in Matthew 28:20 (RSV): " ...obey everything that I have commanded you. And remember I am with you always, to the end of the age."

Are you ready? Fasten your seat belts; let's go!

Money Defined

Money is a *means of exchange* that replaced the barter system[2] centuries ago. The NIV Bible mentions money 112 times—52 references in the Old Testament and 60 in the New Testament. We use these items as money to pay for stuff we buy:

- Cash
- Cheques
- Credit cards
- Charge cards
- Debit cards
- Bank loans
- Other loans from private sources, merchants, and others

In the future, money will be different. You might not see coins, paper or bankbooks. Rather, you will use *electronic money,* chiefly *smart cards* that work like today's credit and debit cards.

In contrast, wealth represents money build-up and, or stuff amassed. With a million dollars in cash, investments, or paintings, folks will say you are rich or wealthy, meaning you have access to much stuff you could convert to money to get different belongings. Probably you used money to get many of those objects. In some countries, wealth means influence, access to people, access to places and services.

Money is for convenience[3] with no intrinsic value. Rather, you value objects money buys. Sometimes you don't need stuff you buy and value; sometimes you can't use them. On a deserted island alone with a million dollars but no food, clothing or shelter, you would starve and die leaving much money because you need food, relationships, clothes, and shelter.

I like this Colonel Sanders' quote: "There is no need to be the richest man in the cemetery." Then again, in Luke 12, Jesus' warning against putting your security in wealth is even more dramatic.

> "...I will tear down my barns and build larger ones, and there I will store all my grain and my goods. 'And I will say to my soul, "Soul, you have many goods laid up for many years *to come*; take your ease, eat, drink *and* be merry."'" "But God said to him, 'You fool! This *very* night your soul is required of you; and *now* who will own what you have prepared?' "So is the man who stores up treasure for himself, and is not rich toward God." (Luke 12: 18-21).

God alone knows the future. Money, wealth or possessions cannot secure it. When we grasp this view, we will stop striving to get money, draw closer to God to know His will, to experience the present with Him, and to value relationships He brings to us.

Money and Happiness

Though work is God's gift to us and is the main money source for most people, many folks get money from several sources other than work:

- Gifts
- Inheritances
- Loans
- Gambling—many lose money this way.

Many people strive to get money because they believe it is the key to happiness. They run ahead of God to borrow or gamble to try to get what they want. But they don't realize these actions show dependence on banks or luck, rather than on God to supply their needs. Some get thousands or millions of dollars but find that is not enough. As you go through this book, keep in mind this prizewinning definition of money:

> A London Newspaper offered a prize for the best definition of money. The prize was awarded to a young man who sent in this definition: 'Money is an article which may be used as the universal passport to everywhere except heaven and as a universal provider for everything except happiness.[4]

The late American cartoonist, humorist, and journalist Kin Hubbard once said, "It is hard to tell what does bring happiness; poverty and wealth have both failed." Research on money and happiness state consistently more money doesn't give happiness, yet folks continue to chase money even though during the *chase* their health and family relations suffer.

Research led by University of Missouri's Kennon Sheldon found that "people who say money is most important to them are the unhappiest.[5]" Princeton University's Daniel Kahneman et al's research[6] titled, "Would You Be Happier If You Were Richer? A Focusing Illusion," should cause you to stop and look at your priorities. These are some findings:

1. Most people believe they would be happier if they were richer, but survey evidence on "subjective well-being" is largely inconsistent with that belief.

2. Using their "Day Reconstruction Method," they found income was hardly a factor with people's moment-to-moment daily experiences.
3. Many people are "highly motivated" to increase income despite the weak relation between income and experienced happiness.
4. People with higher incomes tended to devote more of their free time to tasks involving tension and stress.

To be sure, how can you be happy with the *means of exchange?* Besides, how do you find lasting peace and happiness in possessions? Do you remember your first toy, first bike, or first car? You got major joy for a time, but later the novelty waned, your reaction changed, and you wanted something else, didn't you? God created you to be in a personal relationship with Him, not with belongings.

In Matthew 5:3-12 (NIV), Jesus presents a sermon on happiness called the Beatitudes, which highlights the difference between God's views of happiness and man's views:

- "Blessed are the poor in spirit, for theirs is the kingdom of heaven.
- Blessed are those who mourn, for they will be comforted.
- Blessed are the meek, for they will inherit the earth.
- Blessed are those who hunger and thirst for righteousness, for they will be filled.
- Blessed are the merciful, for they will be shown mercy.
- Blessed are the pure in heart, for they will see God.
- Blessed are the peacemakers, for they will be called sons of God.
- Blessed are those who are persecuted because of righteousness, for theirs is the kingdom of heaven."
- "Blessed are you when people insult you, persecute you and falsely say all kinds of evil against you because of me. Rejoice and be glad, because great is your reward in heav-

en, for in the same way they persecuted the prophets who were before you."

The Greek word used for blessed, *Makarios*, means *happy*— happiness that's independent of circumstances. Jesus' message in these Beatitudes contradicts the world's view. His message starts with you accepting your *spiritual poverty*— your need for Jesus. Then it builds progressively to the happiness you will find when standing for Jesus leads to your persecution. You can't get this happiness or blessedness on your own,[7] from religions, denominations, family history, money or stuff. You and I need Jesus! When He is *in* you, you can walk *with* Him as your guide, confident you can do everything He brings your way. You do not need to *follow* anything or anybody, only Jesus!

The crucial message to each of us is this: Stop striving to get stuff or to do tasks to *make us happy; it* doesn't work! Rather, start investing time with Jesus. Then we will be able to rest in Him, worship Him unreservedly, become more productive in our jobs, and begin to apply our energies to do His priorities. True happiness is a deep state of contentment based on a secure personal relationship with Jesus Christ. It's not a superficial feeling.

You will see money's place more clearly—a means of exchange, a bridge—when you look at the *money triangle.*

The Money Triangle: 3Ms of Money

Each money transaction involves a *merchant, money,* and *me*—the money triangle or 3-Ms of money. The *merchant* buys or produces goods or services to sell to me. Through clever, seductive advertising, he entices me to buy. Previously his sales pitch would highlight product features only, but not today. These days, he presents attractive financing as *bait,* hop-

ing *I* will buy the product or service even if I don't need it.

If I buy the product or service, I will use money as the means of exchange —in essence, as a bridge. I could use cash, cheque, debit card, credit card, IOUs; I could use anything the merchant will accept to exchange for his goods or present his services. Today, many TV evangelists and Christian ministries behave like merchants and use the bait technique to get you to give them God's money!

So which of the three Ms can I manage? I can't manage the merchant who decides the product, service, and bait. His purpose is to get me to buy.

I can't manage money; it's the bridge to get goods or services from the merchant to me. It is lifeless; it won't respond to me. That leaves me. Yes, I can manage me only.

Sadly, society focuses on money, the bridge, which gives me an excuse to blame money (specifically a lack of money), and the merchant's bait for my poor choices. Have you noticed we don't accept responsibility for our actions? The Government, parents, merchants, the Devil, somebody made us do it! We eat junk food, don't exercise, get overweight as the natural effect, but it's not our fault that we are overweight; rather, we need medication for a disease or illness!

We must learn to take our eyes off financial solutions to attitude and behaviour challenges. When we take on debt to get out of debt, understand we are seeking solutions that do not address the main cause, our decisions—our attitudes, behaviours and choices *(ABCs)*. So, if we consolidate loans, refinance mortgages, extend credit terms but end even deeper in debt, accept this result as unavoidable since we dealt with symptoms only rather than the cause: our ABCs.

Know Your ABCs

If I must manage *me* because money isn't manageable, what about me should I manage? I must understand my *attitude* to money, because it decides my *behaviour* and sources from which I *choose*. My attitude is my world-view, my beliefs. It leads to my decisions to buy or not. My ideas about credit and credit cards will decide how I spend. My position about savings will decide how I spend. So too, my stance on home ownership will decide how I spend.

I must surrender my life to Christ to get to know right ABCs. Then I will be able to distinguish wants from needs. That's why the Bible teaches so much about attitudes to money. In Luke 16:13, Jesus tells us to choose between Him and money (mammon[8]). Other teachings show the right attitude is to use money for God's glory[9] and the wrong attitude is to love money.[10] Nothing is wrong with money itself; it is my attitude to it that is an issue.

You and I must learn and follow the many truths in the Bible about our ABCs and money so money doesn't enslave and control us. Will we get rich if we learn and practice biblical financial truths? It depends on how we define rich. People lift Bible verses out of context to tell us God wants everybody to be healthy and wealthy. Some preachers tell us we are not rich because sin is in our lives. Remove the sin, they say, and you will become rich. Sure, we should confess our sins and turn from them (repent), but that alone will not cause us to become rich.

Jesus tells us the *poor* we will have with us always.[11] We don't know why some have much stuff and some don't. Though everyone faces trials, we don't know why some people experience more severe and longer lasting trials than others do; but we know Jesus allows trials in our lives so we might learn to depend on Him and grow closer to Him.

Those of us who choose to become Jesus' disciple have several promises from Him, including this: To follow Him, be ready to give up everything, including our lives.[12] In addition, when we surrender everything to Him, we know we will have abundant lives.[13] Jesus wants us to be ready to follow Him at any cost. Listen, as He reminds us in Luke 14:26-27 what it means to be His disciple:

> "If anyone comes to Me, and does not hate his own father and mother and wife and children and brothers and sisters, yes, and even his own life, he cannot be My disciple. "Whoever does not carry his own cross and come after Me cannot be My disciple."

As you start this journey, stay focused on Jesus; in Him, you will find hope as you learn right attitudes to money. Two words capture riches coming from a life surrendered to Christ: *eternal life.*

Come as you are on this special trip to get freedom from financial stress. Jesus loves you so much He died for you. Besides, He assures you, everything is possible for Him who believes. Do you believe?

You need help to cope with merchants' onslaughts. The family and the church must provide this help. In chapter 12, I discuss the *Family Council* as the family's main learning and teaching centre. But the church has a part too. It must accept its role to lead people to God's agenda, and work with families to help them cope with materialism. To do this, spiritual leaders need confidence to handle money God's way. They must learn, practice, and teach regularly, Jesus' messages about right money attitudes such as these:

1. *Discipleship:* They need to help us put time, talents, and money at Jesus' disposal, which will lead to decluttering our lives (Luke 14:25-33; Luke 18:18-25).

2. *Greed:* Jesus tells us to beware; lives are more important than possessions (Luke 12:15). Church leaders should show this by their example.
3. *Needs:* Jesus assures us that He will provide for our needs always, in His way and His time (Matthew 6:24-34). Pastors and ministry leaders should heed and practice this.

Individuals who learn right *attitudes*, practice right *behaviours* and *choices* from His Word, will avoid bondage to consumer debt. I repeat; your attitude is your worldview that leads to behaviour that decides spending—if you believe a credit card is a funding source, you will choose to live beyond your income. Billy Graham says, "If a person gets his attitude toward money straight, it will help straighten out almost every other area in his life." I think it would straighten out every area! Do you believe this?

Three Key Truths from the Bible about Money

To manage God's money well, (meaning to manage your lifestyle—wants, needs, greed), besides knowing right ABCs, apply *Three Key Truths* from the Bible that collectively I call the *GAS Principle:*

Key Truth #1: **G**od Owns Everything

Key Truth #2: **A**ccept What You Have

Key Truth #3: **S**eek First His Kingdom,
       and Submit Your Requests to Him

Key Truth #1: God Owns Everything

- The earth is the LORD'S and all that is in it, the world, and those who live in it; for he has founded it on the seas, and established it on the rivers.[14]
- For in him all things in heaven and on earth were created things visible and invisible, whether thrones or dominions or rulers or powers—all things have been created through him and for him.[15]

Implications of Key Truth # 1: God's Owns Everything:

You own nothing; you are God's manager or steward, and so, it's essential you know who is a steward:

A steward is someone who gets responsibility and authority from an owner to look after the owner's property in the owner's best interest. In return, the steward agrees to account to the owner regularly for his performance compared with the owner's standards.

God's steward needs to know Him, know His Word, obey Him and obey His Word. God's steward needs to know he will account to God for his stewardship. When you accept your role, you know you own nothing and so you must spend only under Jesus' direction. Therefore, "count the cost" before spending, listen for His voice and He will lead you to His will compared with your wish. Are you ready for this? It's not easy, but He is faithful, kind, compassionate, and He won't leave you.

Key Truth #2: Accept What You Have

- For we brought nothing into the world, so that we can take nothing out of it; but if we have food and clothing, we will be content with these.[16]
- Keep your lives free from the love of money, and be content with what you have; for he has said, "I will never leave you or forsake you."[17]

Implications of Key Truth # 2: Accept what You Have:

Start by accepting *whom you are*—fearfully and wonderfully made,[18] *where you are*,[19] and *what you have*.[20] Don't look at folks on TV with "perfect bodies" and start beating up yourself. You are who you are! If you need to change your lifestyle, God can handle that. Ask Him to show you what to do.

Accepting what you have means living *in your circumstances* but not allowing them to take your eyes off God. Recall the widow in 2 Kings 4:1-7; she had a little oil only, but with Elisha's guidance, she saw she had more than enough. As well, so preoccupied was Elisha's servant with his circumstance, He could not see the victory God prepared until Elisha prayed to open his eyes.[21]

Each believer in Christ should understand that God is faithful, keeps His Word,[22] and His divine power has granted everything the believer needs for life and Godliness.[23] A believer can do God's wishes because God's Spirit lives in him. Do you believe this?

Key Truth #3: Seek First His Kingdom and Submit Your Requests to Him

- But seek first His kingdom and His righteousness, and all these things will be given to you as well.[24]
- Many are the plans in a man's heart, but it is the LORD'S purpose that prevails.[25]

Implications of Key Truth # 3: Seek First His Kingdom and Submit Your Requests to Him:

Do you believe Jesus is who He says He is? Do you believe He will do what He promised? Are you ready to seek first His kingdom and His righteousness? When you seek first His kingdom and His righteousness, you must seek second, third, fourth ... your wants. He will provide your needs. Did you get that? Have you ever seen a sparrow begging for food?

The Three Key Truths are not subjective, changing principles, but eternal. Seek continually to understand them; find what pleases God by studying the Bible to become like Jesus, not to become theologians. In the Bible, you will uncover lasting guidelines for daily living. God, the creator of the universe, owns everything. The Bible shows this clearly in the verses that explain the GAS Principle, and elsewhere. Accepting the GAS Principle will change your life, change your views, and change your role about stuff you "own" as His manager. It will cancel the need to borrow, except to buy a home, and you will be able to do the following:

- Be more alert with spending decisions—allowing Him to lead you.
- Accept you own nothing but you are responsible to God as His manager or steward for everything He allows

you to have while you are here on earth—time, talents, money, family, the environment.
- Realize that later you will account to the Owner of everything, Jesus Christ, for your stewardship.

While jogging one morning, this picture came to me. It reinforces my view of the practical application of Key Truth # 3: Do your best as you seek first His kingdom and righteousness and leave the rest to God.

You are on a plane going from Montreal to Toronto, normally a one-hour flight. Your son Jesse, the First Officer, invites you to sit on the flight deck in the Jump Seat directly behind the Captain. Flustered, you know you will be late for your first meeting in Toronto because a major snowstorm in Montreal delayed the flight.

As the plane takes off you close your eyes and try to relax. After what seemed like two hours, you open your eyes and see the plane has not landed. You say to Jesse, 'Normally, the flying time is around an hour, why have we not landed in Toronto after flying for two hours?' The Captain replied, 'don't worry, relax, and we will take you to your destination.' Stressed, you whisper to yourself, 'Oh God help me please, I am so late for my meetings!' Again, you close your eyes and you notice your heart races as stress rises.

After about five minutes, opening your eyes, you utter 'Captain, what is the problem?' The Captain turns and looks at you. There is a glow around Him. He smiles and says calmly, 'Son, here I am:

- Call and I will answer (Jeremiah 33:3).
- Ask and you will receive (Matthew 7:7).
- Trust in Me, I will make your path straight (Proverbs 3:5-6).
- Enter My presence daily (1 Thessalonians 5:17-18).
- Rest I will give you, just come (Matthew 11:28)."

Overcome with joy, you close your eyes, smile and mutter, "Jesus, take control, I surrender all to you. Where you go, I will go."

This is the essence of money management; turning over your life to Christ and allowing Him to lead all areas of your life.

Summary

Folks behave the same with money as they do with their health. Pharmaceutical companies know this, and so they prey on us. Rather than finding out the cause of the headache, backache, stomach pain, or other ailment, Pharmaceutical companies tell us to ask our doctors about medications that treat symptoms but not causes.

In the same way, financial people tell you to refinance, fix your credit, and do everything except deal with the cause—your behaviour.

Accept you can't manage money, but you can change your attitude, leading to behaviour change, and spending control. As well, trust Jesus to fill your needs according to His will. Remember; it is not *your wish* but *His will!* Ask Him to show you how to react to the *money triangle* and the *Gas Principle*.

Beware, many Christian ministries, and TV evangelists behave like merchants and use seductive, manipulative baits to get you to part with God's money.

Think About This

 We must admit that we spend more of our time concentrating and fretting over the things that can't be changed in life than we do giving attention to the one thing that can, our choice of attitude.[26]

Chapter Notes:

1. Jeremiah 32:17, 27; Luke 18:27.
2. Barter means exchange. Before money, folks traded one item for another. A person with cows who needed fur might trade his cows for furs based on relative values.
3. I can imagine you saying, "Right, give me more convenience!"
4. Glen V. Wheeler, *1010 Illustrations, Poems and Quotes,* (Cincinnati, Ohio: Standard Publishing, 1967), p. 265.
5. Article: *"What Is Satisfying About Satisfying Events? Testing 10 Candidate Psychological Needs,"* Kennon M. Sheldon, Ph.D., University of Missouri-Columbia; Andrew J. Elliot, Ph.D., and Youngmee Kim, Ph.D., University of Rochester; and Tim Kasser, Ph.D., Knox College; *Journal of Personality and Social Psychology,* Vol. 80, No. 2.
6. Article: *Would You Be Happier If You Were Richer? A Focusing Illusion* Daniel Kahneman, Alan B. Krueger, David Schkade, Norbert Schwarz, Arthur A. Stone *Science* 30 June 2006: Vol. 312 no. 5782, pp. 1908 – 1910, DOI: 10.1126/science.1129688
7. John 5:30.
8. The Hebrew word used here is *Mammon* that refers to wealth. Jesus is telling us not to worship wealth, not to see it as an end in itself, but to depend on Him to supply our needs.
9. Mark 12:41; Luke 22:35; 1 John 3:17.
10. Ezekiel 7:19-21; Isaiah 55:2.
11. Matthew 26:11.
12. Luke 14:25-33.
13. John 10:10.
14. Psalm 24:1-2, NRSV.
15. Colossians 1:16, NRSV.
16. 1 Timothy 6:7-8, NRSV.
17. Hebrews 13:5, NRSV.
18. Psalm 139:14.
19. Jeremiah 29: 1-32.
20. Luke 3:14.
21. 2 Kings 6:17.
22. Isaiah 46:11; Psalm 37:25
23. 2 Peter 1:3.
24. Matthew 6:33, NIV.
25. Proverbs 19:21, NIV.
26. Charles R. Swindoll, *Wisdom for the Way* (Nashville, Tennessee: J. Countryman, a division of Thomas Nelson Inc., 2001), p.238.

2

Why Don't We Manage Money Well?

W hat's the problem? Why don't we apply the GAS Principle to help us manage money? When we think we need more money, before we take on debt, why don't we look at our attitudes, behaviours, and choices, rather than look to get more money? Most folks tell me they know what to do—and they do. But they say it's not easy—and it isn't. Learning to wait, to delay a want, to invest time at Jesus' feet to learn right attitudes to money isn't easy or natural. Rather, it's easier, more natural to react to merchants' enticements and deal later with credit card debt.

After knowing what to do, how do we "just do it"? This is the conflict between our sin nature and our lives in Christ. Coming from the "fall", it's a struggle that won't go away that Apostle Paul writes about in Romans 7:14-20. Sadly, we must learn to deal with it again and again.

Many North Americans accept as normal, living pay cheque-to-pay-cheque. Some don't realize their drift deep in debt. Unconsciously, they accept their circumstances as unavoidable and natural. Meantime, businesses study our habits and use outrageous advertising to promote easy debt as *bait* to get us to buy stuff. Recently, an advertisement for a car appalled me. Directed at people with poor credit whom other merchants refused, the advertisement promised a car for no down payment, no credit check, no doubt, at high interest rates.

What does this advertisement imply? You are in debt, under severe stress, but a merchant wants to give you more credit because *he knows* a new car is too much for you to resist. The merchant benefits because when you buy his car, you move his inventory; he charges excessive interest rates knowing enough people will repay in full to give him a reasonable profit. Meanwhile, you take on more debt, remain under relentless stress, stuck in a debt cycle and, if married, your relationship with your spouse worsens.

Why do believers go against God's Word, take on consumer debt that robs the Kingdom, add stress to our families, and yet accept this state as unavoidable? I suggest *FOG* overwhelms and keeps us looking at our circumstances rather than at God. Let's look in the FOG to see what we can learn:

- Faith
- Obsolescence
- Greed

Faith

Simply, we don't believe the GAS Principle: we don't believe God owns everything, we don't accept what we have, and we don't believe God will provide for our needs. Actually, that's not correct! Let me restate it. We believe in our heads, but we do not believe with our *legs*. Unwittingly, we use Scripture to support our unbelief! Without understanding it, we accept parts of the Old Testament teaching on giving to God, and so we think we own and control 90% of funds we get provided we give God His portion of 10% (a tithe). As well, we do not study and try to apply *grace giving* that early believers taught and practiced. I will discuss giving in chapter 9, but in the meantime, think about this: If you accept God owns 100%, how can you control 90% on your own?

The believer's challenge isn't a lack of faith. Read what Dr. Ken Hutcherson in his book, *Enough Faith*,[1] says:

> *It's not the amount of faith we have that matters.*
> *What matters is what we do with the faith God has*
> *given us.* What matters is putting the faith we have—
> be it great or small—in a big God knowing He will
> keep all His promises and do what He says He will do.

Still, often people say they don't have *enough faith*. Have you ever seen a mustard seed? It is small, smaller than a pebble. And Jesus says if you have faith that small, nothing will be impossible for you.[2] The Bible tells us faith is, "…the assurance of things hoped for, the conviction of things not seen."[3] Keep in mind, *hoped for,* and *not seen.* If we can see results, we don't need faith; that's *walking by sight!*

Hebrews 11: 6 tells us that without faith it is impossible to please God who rewards those who seek Him diligently. Believers *walk by faith, not by sight*,[4] so our challenge isn't insufficient faith, but no faith in God. Simply, we don't believe God will do His promises—we don't trust Him to do what He says.

But to believe, we like to see. Unless we see something tangible, we won't step out, confident we will get Jesus' promise to meet our needs. Before we believe, we need signs that God has *started* to do His promises; but that's not faith! Faith is doing our part, and then "going to the Jordan River at high tide, placing the soles of our feet on the water," confident God will part it.[5] That's faith! Tough to do, but that's what we must do—step out, even though we don't see the solution.

When we seek first His Kingdom and His righteousness, and leave results to Him, His *will* becomes our *wish*. Psalm 37:10 reminds us to "delight yourself in the LORD; and He will give you the desires of your heart." Simply, our hearts will want the things God knows are best for us.

Daily we put faith in *things, confident* they will do as we expect. We enter the first of eight floors in a shopping mall, and we don't expect higher floors to fall on us. But when Jesus says to seek first His Kingdom and His righteousness and all *these things* will be given to the believer, we don't wait for Him to supply *these things* —food , clothing, and life. Why? First, we don't believe Him. Second, we confuse wants and needs. Third, we seek *first* our wants, not His kingdom that falls to second, third, or fourth priority. Still, God gives His children what we don't deserve.

Faith "comes from hearing" God's Word.[6] To hear God's Word, someone must preach it! So we need to be available and alert to God. Faith in Jesus is the antidote for worry. Worry and faith cannot co-exist. Still, folks who confess with their mouth, faith in Jesus, worry, and rather than listen to Jesus, look to prosperity teachings and other sources for debt, stress and other relief. Many believers do not realize:

(a) Without a personal relationship with Jesus Christ, circumstances will overwhelm them and money will control them.
(b) They earn God's money, so He must direct its division.
(c) They should wait to pay cash for stuff they buy (or use a credit card, but pay the balance in full).
(d) If in debt, they can draw close to Jesus and that will show others His faithfulness in their lives.
(e) They can trust Jesus to do as He promises. He will supply their needs, His way and in His time.

Have faith in Jesus; do your part—meet conditions in His promises—and then *expect* to get stuff *prayed for,* and *hoped for*. But remember, don't "name it and claim it," because your heavenly Father knows what's best for you and your *wish* might not be His *will*. Ask His Holy Spirit to direct you when you ask for stuff. *You might get what you want,* to your regret, like King Hezekiah, who asked for and got extra years that he and others would have been better without.[7] That's why God says; ask according to His will.[8]

Stop, mull over this: do you believe God owns everything, you own nothing, but you are His manager for 100% of funds you use? Do you believe Jesus will do as He says and provide for your needs? Do you believe Jesus will give all you need for "life and godliness"? Can you see your beliefs in how you handle your financial affairs?

Jesus knows what you need, you don't, so when you don't get what you asked for, first, look at your life. Have you done the conditions to claim His promises? Second, ask Him to show you what to do and don't stop looking to Him and listening to Him.

Some folks don't accept Jesus as Lord and Saviour. Some say they surrender to Him, but haven't learned His Word or His ways, so they don't know, understand or believe His promises; still they claim them, complain, worry and become anxious when they don't get what they want. In Matthew 6: 25-26 and 34 (NIV) Jesus says to His followers:

> **25-26"**... do not worry about your life, what you will eat or drink; or about your body, what you will wear... Look at the birds of the air; they do not sow or reap or store away in barns, and yet your heavenly Father feeds them. Are you not much more valuable than they...?"

> **34** "So do not worry about tomorrow; for tomorrow will care for itself...."

When your next financial challenge comes, look away from money, look to Jesus and ask Him to show you right responses. Believe Him; stay close to Him so you can hear Him. God spoke the following verse to Israel, but when you stay alert to His presence, His Holy Spirit will prompt you to stay on the right course: "Your ears will hear a word behind you, "this is the way, walk in it," whenever you turn to the right or to the left."9

Planned Obsolescence

So far, it should be obvious the main influence that causes us to spend funds we don't have to buy stuff we don't need is our disbelief that God owns everything and He will provide for our needs. Merchants have figured out why we spend and devised *product Obsolescence* as a key strategy. To raise sales, they build products with short life cycles and often they release new improved versions. Each introduction perks up current versions, producing better and faster (where relevant) products. Ironically, improvements designed to help us be more effective, cause the opposite. We become *slaves* to the new gadgets that grab our attention continuously: cell phones, small music gadgets, faster computers, and the Internet. Yet, have you noticed, we spend more time on these gadgets than the time they freed?

To support this rapid obsolescence pace, corporations use aggressive and sophisticated marketing to convince us to buy their goods and services. They supply expensive credit, and convenient shopping by the Internet, telephone, television, and direct mail. They capture our imagination and their sales soar!

Merchants study our buying habits then gear their marketing to get us to buy. According to "Science of Shopping" guru, Paco Underhill, merchants have over-retailed us dangerously—too much for sale through too many outlets. And he says they produce stores faster than we produce new baby shoppers!

Why do we respond to merchants' dazzling advertising campaigns with credit we can't afford for stuff we don't need? Why do we upgrade stuff when merchants put out later models? We had no problem with our computers, cars, and "grown-up toys" before merchants convinced us we had to change them. Still, we bought newer models with expensive credit, and so robbed the Kingdom. We acted because the FOG trapped us.

Greed

Product obsolescence is the *external influence* that leads us in debt. But as we said earlier, it works because we don't believe God owns everything. Unlike early believers, folks practice tithing and claim ownership of 90% of God's money for their purposes. This tithing mindset creates the illusion we are in charge of spending 90%, which feeds on our *greed* nature, the driving force behind our falling in debt. Greed causes us to look away from God, look to our circumstances, and rationalize why we shouldn't trust God. Commercials and infomercials attract us because of greed.

The Concise Oxford Dictionary of Current English, 9th Edition, defines greed as "Intense or excessive desire especially for food or wealth." We display this excessive wish for wealth when we:

- Give telephone-marketers our bank account or credit card numbers in exchange for prizes that never appear.
- Attend seminars teaching us how to get rich quickly and effortlessly.
- Buy lottery tickets and other gambling forms.
- Buy stocks on *tips* about future prices.
- Speculate in financial markets.

Nobel Prizewinner, the late Milton Freedman, said, "The problem of social organization is how to set up an arrangement under which greed will do the least harm, capitalism is that kind of a system." But Mr. Freedman, capitalism or other economic arrangement doesn't *cause* people to be greedy! Greed results from the *fall;* people are born with this tendency.

William Wilberforce the Philanthropist and Reformer who led the fight to abolish slavery in Britain got it right when he said, "I continually find it necessary to guard against that natural love of wealth and grandeur which prompts us always, when we come to apply our general doctrine to our own case, to claim an exception." [10]

That's why Jesus said this about greed in Luke 12:15 (RSV): "... Take care! Be on your guard against all kinds of greed; for one's life does not consist in the abundance of possessions." We must be on guard and lean on Jesus continually because greed comes to us naturally. Apostle Paul's message in Colossians 3:5 (RSV) also is deep: "Put to death, therefore, whatever in you is earthly: fornication, impurity, passion, evil desire, and greed (which is idolatry)."

I spend hours at international airports, and I see many books proposing the formula to get rich quickly and easily. Equally, I see advertisements for seminars where presenters claim to have the get rich quickly and effortlessly recipe. Regrettably, people buy these books, attend similar seminars, but lose their small savings along the way. These books and seminars appeal to our greed nature!

The 12 November 2005 New York Times ran an article titled "Get Rich Quick, Write a Millionaire Book," that stated:

"The Bottom Line is: save your money by not buying these books.[11] At about $25 a book, buying one each year probably will not decimate your retirement fund. But if you don't, you'll have at least $2370 in 40 years."

Still, wittingly and unwittingly, some folks see greed as positive. Consider these three post-1980's greed-related comments:

First, in his 1987 book *Just Rewards*,[12] David Olive wrote: At a conference on Native Canadian business enterprises in 1986, Barbara McDougall, then minister of state for finance, celebrated the rise of Native-owned businesses. 'There's one underlying motive in business shared by all – it's greed,' said McDougall, who once worked in the securities industry....

Olive mentioned business executive and British House of Lords member, Conrad Black too. Black told Peter Newman "greed has been severely under-estimated and denigrated. There is nothing wrong with avarice as a motive, as long as it doesn't lead to anti-social conduct." Olive commented on these and other statements, "greed does bring out the worst in people – and in corporations." To be sure, it does.

Second, the 13th September 1999 *Business Week* edition carried an article titled "US$ 276 million: Now that's Motivation", which states:

> " ... No doubt there is potential to be mined in self-improvement and personal enrichment—the market accounts for more than US$ 7 billion in video, book and other sales...."

Third, in the 17 April 2001 Boston Globe, MIT professor Lester C. Thurow commenting on stock markets' rise and fall, said this about greed:

> "Capitalism taps into the greed that seems to be built into human beings. The desire to have 'more,' however much one already has, is the human desire that makes capitalism work ..."

Greed causes us to want more. We go to the store to buy one pair of shoes but leave with two because the extra pair was *only* half price! We spent *half price* too much because we did not need the second pair! We couldn't afford it, but we used available credit!

Let's remember Jesus' warning: beware; your life does not consist of the *abundance of possessions*. When tempted, God shows a way out always.[13] So, the next time a seductive advertising tempts you, ask Jesus to show you His *way out*. Also, decide never to buy impulsively. When the urge comes to spend impulsively or to use spending as therapy, pray; wait at least 24 hours, by then you will see God's way out!

FOG, not exercising *faith* in Jesus, *planned obsolescence*, and *greed* distort reality and we spend without assessing the effects. Rather than deciding if we need an item and if we can afford it, we ask about available payment terms. Usually, we decide to buy based on available financing terms, even if expensive—and normally, it is expensive. Merchants use these terms as bait to get us to buy stuff: "no down payment", "zero percent" financing, and "no payment until..." much later. Some Christian ministries use these terms as bait: "sow in the ministry, and you will reap ..."; "send for this healing cloth, bottle of Jordan River water ..."; "give a special gift this month and get a double blessing."

It gets worse. We encourage our children to get credit cards to get *credit ratings,* rather than encourage them to save, wait on God, before buying stuff. Still, we don't teach them to manage money—their wants, needs, and greed—for God's glory. If we want them to have credit cards, we must teach (our actions speak loudly) them[14] to use these cards properly—like cheques. If we don't teach our children, they will get credit ratings but with much debt.

FOG produces dire, potentially lasting, effects:

- FOG blinds us so we don't realize interest we pay could go to fund God's work.
- FOG leads students to take student loans without considering later repayment.
- FOG creates an urgency to upgrade homes, cars, and other items on credit and ignores the emotional, personal, family, and financial costs.

- FOG causes a vicious debt cycle that keeps our eyes on our circumstances so we don't see our poor family relationships, depression, cynicism and our distance from our heavenly Father.
- FOG causes us to forget God's ownership and our stewardship, and so, at best, we *tip* God with a *tithe*[15] while spending hundreds and thousands of dollars on loan interest. When we tithe, we give God 10% or other amount (offerings), and spend the rest of His money our way.

Slow Burn Principle

Sadly, the FOG moves in slowly. Like a frog in a beaker of water with a flame lit below, we fall deep in debt, slowly and unintentionally. For some, skipping the first credit card payment was difficult: a big deal! The second was less, and so on: A *toehold* became a *foothold* then a *stronghold* and later a *stranglehold*. James puts this regression succinctly:

> "But each one is tempted when, by his own evil desire, he is dragged away and enticed. Then, after desire has conceived, it gives birth to sin; and sin, when it is full-grown, gives birth to death." (James 1:14-15), NIV.

Here are seven signs you are in the FOG, in the debt-beaker with rising heat. These events come from my experience with individuals and couples. If one applies to you, beware; you might be insensitive to the *reality* that your finances control your life. Seek God's peace as you answer the *GIC DIES* questions:

1. Giving to God stopped or lowered?
   - Giving to God should flow from your stewardship role. Do you believe God owns everything and the funds you earn go to *"God's bank account"*? When you change

your giving to God without His guidance, you control His money; He doesn't. Watch out! Are you feeling the heat?

2. **Income rises but your debt rises too?**
   - This happens naturally. Many people say they have more income today than five years ago, but they feel worse off, and they are; they fulfilled wants on credit, not thinking about later payment. Or, they planned to use expected future funds they never got. They assumed the promised bonus, promised overtime, and the promised raise would come, but none happened. Meanwhile, they *bought to pay later*. Even if you are hurting from rising heat, it's never too late to turn to God for help.

3. **Credit card balances unpaid routinely?**
   - *A credit card is a cheque,* not a funding source. If you cannot pay your balance in full monthly, you cannot afford to keep a card. Use the card only when you have matching funds in the bank. If you can't pay monthly balances fully, cut up your cards. If you want to put them aside temporarily, put them in a freezer bag and put the bag in the freezer.

4. **Debt consolidation being considered or done?**
   - Debt consolidation does not work unless you change your attitude and behaviour. Indeed, likely you will be worse off if you consolidate without changed ABCs. Thinking about debt consolidation, is a sure sign the heat is on. Check your spiritual life.

5. **Insurance policies cashed to pay debt?**
   - Cashing an insurance policy alone is not an issue. If you do not need insurance, it might be good to cash the policy and redirect funds. Still, if you sense the need to cash the policy to repay debt, the heat is on, and you have an issue.

6. **Extending credit terms or juggling bills?**
   - Paying bills partly and wanting more time to pay bills fully are two key signs your financial picture needs attention. Ask God to show you how to overcome anxiety about your bills.[16]

7. Savings used to pay bills?
   - Using savings to pay regular bills is an early slow burn indicator. Plug leaking expenses.

Summary

Thank God for blessing you with what you have; you have more than you think. Ask Him to teach you to appreciate and use what He has given you to glorify Him and further His kingdom. When you feel sad, lonely, depressed, turn to God, don't spend as therapy for emotional relief; you know it doesn't work.

Ignorance of biblical teachings on giving to God leads folks to practice tithing and so they try to spend on their own 90% of God's money, rather than allowing God to help them spend 100%. This results because they don't believe God owns everything and will do as He promised, supply their needs.

Stay in the Word to develop a strong, personal relationship with Jesus Christ and to escape the FOG. You have *enough faith* to do everything God wants you to do; believe Him. If you don't soak yourself with Jesus, surrender 100% of His funds to Him, you will continue to react to merchants' seductive appeals and later you will lose your way in the FOG, falling in the erupting debt volcano!

Think About This

 Be anxious for nothing, but in everything by prayer and supplication with thanksgiving let your requests be made known to God. And the peace of God, which surpasses all comprehension, will guard your hearts and your minds in Christ Jesus.[17]

Chapter Notes:

1. Dr. Ken Hutcherson, *Enough Faith*, (Oregon; Multnomah Publishers, Inc. 2006), p. 19.
2. Matthew 17:20.
3. Hebrews 11:1.
4. 2 Corinthians 5:7.
5. Joshua 3:13.
6. Romans 10:17.
7. 2 Kings 20; 2 Chronicles 32:24-31.
8. Psalm 23, John 16:24.
9. Isaiah 30:21.
10. William Wilberforce, *Money in Christian History*, (Christian History), no. 14.
11. The article mentioned these and other books: Automatic Millionaire and Rich Dad, Poor Dad.
12. David Olive, *Just Rewards*, (Toronto, Canada: Key Porter Books Limited, 1987), pp. 23-24.
13. 1 Corinthians 10:13.
14. See chapter 12 for full discussion of Family Finances.
15. In chapter 9 we will discuss tithing, including why it does not apply today.
16. Romans 5:8.
17. Philippians 4:6-7.

3

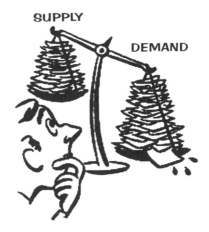

SUPPLY

DEMAND

Quick Start Action Plan— Learning Your ABCs

In chapter one we realized money isn't manageable. In chapter two, we saw the FOG that swallows up folks who fall deep in debt slowly and unconsciously. This chapter is a *station stop*. In it, I introduce practical steps for you to climb today to help control the key variable in the money triangle—you.

Often, to get to the *quick start* action plan, you might need to receive an SOS[1] to help adjust your attitude and behaviour to God's plan for you. You might not be in distress, but periodically, you need to accept and test the *signal* by checking your reaction to these three questions; do you need to:

- Stop striving for more and accept what you have?
- Own your present circumstance?
- Start playing *offense* with merchants today?

Stop Striving For More and Accept What You Have

Stop striving for more and accepting what you have is the *A* in the GAS Principle. It gets to our greed nature. It is easy to say, but difficult to do. Still, *decide* today to *stop* buying goods or services unless first you follow spending decision procedures we discuss in chapter 11, or other procedure that God directs.

Stop thinking, saying, and then spending because an item is *only $10* or other small amount. Get a piggy bank and label it "ONLY." When you say something is *only $x*, don't spend, put *$x* in the ONLY piggy bank. Each Christmas, give away amounts in the Piggy bank as the Lord leads.

Stop *tipping* God with a *tithe* and *offering*. Start presenting 100% to Him and let Him, as Owner, guide you to share His money (100%) that you control as His steward. In chapter 9, we will discuss tithing and giving. There you will see the Apostles and early church did not practice tithing, but grace giving (2 Corinthians 8 and 9).

Stop allowing merchants to decide when, how much, and why, you spend. As well, stop reacting to their sales seduction; learn what savings look like. You save when you do not spend! Merchants tell you about their sales, confident when you spend you will believe you save amounts they tell you. Don't believe them! Study these two messages about sales and deals, recall them when you think you should buy items on sale:

1) Sales
   a. You benefit from a sale when these conditions exist:
      i.   You buy an item you *need*
      ii.   You do not borrow
      iii. You spend less than you planned

Fifty percent off is fifty percent too much if you did not need the item, did not plan to buy it, had to put it on your credit card but did not pay the full balance.

2) Deals
   a. Someone told me this gem at my seminar: a deal is a debt-enhancing act of lunacy. To this, I add; it leaves you depressed, empty, anxious, and lonely.

In January, I see many folks who show *deal reaction symptoms* after spending in response to merchants' Christmas enticements. How do you celebrate Jesus' birthday by spending money you don't own, to buy stuff you don't need that doesn't glorify Him? To this point, one Christmas, my 10-year-old grandson and I discussed Christmas giving like this:

> "Dylan, on your next birthday, I think I should buy each of your friends a present, rather than buying a present for you." I said.
> "Papa, that's not fair!" Dylan replied.
> "Why not, that's what you want to do for Jesus' birthday; you want to get all the presents, while He gets none." I explained.
> Dylan, pondered, and then said, "I see." He got the message; at Christmas, using time talents and, or money, we need to give gifts to God. Dylan and the rest of the grand kids each gave gifts to God by Papa and Grandma donating to a Christian charity that clothed, fed, housed, and taught children, funds they would normally spend on the grandchildren's gifts.

Stop; don't let merchants control your actions! With Jesus' help, you decide, not merchants:

- What you need
- Why you need it

- When you need it
- How you will pay for it.

Proverbs 3:5-6 says," Trust in the LORD with all your heart and do not lean on your own understanding. In all your ways acknowledge Him, and He will make your paths straight." What's a straight path in your life? God's best for you might not look good to you at the time He presents it. In the same way, your best for your three-year-old might not seem good to her.

Own Your Present Circumstance

Own your present financial position, apply self-control, be content with what you have, also is in the GAS Principle's A. God knows your possessions and where you are in life's journey. You cannot surprise Him. He does not sit in heaven worried because you think you live in difficult circumstances. He allows every-thing in your life for a purpose. So accept your circumstances, try to *see in them* messages He wants you to learn as you walk *with Him* through them. Read in the Old Testament, Job chapters 40-42, and camp on discussions with God and Job. What can you take from this and use in your condition?

As friends tell you how to deal with your circumstances, turn again to Job and look at bad counsel from his friends.[2] Only with eyes fixed on Jesus will you own your condition, and lean on Him as you walk through the valley.

Pastor and Bible teacher Chuck Swindoll says, the grass is greener on the other side but it needs mowing. Don't look at your neighbour's living standard. You don't know how he financed it. Stay where God puts you and do as Apostle Paul suggests, "...whatever is true, whatever is honorable, whatev-er is right, whatever is pure, whatever is lovely, whatever is of good repute, if there is any excellence and if anything wor-thy of praise, dwell on these things.."[3]

Often we blame others for our poor choices that caused our financial challenges. We forget we signed the agreement but didn't read the *fine print*—where merchants put their agreements' negative parts. You would do well to remember this anonymous quote: "What the large print giveth, the small print taketh away."

Still, we buy stuff on our credit cards but don't think about repayment. We take student loans because we want to finish college our way, in our time. We don't ask God how to help us distinguish our wants from His best. Are you there? Have you been there? I have.

Thank God for your circumstances. If in debt, draw close to Him, listen to Him, and let Him guide you to changed attitudes and behaviours. God owns everything, doesn't need debt, but wants you to give him the burdens you carry from your debts. Accept your financial debts, give Him the burden (the stress), and He will work with you to help you clear them. In chapter 5, we will discuss a Christ centred approach to getting out of debt.

How can you be content where you are when you face difficult circumstances? Read aloud Philippians 4:12 and listen to Apostle Paul, who was a human with access to Jesus, like you and me:

I know what it is to be in need, and I know what it is to have plenty. I have learned the secret of being content in any and every situation, whether well fed or hungry, whether living in plenty or in want (Philippians 4:12), NIV.

These are potent words from Paul—being *content in any and every situation*. To be sure, only a few practice or teach this idea today. In my seminars, folks tell me it's wrong *to be content with what you have and with whom you are,* as this state suggests you lack ambition. They argue you cannot excel when content because you'll accept mediocre standards. They point to many professional athletes who reject current performance as the basis to propel them to perform at higher levels—*push the limit and beyond to get to the next level,* they propose. Some athletes don't accept their gifts, with their limits, from God. Could this be a major reason drug abuse is such a central issue in professional sports?

What is *contentment?* The Greek word for contentment in Philippians 4:12 connotes *sufficient, satisfied, or enough,* as opposed to lazy, mediocre or complacent. In the following verse, Philippians 4:13, we read Paul's bold statement that he can do all things through Christ who gives him strength. Folks *claim* this passage and expect to do everything they want. But that's interpreting it separately. Believers can't do everything they want; rather, they can do everything He wants done.

Jesus does not give us superhuman skills to do anything we can imagine. He calls and equips us to do His plans. As we travel on our journeys, we will face troubles, pressures, and trials. Apostle Paul reminds us to ask Christ to strengthen us to do His will. But to be able to see and hear Him clearly, we need to be content with what we have and not be looking elsewhere for what we want.

Paul was confident and secure in his relationship with Christ. He knew when trials and difficulties stretch Christ's followers, we can be confident Christ will drench us with enough strength to carry out His will. Besides, he understood it's through Christ's strengthening we can get to the next level to become content—but only according to His will. Listen to prophet Isaiah as he describes this condition in Isaiah 40:29-31:

> He gives strength to the weary, and to *him who* lacks might He increases power. Though youths grow weary and tired, and vigorous young men stumble badly, yet those who wait for the LORD will gain new strength; they will mount up *with* wings like eagles, they will run and not get tired, they will walk and not become weary.

Contentment is intangible and hard to understand. Folks seek unsuccessfully to find it in money, fame, work, prestige, and possessions. Not finding it here, they become frustrated; they reach for drugs, sex, gambling, or other addictive behaviours that continue the downward spiral.

Contentment doesn't mean good-bye to difficulties; we will experience trials and challenges to raise our faith and draw us closer to the Lord. It's our response to our conditions that's crucial—by God's grace, leaning on Him as we go through and move beyond them.

To gain contentment, we need to surrender—let Christ control— all areas of our lives; letting Him be Lord and Saviour. We need to accept who we are—warts and all—and what we have. Sometimes our trials result from our poor choices. Yet, God is faithful, kind, merciful, gracious; He will guide us through these trials. We need to obey His teachings and live *in* our circumstances, confident Christ will see us *through*. In this way, we choose to live Christ-centered, rather than me-centered lives. Apostle Paul describes this lifestyle in Galatians 2:20:

"I have been crucified with Christ; and it is no longer I who live, but Christ lives in me; and the *life* which I now live in the flesh I live by faith in the Son of God, who loved me and gave Himself up for me."

Imagine Jesus is the composer and orchestra conductor, and you are playing a complex arrangement that needs you to keep your eyes riveted on His every move. Keep your eyes on Him and you will find contentment.

Meanwhile, mull over Galatians 5:22-23: "But the fruit of the Spirit is love, joy, peace, patience, kindness, goodness, faithfulness, gentleness, self-control; against such things there is no law." If you don't have the fruit of the Spirit, it will be difficult to stay *in* your circumstances. In the next chapter, you will see how to get the fruit of the Spirit. Today, decide in your head, and then ask the Lord to help you believe in your heart:

- You *own* and understand where you are in life's journey.
- You *own* your mistakes—don't rationalise and excuse your circumstance.
- You *own* your behaviour—don't blame anyone.
- You *own* your decisions—decide to change as needed.
- You *own* your financial debts—don't borrow to hike spending as a way out.

Believe Jesus' words in Matthew 11:28: ""Come to Me, all who are weary and heavy-laden, and I will give you rest."
Let's look at other practical steps to get you going.

Start Playing *Offense* with Merchants Today

Start playing *offense* to become and remain debt free in this vicious contest for God's money. How? First, know *your views* about money, especially about these two myths:

1. You need a special gift to handle money.
2. If you get more income, you will stop living pay-cheque-to-pay-cheque.

Myth # 1:
You Need a Special Gift to Handle Money

No, you don't need a special gift to handle money! Many people say they do, but the money triangle—the 3Ms—we discussed in chapter one explodes this myth. We must manage our wants and needs—our attitudes and behaviours—not the bridge, money. That's why Jesus spoke often and poignantly about needed money attitudes. People who blame their poor financial condition on the lack of gifts, ought to look in the Bible to see what it says about right and wrong attitudes to money. This is the crux: Tools and techniques we discuss later in this book will help only with right biblical money attitudes. If you know how to prepare and use budgets, spending plans, cash flows, but still you can't resist merchants' enticements to spend, money will strangle you—stress from poor attitudes will overwhelm you.

Myth #2:
If You Get More Income You Will Stop Living Pay-Cheque-to-Pay-Cheque

Wouldn't it be good if when you got more income you stopped living pay-cheque-to-pay-cheque? Sadly, that's not the case for most folks. They do not limit spending to their incomes. Research shows seductive marketing, easy credit, and insatiable appetites, drive consumer spending. That's why the more income you get the more you spend. You must learn to apply biblical ABCs and follow Christ-centered procedures before spending. As well, you need to use a spending plan, and decide not to succumb to tempting advertising that merchants use to get you to spend, and so fall deeper in debt.

Learn to handle present income. If you have difficulty living on what you have, you will have difficulty with more! If you have difficulty giving from where you are, you will have difficulty giving when you get more! Giving means opening your palms and letting Jesus tell you how much He wants to stay in His kingdom. It doesn't depend on you. Already, He has 100%!

What should you do today? *Accept* you can't manage money. *Admit* you don't need special gifts to *grip* household finances. *Ask* God to give you His *PhD:*

1) Patience
   a. As God's steward, don't borrow except for a home. Before buying a home, seek His timing, and His place. He will provide the down payment and mortgage that fits your budget.
2) Humility
   a. When you don't have, ask Jesus how to *adjust your lifestyle.*
3) Dependence
   a. Ask Jesus to help you learn to lean on Him in the valley—when the car breaks down, the roof leaks, bills become due. If you know Jesus as Lord and Saviour, you have enough faith to do everything He wants you to do.

Five Practical Steps to Start Today

Here are five practical steps you can start today to thrust you on your journey:

1. Start to record your spending, continue for at least one month.
   a. Get a notebook with columns as in Appendix 2 and start to record every cent you spend. Yes, every cent. Do this for at least one month. What you see will shock you. I know folks who found $400 waste in the first month. Your spending record will show *why* you spend, *when* you spend, and for *what* you spend. Today, if you are like most folks I counsel, you don't know this information, but you think you do. Look for and learn:
      i. Where are the leakages?
      ii. What's your spending pattern? Do you spend more on Fridays? Or on Mondays? Evenly during the week? Do you spend to lift your spirits?

b. In chapter 8 I suggest a *quick start budget kit* that includes recording your spending. If you get familiar with your spending now, later you will be well on your way to doing your budget.

2. Start a *spending fast* the *month after you start to record* spending.

   a. During a spending fast, spend only for items legally, morally and ethically needed. When the urge to spend comes, wait at least 24 hours. Meanwhile, pray and seek God's help.

   b. Record spending while on the *fast;* compare it with spending in the first month. You will notice you spend loose change without thinking, and it adds up. So, stop spending coins you get as change and put them in the *ONLY* box.

   c. Ask the Lord to show you needed attitude and behaviour changes.

   d. Note the following:

      i. Difficulties you meet during these two months.

      ii. Spending that could and should have waited until you got funds.

      iii. Spending you didn't plan.

3. Start noting the procedure you follow before you spend.

   a. How do you decide to buy an item in a mall? At a fast-food store? Do you buy because you have cash, funds in the bank, or because the merchant entices you to buy? Note your reasons.

   b. If you choose to spend cash and not use a credit card, you will spend less; be alert to spending because you have a credit card.

   c. Husbands and wives, do you consult each other? Do you think you should? See *Family Finances*, chapter 12, for more on this.

   d. Do you distinguish a financial salesperson from a financial advisor or planner? See chapter 18 to help you select a financial advisor.

4. Start living in your income.
   a. Ask God to show you a *living standard* to uphold. This could be your current or future income level.
   b. Limit regular spending to the level the Lord tells you. Give away all income beyond that level.[4]
5. Start an accountability program.
   a. Ask God to bring a strong Christian brother (if you are male) or sister (if you are female) to encourage your walk with Him[5] and to help you stay with these quick start items.

You are ready to enter the critical stage of your journey where you will see ...

The

Shepherd

gives

Gas

for

Peace[6]

on the

Plane[7]

Summary

Periodically, each of us needs to accept an SOS to see how we are doing with God's money, time and talents. Are you content with what you have? If not, ask the Lord to show you how to accept who you are and what you have. Only when you become content will you be able to look away from your circumstances and merchants, and direct funds hilariously to God's work.

Tracking spending routinely is a good habit that will teach you about you and your spending habits. It will prepare you to budget, and help you honour God with His finances. You can start today to learn about your finances; you do not need special gifts to manage money, you need a close personal relationship with Jesus Christ. That's why more money is a band-aid for personal debt problems. Changed attitudes will solve them.

Think About This

The truth is, God always responds to our prayers. The way he does so reveals as much about us as it does about God. We can become frustrated when we pray for one thing and receive another. But we are wise to look beyond God's answer to see His message behind it.[8]

Chapter Notes:

1. The description commonly used for the International Morse code distress signal (· · · – – – · · ·)
2. Job 6-27.
3. Philippians 4:8.
4. Matthew 25:14-30.
5. Proverbs 27:17.
6. *PEACE Budgetary Control* , Copyright © 1994-2007 Michel A. Bell
7. *PLANE Spending Analysis*, Copyright © 1997 Michel A. Bell
8. Henry and Richard Blackaby, *Hearing God's Voice,* (Nashville, Tennessee: Broadman & Holman Publishers, 2002), p. 123.

4

Three Essential Financial Planning Steps

As you enter this important journey stage, you need to know where you are and where God wants you to be. Do you know your financial picture? Do you live a debt free lifestyle?[1] Do you live pay cheque-to-pay cheque, barely paying bills? Do you want to be rich and stash away millions?

My goal as your guide is to help you assess your position compared with where God wants you to be. And if there is a gap, help you bridge it. But beware; bridging could entail life style changes. Your goal is to ask God to confirm your condition and lead you to His path at His pace, in His way.

To continue the trip, decide three matters that will affect how you live. Climb these stairs, get His peace, and watch Him provide for your needs:

1. Settle your *eternal worth:* Where are you with the Shepherd?
2. Find out your *material worth:* Where are you with His possessions you manage?
3. Find out your *life goal* from God: What's your purpose in life—your destination?

The 1st Step: Settle Your Eternal Worth

In the previous chapter, how did you react to the SOS distress signal? The first matter I should have asked you to deal with was your eternal worth; but I didn't. When I suggest this crucial first step to folks I counsel, usually I don't get their attention. They become preoccupied with money issues, so they don't see and hear what God prepared for them. Only after a brief reply to the SOS call, as I explained in chapter 3, do they see clearly the need for the eternal worth check.

Go to a quiet place to deal with your eternal worth. As you think about it, I will share my story, briefly. I grew up in the church, but didn't know Jesus as Lord and Saviour. I walked away from church when I went to college at age 19. I didn't need God; I thought I had it all. I sailed through college at the top of my class, climbed the corporate ladder rapidly, and I controlled me. Who needed God? Along the way, I picked up two ulcers—age 29 and age 35—had the world's success trappings, but was in turmoil continually.

Then it happened! My 12-year-old daughter became a believer; I thought she was crazy. Why would an intelligent, educated person do such a *stupid act?* I insisted she shifted effort from studying the Bible to studying *stuff that mattered*—math, science, and other schoolwork. During many *debates,* she challenged me to learn about Christianity. "How can you discuss this topic when you know so little about it?" She asked repeatedly.

I accepted her challenge confident I would prove her wrong. Later at age 38, after a two-year journey trying to disprove Christianity's soundness, God's creation overwhelmed me and I knew I didn't have *enough faith* to believe everything in the universe came from nothing.

As God opened my eyes and my ears, I saw His hand in my daily actions, and later I surrendered my life to Jesus. From His Word, I knew His Holy Spirit came to live in me, so I asked Him then to help me live the victorious life wherever I went. Over twenty years later, I look back and marvel at His devotion, consistency, and His love. Though I stumble often, He picks me up and puts me back on His trail.

Where are you? *Are you playing church?* Is Jesus your *Saviour?* Is He your *Lord and* Your *Saviour?* Did you *surrender,* and then walk away? Wherever you are, stay with me, and after this section, answer these three questions:

1. Are you content with your life?
2. Is God's Spirit directing your life?
3. If you died tonight, are you 100% sure, you will go immediately to Jesus?

Jesus wants you to be His Chief Financial Officer (CFO) to handle His money, His way. In my role as CFO of different *Alcan* subsidiaries, I had to know and then carry out *Alcan's* principles, policies and practices. I couldn't be successful otherwise. Similarly, to manage God's money well, you must know Jesus and His Word—know His teachings.

Managing God's money is a part of the believer's journey to heaven. Part of learning to be Jesus' disciple, you cannot isolate it from the rest of your life. How you spend money, helps define who you are, what you believe, what's your relationship with Christ.

Look at last month's financial transactions: credit card charges, cheque stubs, and other financial matters. What do they tell you? When you review these papers, a good reality check to

confirm where you are today is to ask Jesus to help you see as He sees. If you are uncomfortable with your findings, look in the mirror; answer this question: Do you need to change your attitude and behaviour toward money?

You spend money based on your attitude (beliefs), so it's essential you know what you believe. How do you know truth from lies? Jesus is truth[2]—His Word contains unchanging truths.[3] Unless you know Him, you will be in bondage striving to fill a void in your life.

Jesus is love. He is the perfect Father who calls us to a personal relationship with Him, to a *forever to remember*—everlasting life with Him in heaven.[4] He told the well-known Jewish teacher Nicodemus that Nicodemus needed a spiritual rebirth to gain eternal life.[5] As well, He told his disciples, "...unless you are converted and become like children, you will never enter the kingdom of heaven".[6] We experience the *kingdom of heaven* when we let Jesus work in us and we do everything through His strength.

Listen to Jesus' call and accept His invitation for this *forever to remember*. Apply the faith, sincerity, humility a child shows to her parents as you respond. Ask Jesus to remove your unbelief and tell you who He is.

Deciding to surrender your life to Christ will be your most important lifetime decision. Jesus invites you, and you respond. It's deep with lasting effects; it is the start of your journey to heaven. Do you accept these truths?

- Jesus Christ lived on earth, died, and then rose from the dead.
- He is the only true and living God.
- The Bible is God's Word (inspired) and is without error (infallible).
- You are a sinner, and you need to seek forgiveness.

Apostle Paul tells us in Romans 10:9 (NIV): "... if you confess with your mouth, "Jesus is Lord, and believe in your heart that God raised him from the dead, you will be saved." From your heart, will you take these actions?

- Ask Jesus to forgive your sins (confess).
- Decide to turn away from your sins (repent).
- Ask Jesus to control your life (receive Jesus as Lord and Savior).
- Ask Jesus to show you how to live as His disciple wherever you go (so you walk with Him always).

When you surrender your life to Christ, He gives you His Holy Spirit to teach and guide you, and you become His CFO. Besides, He gives you many assurances such as these:

- He will never leave you or abandon you (Hebrews 13:5).
- Nothing is impossible for Him (Matthew 19:26).
- One day you will account to Him (Matthew 25:14-30).

I pray that today you settle your eternal worth—your position in Jesus Christ. If you surrendered your life but walked away from Jesus, turn around and head back to Him. He is waiting to forgive[7] and comfort you. Jesus Christ is the GAS Principle's foundation. Unless you accept the GAS Principle, you will not accept your stewardship role and you will try to manage on your own, and likely you will get lost!

The 2nd Step: Find Out Your Material Worth

You are ready to find out your *material worth*; the net value of *stuff* you hold on Jesus' behalf. Financial people call the statement in Table I a *Balance Sheet* or *Net Worth Statement*; I call it your *Material Worth Statement*.

A still-photograph of your financial affairs at a specific date, prepared today, it would change if you spent or got funds tomorrow. At a precise date, it tells you what you *own* as God's steward, and how you are financing these items.

Table I

Material Worth Statement at 30 June
(Always at a specific date)

Stuff I *Own* at Market Price[8] (Assets) - $

Cash	5,000	2.5%
Personal Effects	15,000	7.5%
Car	9,000	5%
Furniture and Equipment	20,000	10%
House	150,000	75%
Assets	**199,000**	**100%**
Financed by Liabilities and Equity - $		
Family Loan	2,000	1%
Other Loans	2,500	1%
Car Loan	11,000	6%
Credit Card balances	20,000	10%
Mortgage	125,000	63%
Loans	**160,500**	**81%**
Material Worth (Equity)	**38,500**	**19%**
Loans and Equity	**199,000**	**100%**

Essential to start the get out of debt journey, it's helpful to track stuff— value items we call *assets*—and *debt changes*. Notice we show assets at market price, not the price you paid. Note too the caution in the endnote to avoid using the equity value in your home to buy more bits and pieces. I see banks encourage this foolish, rising trend. They raise your mortgage to lend you funds to pay off credit card balances and other consumer debts for short life cycle items;[9] don't do this! If you do, you will carry a loan for a sofa or DVD player for the life of your mortgage!

Often forgotten, the asset *personal effects* could include objects you don't need and you could sell to repay debt, but beware; never sell assets merely to lower debt, always ask Jesus to guide you with this decision that could be irreversible. Unless you change your attitude and behaviour, selling assets to lower debt merely delays the showdown to deal with lifestyle changes.

As well, Table I shows the *owner* used $160,500 loans, and $38,500 *own* funds (equity) to finance $199,000 assets. When you see folks with *nice* homes, *nice* cars, and other *nice* belongings, remember this material worth statement. Often, loans financed these *nice* homes or *nice* cars—probably they carry *nice* mortgages!

Debt Ratios

Set two financial ratio goals as key signposts for your journey: the *Maximum Debt Ratio* (MDR) and the *Debt Repayment Ratio* (DRR). In Table I, the MDR is 81%, representing loans $160,500, as a percent of loans and equity of $199,000 [(160500/199000)*100]. Ideally, loans should be zero, but don't worry if it is not zero; it is what it is. Decide to get it to zero in two stages.

First, repay nonmortgage loans—usually they are more expensive than mortgage loans. Second, repay mortgage loans. Some folks see their mortgages as acceptable to carry for a long time. Let God show you the repayment period; your mortgage is a loan, usually expensive, and you should repay it, not add to it, to get rid of interest charges.

Ask the Lord to show you the period, and lifestyle adjustments needed to become debt free. We will discuss this further when we discuss getting out of debt.

The DRR shows loan payments[10] for the period (one year), as a percent of gross income for the same period. Again, it is what it is; ask the Lord to show how to lower it to zero progressively.

Don't let these calculations intimidate you. For this journey, you need to learn your *ABCs*, not your *123s*. I know you can do it; you don't need to know math, like math, or want to do math! Accept your role as God's money manager and then ask Him to guide you. He will.

The 3rd Step: Find Out Your Life Goal

It's game seven of the Stanley Cup finals at the Bell Centre in Montreal. The Vancouver Canucks meet the Montreal Canadiens with the series tied at 3-3. It's game time, players *face-off*, and Montreal gets the puck. In a series of plays performed brilliantly, a Montreal player prepares to shoot. Abruptly, he and all other players start yelling at the referee. Where is the net? How do we score goals? No nets, no goaltenders; what's this game's purpose?

Until a few years ago, I defined a goal as *my destination,* where *I wanted to go,* or what *I wanted to do.* I said, I want to go to Bible College, or I want to start a business. Rather than, God, where do you want me to be? What do you want me to do?

As I dug in God's Word, I started to understand my discipleship and stewardship roles better. The Word convicted me about me-centeredness; unconsciously, I wasn't seeking God's best, but my best for me. I was looking from my view, at my wants.

Jesus teaches us in Matthew 6:10 to seek His will, and in Matthew 6:33, to seek first His kingdom. So, our main goal must be to find out and then do His will. Not only did Jesus teach us to do His will, but also He modeled it with His Father.

Life Goal

The third step to managing God's money is to *find out your personal life goal—* God's purpose for your life. I like Richard Foster's quote: *Goals are discovered, not made.* When we go through life with *our* goals or *no* goals, we miss *God's goals,* and *we get lost!* Usually, I think about two types of goals: *personal life goals and material goals.*

A *personal life goal* is akin to a company's mission statement; it provides its direction. After defining its mission, to carry it out, the company develops compatible strategies, goals, plans, and budgets.

God gives each believer the *Great Commission* to "make disciples" (Matthew 28:18-20) as the believer's general, on going mission. So, each believer has the same *general life goal;* but God chooses a specific mission for him as his part of the Great Commission. I call this specific mission, the believer's *personal life goal.*

With his personal life goal, God gives the believer daily, weekly, monthly, compatible strategies, goals, and plans. I call these regular goals, *material goals.* Congruent with personal life goals, each material goal teaches us to be more like Jesus. And like personal life goals, we get material goals in God's timing.

Why distinguish the personal life goal from material goals? The first is our mission; it's on going, helps with daily choices, and once we get it, as with Joseph, David, Apostle Paul, and others, it's likely to remain with us during our lifetime.

My *personal life goal* is to teach biblical stewardship of time talents and money. It is on going, and the path God chooses for me to present Christ to others. *Material goals* God gives me include presenting specific seminars, writing specific books, and appearing on identified radio and TV programs. They are independent of my gifts, talents, and skills.

Through my personal life goal, today, God has shown me I should not provide consulting to secular businesses. So, when a business asks me to consult (a material goal), I know that's not in God's path. Without a personal life goal, I would look at my schedule, and if I am available and the price is right, I might do it! But this would distract me from God's call on my life and I would be busy doing my stuff rather than doing God's work.

Busyness and discontent with your job could be signs you need to get off the treadmill and sit at Jesus' feet to learn your personal life goal.

Scripture shows a consistent goal-setting-doing pattern. God gives His people clear, complete, concise (3-Cs) material goals to sanctify them to become like Him. Besides, He defines a plan and then gives us all we need to do it. Still, not one person sees or understands everything at the time, because each time He gives only what we need.

But what about those who do not believe in Jesus? The first special goal God prepares for each person is that he and she get to know Him individually.[11] That's first base! After that, to those of us who surrender our lives to Him, in His time, He shows us the special personal life goal He prepares for our lives. Still, many folks don't get to know Him so they miss their personal life goals. These folks seek to know about Jesus and other religious leaders. They will tell you Jesus was a great prophet, a good person, but this shows they don't understand who He is.

To see two men who knew God with all their hearts, and who sought after Him, read King David's inspired writings in the Psalms, and Apostle Paul's letters in the New Testament.

Do you believe God created you for a purpose? Surrender your life to Jesus, receive His Holy Spirit to teach and guide you in God's truth, and ask Him to show you, your personal life goal. Let's look in the Bible at some Bible folks' personal life goals:

Bible Character	Life Goal
Abraham	Go where God leads[12]
Joseph	Rule over Egypt[13]
David	Be King of Israel[14]
Paul	Take the gospel to Jews and Gentiles[15]
John The Baptist	Jesus' forerunner[16]
The Apostles	Follow Jesus[17]

These folks' personal life goals were not tasks they carried out rarely. Rather, God gave each, specific long-term missions. What can we learn from God's interaction with these folks to help us get and understand our personal life goals?

First, God chose each goal, not one of those folks did.

Second, not one person did anything on his own to prepare for his personal life goal. Rather, God used each, as he was, warts, and all.

Third, apart from Apostle Paul, when He chose these folks, God did not explain why He chose them, or what their tasks might entail. To His apostles, Jesus said follow Me, a clear statement for a journey that would end in heaven.

Fourth, not one asked where he was going—how unlike us! David was a boy when Samuel anointed Him. He didn't ask God about God's plans. After his anointing, David went back to shepherding until God was ready to move him in the king's job. Paul was doing the opposite to what God called Him to do. He was persecuting Christians! God refocused His zeal.

Fifth, though God prepared each person's life goal before He created him, each knew his personal life goal at different life stages. In Joseph's youth, God showed Joseph his personal life goal in dreams but Joseph didn't see it.

Sixth, tasks they did along their trip that seemed unrelated helped prepare them for their personal life goals.

The personal life goal is on going and each person gets it in God's time, for God's lifetime assignment. To seize your personal life goal, you need to be ready to do what God asks even when you think you don't have needed gifts, training, or skills.

Shortly after my wife surrendered her life to Jesus, He started to lead her to teach Bible studies. She felt inadequate and unprepared. Still, she obeyed God, studied, and taught His Word. In the many locations we lived, God led her to teach Bible studies. Looking back, we see clearly God's call on her life—teach His Word.

Do you need to know your personal life goal to be effective for God? No! You will know it when God is ready. Meantime, do as He asks. But when you know your personal life goal, it will provide clear direction for the path God selects for you. Tread it daily! Recall it to guide your actions. If you don't follow this path, you will go the wrong way, your way. You will look for your gifts, find them and they might trap you. To be sure, when you see your gifts, you will try to use them in your way. That's looking backwards; your personal life goal does not flow *inevitably* from your gifts. God gives the personal life goal and then He equips you! Do you see the difference?

How do you get your personal life goal? Be alert to what God is doing in your life and work with Him in those areas. Take your eyes off you, your gifts, and your circumstances. If you don't know your personal life goal that's all right. Simply be alert to what God asks you to do, and do it. You will see a path; follow it. Don't look at your gifts; look at God.

Before she started teaching the Bible, my wife didn't think God gifted her to teach. Had she focused on gifts she would not have taught. Rather, she obeyed God's call, trusted Him to give her what she needed, when she needed it, and He did.

I got my personal life goal from God in my mid 40's, a few years after I surrendered to Christ. After I got it, God led me to start a non-charity ministry, and then led me out of my job as a business executive; this wasn't my goal.

At first, I did not appreciate what God was showing me, and I defined my personal life goal like this: "to serve Jesus whatever the cost," in essence this is part of every believer's general life goal. My executive job fitted that path and I was sure God wanted me to continue my business career until 65. Later, as I listened and did His other matching goals, I realized the personal life goal He gave me was this: "as He leads, teach biblical stewardship of time, talents and money." Everything I do need to show this. At age 55, He led me to my present unpaid full-time non-charity ministry, Managing God's Money.

In summary, God calls each believer to take part in fulfilling the *Great Commission*. Has He shown you your role? That's your life goal, your mission on earth that stays with you until He chooses to change it. Often, like Joseph, you do preparatory tasks, but you don't understand their later effects.

God gives you your personal life goal; you do not choose it. So don't try to find your *gifts* and then try to use them. Rather, ask God to show you what He wants done; He will equip you.

If you feel rushed continually, unfulfilled, dissatisfied with your job, first check your attitude; next, ask God if you are working His goal or yours. Besides, you will have difficulty hearing His material goals.

Material Goals

As I said earlier, your personal life goal is similar to a company's mission statement. *Material goals,* on the other hand, are specific tasks God selects to teach you to depend on Him and draw closer to Him.

You must be open continually to hear, believe, and obey God. Here are examples of God's clear, complete, concise material goals that not one of these folks requested:

- Noah to build the ark[18]
- Nehemiah to rebuild the wall around Jerusalem[19]
- Jonah to go to Nineveh[20]
- Joshua to lead Israel to the promised land [21]

Life and material goals need vision that call for faith that comes from hearing and understanding God's Word. If God's goal isn't clear, complete, and concise to you, ask Him to clarify. A material goal *to attend university* is fuzzy and you can rationalize why you can or can't do it. God's material goals will be specific, such as, university name, particular degree, when, how you will finance it. Look at His goals to people He called. To be sure, if He is your Lord and Saviour, He has called you.

Often His material goals will be beyond your imagination, and will take you outside your comfort zone; but that's all right because they won't fail. Look at Noah and others. They were ordinary humans like us.

Don't confuse the material goal you get from Him with the *plan* to do it. The *goal* is the destination — *where* He wants you to be, or *what* He wants you to do, and it's fixed. The plan, on the other hand that I will discuss in section II, shows *how* to get to the end, or *how* to carry out the goal and can be fuzzy.

You could get from God, material goals with specific details for topics such as these:

- Long-Term Goals
  - Retirement: Does God want you to retire; when; where; and then what?
  - Investments and Savings
- Short-Term Goals
  - Specific vacation
  - Specific education courses
- Financial Health Goals
  - Maximum Debt Ratio[22]
  - Debt Repayment Ratio[23]

It's easy to write material goals but difficult to do them consistently. Do them with God's help. Still, you need a means to track them.

Setting and Checking Goals

Doing God's material goals can absorb you so you forget the greatest commandment[24]—to love Him with all your heart, mind, soul and strength. You do not please Him by doing stuff. You please Him by obeying Him![25] That's it! Everything flows from this! Your emphasis must be on God, not on doing stuff. When you understand this, you will be able to understand and translate His material goals in clear, complete, concise goal statements.

If you were studying for your final math exams, what would be your goal statement? If you were like most folks, you would set a grade level—to pass, or to get at least a *B* or to get an *A*. That's not how God gives His material goals. He wants you to do your best, He will take care of the results, and so your goal for the math exam should be to do your best as you prepare for and write it. You would need to define *best*—such as doing homework, class assignment, studying and reading *X* hours five days a week, attending classes, and so on.

God equips you to do what He calls you to do. Your role: lean on Him and do it. Understanding biblical success will help you see this more clearly. Success[26] is a developing journey with these four parts:

- To know Christ
- To be secure in "who you are," and who you are "in Christ."
- To be the best you can, using your talents to the maximum degree possible and for His glory
- To accept and learn from this effort's results

So, after defining them clearly, how do you track your material goals?[27] Use forms in Appendices 3 and 4—Goal Statement Forms (GSFs) and Goal Tracking Forms (GTFs). *Count the cost* of each goal and check its individual parts—*control items* or *sub goals*— that are preconditions to doing the goal. With God's help, after looking at each goal's full effects, ask Him to show you His plan, His timing and His finance sources. A goal to finish a degree will have preconditions such as these that need separate sub goals:

1. Fulfill academic needs in a specific time.
2. Save fees at specific rate over a set time.
3. If you will be going back to school after working awhile, arrange alternate income—again, over a set time.
4. Arrange to handle family impacts in specific time.
5. Secure available time from work.
6. Identify tasks to *selectively neglect*—show what you will sacrifice and how you will handle their effects.

Often we confuse these preconditions with plans to carry out the goal, not realizing each precondition needs its own plan. In section II, we will discuss the planning procedure.

Use one form for each goal and show its control items. Ask the Lord to help you write each goal on a GTF. Writing it on this form, clearly, concisely, completely, and thinking about its control items, will help you see the full picture and understand more fully what God is asking you to do.

Goal definition can be a big challenge. In my eight years working in Japan, I appreciated the emphasis Japanese businesspeople placed on goal definition. In North America, often we rush ahead without understanding what to do and have to start over. Jesus is the believers' major advantage; before we act, we can ask Christ to clarify His goals. So, don't rush ahead to do the goal without understanding it. That approach will frustrate you and you might miss what God prepared for you simply because you didn't invest time at the start, talking and listening to God.

God needs to be integral to goal setting and doing procedures. A question to ask always is this: Am I working *for* or *with* God? If I work for God, I will be a doer, rushing always. If I work with God, I will be a listener, always wanting to hear before doing. Think about it.

Use Appendix 4 to check progress against each goal. This form is a useful tool, not a substitute for God. Some folks can see the picture and note progress without these forms, that's all right, don't use them. Just ensure you can record, check, and discuss goals and progress with the Lord.

Don't let the procedure become the goal and, or the god. A goal without a plan is like a hockey game without a puck! It won't happen!

Summary

If you haven't done so, settle your eternal worth today. After, look at your financial affairs and ask the Lord to show you how to move ahead.

Do you know God's plan for your life? Have you asked Him to show you? Or, is learning your gifts your focus? God prepared a special life goal for you. Invest time with Him to see what He wants you to do. If you can't see this life goal, just do as He asks and He will lead you where you need to be. He will equip you with time, talents, and money to do His tasks. That's His nature!

Think About This

"A man who was merely a man and said the sort of things Jesus said would not be a great moral teacher. He would either be a lunatic—on a level with the man who says he is a poached egg—or else he would be the Devil of Hell. You must make your choice. Either this man was, and is, the Son of God: or else a madman or something worse.[28]

Chapter Notes:

1. A debt free *lifestyle* means you do not incur debt for consumer items. As well, you do not try to buy a home apart from God. You will get a down payment and mortgage that fits your budget and allows you to give funds to God's work as He directs. You can be in debt today but decide not to borrow in the future and so live a debt free lifestyle after today.
2. John 14:6.
3. Hebrews 13:8; 2 Timothy 3:16.
4. John 10:27-30.
5. John 3:1-17.
6. Matthew 18:3.
7. 1 John 1:9.
8. Market value is the amount someone is willing to pay for an item, not what you think it is worth. Beware; don't use your home's high market value to get more loans. As you reduce your mortgage, don't use the equity released to buy stuff.
9. Short life-cycle consumer items like consumer electronics, clothes, groceries and other items you put on your credit card.
10. Include all loans' principal and interest payments in the period, including your mortgage.
11. 1 Timothy 2:3-4.
12. Genesis 12:1-3.
13. Genesis 41:38-45
14. 1 Samuel 16:1-13.
15. Acts 9:15.
16. Matthew 3:1-3.
17. Matthew 4:19; 8:22; 9:9; John 1:43.
18. Genesis 6:14-22.
19. Nehemiah 2:12-20.
20. Jonah chapters 1 and 3 – Here we see a disobedience-obedience cycle.
21. Joshua 1:2-5.
22. Maximum Debt Ratio represents the total of all loans on the material worth statement ($160,500), as a percent of liabilities and equity of $199,000. For this person it was 81% at 30 June ((160,500/199,000) X 100).
23. The Debt Repayment Ratio is the total loan payments (including mortgage principal and interest) for the period (one year) as a percentage of gross income for the period.
24. Matthew 22:37-40.

25. 1 Samuel 15:22-23, Micah 6:6-8
26. Michel A. Bell, *Managing God's Time,* (Enumclaw, WA: WinePress Publishing, 2004) pages 111-120.
27. Your *life goal* is on going. It ends in heaven. You would not track it except to ensure your material goals do not contradict it.
28. C.S. Lewis, *Mere Christianity*, (New York: The MacMillian Company, 1960), p.40-41.

5

Debt—Costs, Effects, and the Way Out

*A*re you in debt? Do you know the financial cost? The emotional cost? How much interest, including mortgage interest, did you pay last month? Last year? How does this compare with amounts you left in God's Kingdom?

Personal debt is a challenge to many Canadians and Americans. Up to the mid 1990s, Canadians and Americans spent less than their *personal disposable income.*[1] But since 1996, Canadians and Americans spent almost all their disposable income, saving little.[2] Canadians and Americans piled up debt at different rates: Between 1983 and 1991, Americans carried a greater debt load, and from 1992 to 2000, Canadians had the greater debt load. By 2005, for each disposable income dollar, *Canadians owed $1.16, Americans $1.24*[3] To be sure, household debt continues to challenge North Americans.

What's the answer? It's not Government intervention; nor lower interest rates from finance companies or others, neither is it more and cheaper student loans. Rather, it lies with us. Each person needs to accept his and her responsibility, and learn to be patient and humble. As well, we must learn to live on what we earn, save to buy stuff, and stop chasing unaffordable living standards.

Most of all, we must know our views of borrowing. Among Christians, I have noticed two opposing views. One group believes borrowing is not biblical, the other thinks it is normal and unavoidable. Answer? Neither. Still, some folks believe they borrow only when they get funds directly from banks or other financial institutions. They miss non-obvious borrowing forms. To get on the same page, let's define borrowing. *The New Concise Oxford Dictionary*, 9th edition, defines borrowing as follows:

- Acquiring temporarily with the promise or intention of returning
- Obtaining money in this way

Here is my practical money borrowing definition: *You borrow money when you commit to spend future amounts you do not hold today, to use someone's services, goods, and, or money today.* Thus, you borrow when you use a credit card and don't pay the full balance. I want to stress that a credit card is a cheque and *not a funding source.* A quick look at the credit card's evolution will clarify.

Credit Cards

In 1914 Western Union introduced the first *charge card.* Today, charge cards exist but are not popular with individuals. Like a credit card, a charge card is a means to get short-term funds—about one month—to buy goods or services. It's not a loan, so it does not carry an official interest rate. But if holders don't pay the full monthly balances, they must pay a fee of up to 5% of the card's balance, and face possible use limit or card cancellation. The charge card is like a cheque that clears in about one month.

According to *Encyclopaedia Britannica*, credit cards' use started in the United States during the 1920s when individual companies such as hotel chains and oil companies issued them to customers for buys *at those businesses.* Credit cards' use rose significantly after World War II. And In 1950, *Diners Club International* issued the *first universal credit card* that people could use at *selected stores and businesses.* Diners Club charged cardholders a yearly fee that they billed yearly or monthly.

In 1958, American Express introduced another major *universal card.* Later, banks issued their universal credit cards. Today in Canada over 100 million banks and merchants' credit cards exist, and in the USA about 1.2 billion. In Canada, 60% of credit card users pay monthly balances in full compared with 40% in the USA.

To learn to use a credit card, get a card with a low limit, not more than $500, open a bank account and deposit $500. Arrange with your bank to pay the monthly card balance fully from that account. Monthly, top up your bank account with the amount the bank withdraws to pay the previous month's credit card charges. So, if in month one you charged $300, which the bank paid from your account in month two, leaving a $200 balance in month two, deposit $300 to the account to restore it to $500. Repeat the cycle. Beware; unless you use a spending decision procedure similar to the *Affordability Index* in chapter 11, you will spend more when you use a credit card.

When you use a credit card, use it like a cheque or charge card and pay monthly balances in full. When I lived in Japan, I liked their credit card payment arrangement so much I got my Canadian bank to do the same. Over 13 years ago, I arranged with my Canadian bank to pay in full my monthly credit card balance from my chequing account. On the due date, the credit card company gets its money automatically, so my credit card is a charge card, like a cheque.

Returning to the borrowing definition, you borrow when you accept financing to buy items. Though not obvious, you borrow when you lease a car. Leasing and borrowing money have the same effect: to use merchants' goods or services today, you take on responsibility to pay them from future income. Under a car lease, you agree today to a future payment to use the car for a fixed future period.

Co-signing[4] a loan for another person is another borrowing form not recognized readily. When you co-sign a loan you agree to accept responsibility to repay if the borrower can't pay—potentially you become the borrower (until the other party pays the loan) and lender (if the party doesn't repay the loan).[5] Read Proverbs 11:15 about co-signing or guaranteeing a loan: "He who is guarantor for a stranger will surely suffer for it, but he who hates being a guarantor is secure." The same principle applies when you guarantee a loan for a family member. You become the borrower and must repay if your family member can't or won't repay.

When someone asks you to co-sign a loan, reflect on this biblical advice. Don't co-sign unless you accept that if asked, you must be ready to repay the loan. Further, *you shouldn't co-sign if you know co-signing will encourage delinquency.* But as for all decisions, ask Jesus to direct you.

The Borrower is the Servant of the Lender

What else does the Bible teach about borrowing? Scripture does not prevent borrowing, but it shows it negatively. Proverbs 22:7 says, "The rich rule over the poor, and the borrower becomes the lender's slave." But it's clear that when you borrow you should repay.[6] Apostle Paul re-enforces this message in Romans 13:8: "owe nothing to anyone except to love one another; for he who loves his neighbor has fulfilled the law."

Besides reminding us to pay our debts when due, Apostle Paul reminds us of our debt to love one another. As fallen people, we owe a debt we can never repay. Graciously, when He died on the cross, Jesus Christ paid the supreme price for this debt—for our past, present and future sins.

Believers need to start loving each other as Jesus commanded and respond to genuine crises in other believers' lives—not only with money, but also with care and attention. Ask Jesus to help you respond to crises you face as Job did.[7] Jesus will help you live *upside down*[8] in a world where the focus is *on my circumstances and me.*

Can you imagine what would happen, if daily we carried out the greatest and second greatest commandments?[9]

Borrowing Assumptions

Though not dealing with borrowing directly, James 4:13-15 (NIV) shows why it isn't wise to borrow:

> Come now, you who say, "Today or tomorrow we will go to such and such a city, and spend a year there and engage in business and make a profit." Yet you do not know what your life will be like tomorrow. You are *just* a vapor that appears for a little while and then vanishes away. Instead, *you ought* to say, "If the Lord wills, we will live and also do this or that."

This passage shows at least three false borrowing assumptions:

1. The future will resemble the present.
2. You have no alternative.
3. Jesus sees as you see.

How do you react when your car stops working? Normally you borrow based on these three false assumptions.

First, you *assume the future will resemble the present,* so you borrow to repair or replace the car, assuming you can repay the loan from future income. But Apostle James says,

"...you do know what your life will be like tomorrow"! Will you have a job? Will there be another crisis? God alone knows the future, so you must consult Him before acting.

We see the second false assumption—*you have no alternative*—in this statement: "I must repair my car to go to work." You overlook the *wait; seek God's solution,* alternative that's available always. So you panic, and place your eyes on your circumstances, away from God and His solution. In this assumption, you act like God is asleep and doesn't know your condition. You forget you don't know, but He knows the perfect solution. Is there a message in the broken car?

The third assumption, Jesus sees as you see, *puts God in a box,* and is the most destructive. When the car breaks down you want to replace it today. But is the car the right transport? Do you try to understand your transport needs? Replacing a car with a car assumes you need a car. But you don't need a car; you need transport that might not be a car! So you need to ask God for His solution that could exclude money. Perhaps you should carpool until you save funds. Or, God might be teaching you humility and dependence on Him!

James reminds us to look to the eternal and seek God's will. Don't lean on you, lean on God! Faced with challenges with the car, washing machine, stove, how do you act? Do you seek God's peace and ask Him to show you His path? Scripture tells us to seek God's peace. Philippians 4:6-7 affirms this:

> Be anxious for nothing, but in everything by prayer and supplication with thanksgiving let your requests be made known to God. And the peace of God, which surpasses all comprehension, will guard your hearts and your minds in Christ Jesus.

When we seek and get God's peace, we will see solutions He prepared and then we will trust Him for His results.

Praying for a Financial Miracle

Praying for a *financial miracle* tells God the *results you want,* which suggests your solution is best. Yet, only He knows the future. To learn humility, dependence, sharing, caring or other trait, you might be better off without a car! After my wife reflected on her bad car accident, she learned:

1. God did not cause the accident, but He allowed it.
2. He wasn't ready to bring her home.
3. God wanted her to learn from this accident. Before the accident, many tasks occupied her, including finishing a degree at *Briercrest Bible College*; she needed to slow down. She heard, thanked God for His love, and slowed down.

When you ask for a financial miracle, you take your eyes off God and His message in the broken down car, washing machine, or other item. It is like giving your sick five-year-old child, candy because she asks for candy, rather than giving her the prescribed medicine. You would never do this, yet this is what you expect from God!

Your heavenly Father wants you to bring your needs to Him. The need is not money but stuff like food, clothing, shelter, or transport. Besides, you must understand that to grow closer to Jesus, you need to bear results of poor decisions, and the effects of your disobedience.

Don't put Jesus in a box. Rather, expect Him to treat you much better than you would treat your five-year-old child or grandchild. In John 14:14, Jesus said, you may ask Him for anything in His name, and He will do it. Ask Him to give you what He knows is best for you.

When you think you need to borrow to buy a *needed* item or service, stop, ask God to show you if you are working His goal or yours. Recall David's words in Psalm 18:30, ask Jesus to help you understand His plan to reach His goal. David said,"As for God, his way is blameless; the word of the Lord is tried; He is a shield to all who take refuge in him."

Not enough funds might be God telling you to turn away from what you are doing and do what He wants done. Then again, it might be the results of your poor choices, so you need to live with and learn from your condition. Often, folks will tell you to "rise above your circumstances"; don't, you need them to grow, but you need Jesus' help to *walk through them.*

These days, society defines results of many *sinful actions* as *medical conditions*—gluttony is sinful, obesity is the result; spending God's money wastefully to *feel good* is sinful, debt is the result. As well, society encourages *deflection speech* to remove responsibility for actions. Folks blame parents, teachers, siblings, merchants, Governments, and others for different behaviours. Have you noticed? Many say they don't have time, a silly deflection meaning they have not performed well in available time—they failed to work with right priorities. Then again, some folks borrow to buy stuff, fall deep in debt, blame merchants, and then pray for a financial miracle. They want God to give them money to pay off their debts. They don't want to deal with behaviour issues.

God is gracious and merciful, but He is just. Why should He give you money to allow you to continue bad practices? He loves you too much to give you your *financial miracle;* instead, He will be with you to help you learn from your circumstances.

Financial Cost of Borrowing

Interest has been around a while. Ten Old Testament references (in the NIV) counsel lenders against either charging interest on loans to the poor or charging excessive interest. The only New Testament reference is in the parable of the *Talents* in Matthew 25:27 and Luke 19:23. The essence of this parable is neither about money nor banking.

Warren Wiersbe in his *Be Series*[10] on the New Testament states that Talents represent opportunities to use our abilities.

The servant in the parable did nothing with his Talent, probably thinking it was so small it would make no difference. In God's eyes, nothing is too small. So, the master in the parable told the servant who hid his one Talent in the ground: "Then you ought to have put my money in the bank, and on my arrival I would have received my money back with interest." In essence use what God gives you, don't hide it!

Back to interest; it is the cost for money someone (or institution) lends you. Long ago, the lender was a bank, but not today. Merchants earn huge profits from interest, but often what they tell you is not what you get. To move their inventories, merchants seduce you with slogans such as, *no payment until …* months or years ahead. You rush to get products. When the payment date comes, you don't have funds and you decide to ask the merchant for a loan. Gladly, the merchant gives you the loan with interest starting from the date you took the product! Did you get that? Let me repeat:

January 1st you get furniture for *no payment until December 31st"*	Cost $5,000
December 31st you can't pay, so the merchant gives you a loan	Loan $5000
Interest on the loan for one year will be around 30% *before taxes*	Interest $1500
The loan at January 1st Year 2, grows rapidly to $6,500: Cost $5000 and interest during the *no payment* period $1,500.	Loan $6,500

If you thought you got a good deal because you used the furniture for one year at no cost, think again! Sadly, you would not see this clearly when you took the furniture. The merchant will not be out-of-pocket. Imagine if funds spent on these transactions went to the kingdom!

Then again, some folks' loan payments never lower their loans because they pay less than interest charges. If you paid $100 monthly, you would never repay this $6,500 loan at 20% (or higher) yearly interest rate.

As well, some folks do not understand loan terms: "a.p.r," compounding period, and so on. APR means *annual percentage rate*—the interest rate percent that applies for one year. So 18% a.p.r on your credit card balance means 1.5% monthly (18 divided by 12). This is important because some merchants quote the low number, 1.5%, and you might not understand it means 18% each year.

Borrowings' financial costs aren't obvious in other ways: To pay interest costs, first you earn income, pay taxes, and then from the rest, you pay interest. Most of us don't know the effect of paying interest from after-tax funds. Strapped for cash you borrow, considering the repayment amount only, rather than the full cost. So, when you charge an item on your credit card, you think it's all right to leave a balance and pay interest that could go instead to fund God's work.

Let's look at the true cost of a typical departmental store credit card (see next page):

The cost on the credit card might be 28.5%, but to this person whose top tax rate is 30%, it is 40.7%. So, to pay $ 28.5 interest, this person must earn $40.7, pay taxes at 30% ($40.7*.30=$12.2) and then pay the credit card interest of $28.5. Since you spend after-tax dollars, you spend more than you think.

Department store credit card interest charge	28.5 % (after-tax)
Top personal tax rate *assumed* at 30%. So you take home 70% of your gross earnings. You get the true cost by dividing 28.5 after-tax by your after-tax percent (70%) that applies to your income. So, if you take 30% of 40.7, you get to the after-tax cost of 28.5.	40.7% (28.5/0.7)
So, to pay $28.5 in interest, you must earn this amount before tax	$40.7
Pay taxes at 30%	12.2
Take home after-tax (to pay the credit card interest)	$28.5

Emotional Cost of Borrowing

Perhaps the most significant borrowing cost is the effect on the family. Folks don't realize families' debts can create a major emotional burden on husband, wife, and children. As loans rise, so do family tensions, tearing apart families. That's why research shows consistently, money triggers most arguments in marriages. I know families where one spouse has not had a good night's sleep in years because she worries about their deepening debts!

Still, folks take on extra debt without thinking about its impact on present financial commitments. Later, monthly spending seems heavier than imagined, causing even greater emotional turmoil. The emotional cost saps their energies, causing them to take their focus from God—they stop communing with Him, and stop doing His work.

For your personal health and family's sake, get a grip on personal finances!

Interest Income

The other side of interest on loans is interest on deposits. You deposit funds with institutions, confident the funds are safe. You do not care (most people do not know) that banks do not keep deposits in their vaults. They lend more money than they take in. When the bank or financial institution gets a deposit, by law, it must keep a small percentage, but it will lend more than it has to you, someone else, or me (borrower). To the depositor, the bank will pay an interest rate (say 5%) lower than the interest rate it gets (say 9%) from the borrower. The 4% difference is the *spread* the bank keeps as a profit.

Besides the spread, the interest rate financial institutions charge on loans, comprise some of these items:

- Their cost and profit
- Their estimate of the risk of non-payment (the higher the risk the higher the interest rate charged)
- Their view of the quality of security provided by borrower (the closer to cash the better for them)
- Your credit history
- The loan's purpose

Good News

You don't have to borrow; you can save to buy stuff. Be patient; God is faithful and will supply your needs. What about a house, do you borrow? You can select the timing to buy a house.

Save an affordable down payment, get an affordable mortgage, and get God's timing—buy it in God's time using a down payment that fits your budget and removes the need for *mortgage loan insurance*. As well, ensure buying the house, doesn't lower funds God tells you to give to His kingdom. I discuss buying a house in chapter 14.

Strive to be debt free. First, pay off consumer debt, and then mortgage debts. Each believer knows what he needs to do to live debt free:

1. Get Jesus' PhD[11]
2. Trust in the Lord
3. Don't borrow except for a house
4. Spend less than you earn
5. Work with a budget
6. Start a *Capital Fund* for major buys and for emergencies.

Do you have the courage to go against *me-centered* Christianity and exercise radical obedience to Christ? Can you hear Jesus calling you? Slow down; don't let *hurry-sickness* trap you.

If you have no debt, rejoice! But beware; predators will entice you to spend wastefully. Hold Jesus' money with open palms as you seek His direction to give it away.

Sometimes you think you must borrow to provide for your family. I urge you strongly never to borrow as a first choice. Review the *GAS Principle*, the *money triangle* in chapter one, and *seek earnestly* to know God's will for you. He may be taking you and your family through the *refiner's fire* to *purify* you.[12] You wouldn't want to miss the resulting benefits, would you?

Getting Out Of Debt

Jesus Christ owns everything and never needs financial debts. Still, He will guide you to get out of debt. Believe with your pocketbook that Jesus owns everything and has promised to take care of your needs. As well, believe that nobody's circumstance is too big for Jesus. Start today to believe Jesus and be ready to accept your circumstance, especially the effects of poor judgment.

Jesus might not remove your financial debt in your timeframe, but He will remove the *financial burden* today; just ask Him! Then you will be able to look away from your circumstances and to Him.

The Case of the Vanishing Dollars

Step one toward financial debt relief is to remove the *debt burden*, transfer it to Jesus. Then, the financial stress will go and you will be able to focus on Jesus to hear His solutions to work off the financial debt that you must keep. Do you understand you can and should separate the financial debt from the emotional, mental, psychological, and sometimes physical burden? This is the first goal of the getting out of debt procedure: giving Jesus the debt burden. Only then will you be able to move to the next step to solve the *case of the vanishing dollars*. As you solve this case, Jesus will help you develop right ABCs about money.

If you are ready to surrender all to Christ, probably being in debt is the best place to be. It will not feel this way, but in hindsight, you will see God's hands and will marvel at His greatness! But beware; you need patience. Normally folks get in debt slowly, so it's reasonable to expect getting out will be slow. Slow down; don't miss lessons God will teach you as He guides you through the debt elimination procedure.

At this stage, the goal for an individual or couple is to learn *where* dollars went, *how* they got there, and then set up a procedure to prevent a recurrence. In essence, you want to answer these three questions:

1. What did I[13] buy?
2. What procedure did I follow *before* buying?
3. How can I prevent a repeat of getting into debt?

The getting out of debt procedure is *fact-finding,* not *finger pointing.* It needs husband and wife's commitment. You don't need to know *why* you spent funds. Each of us has a *good* reason he did it—don't go there, especially couples—please don't camp here!

Three preconditions must exist to follow the proposed Christ-centered approach. Ask Jesus to help you:

1. Focus on *changing you* rather than *changing* your condition or other folks.
   a. Entering this challenge willing to *learn* and to *change* will help you see clearly God's best.
2. Accept your condition. If you don't, you won't be able to see opportunities and blessings God prepared for the way out. You don't want God to lift your condition; rather, you want Him to guide you through them. That's how you will learn. Think about it!
   a. Many folks blame others, rather than see their roles as they drifted in debt. Usually folks get in debt because they lacked patience, faith, were too proud to seek help, were greedy, or a combination.
3. Try to see your condition as Jesus sees them.
   a. After you accept where you are, ask Jesus to show you the lessons He prepared for your growth. Ask Him to let you see and hear Him clearly.

You are ready to follow the Christ-centered procedure to help you understand *how* you got into debt, to prevent a recurrence, and to draw you closer to Jesus. Ideally, couples should work together as one unit as they take this journey. But, husband and wife do not grow at the same rate, so each family must decide how they will approach solving this case:

1. Get a special notebook; label it, the *Case of the Vanishing Dollars.*
2. Set a time—maximum one month—to discover *how*, not *why*, you got in debt. A key question will be this: before spending, what decision procedure did I follow?
3. Review sequentially, your spiritual life, ABCs, and financial affairs.
4. After each stage, write a *one-sentence conclusion* for that phase. After all three stages, list main categories *where funds went*, and then answer this question with yes, or no: *Did I spend most of the funds on needed items according to Matthew 6:33?*

My Spiritual Life: Has it been FLAT?

Prayerfully think about your present and recent spiritual life by asking: *Has my spiritual life been FLAT?* This is not a mechanical exercise; do it prayerfully, earnestly seeking to hear from God. Each person should answer these personal questions:

1. Have I been **Feeding** on Jesus' Word? (Hebrews 5:12-14).
   a. The issue is this: Have I been studying God's Word consistently, not merely, reading a two-to-three minute daily devotional, but investing time in His Word learning and growing closer to Jesus.
   b. Have I been seeking to be His disciple, wanting to follow Him and willing to give up all?
2. Have I been **Listening** to His voice? (Luke 10:38-41).
   a. Have I been investing time with God learning His goals and plans for my life?
   b. Have I been seeking His guidance over all areas of my life?
   c. Have I spent quantity time with Him routinely?

3. Have I been **A**way from church or home fellowship, and Bible study? (Acts 2:41-44)
   a. Have I been attending a Bible believing home fellowship or church where I am fed? Or have I been attending a church or home fellowship where the teaching is not biblical, but *tickles* my ears?
   b. Have I been studying the Word with a group seeking after Jesus?
   c. Have I been absent from church or home fellowship and Bible study routinely?
4. Have I been **T**alking to Jesus regularly? (Matthew 11:28-29; 21:22; Psalm 5:1-3; 1 Thessalonians 5:16-18)
   a. Have I been praying regularly, not asking for stuff, but trying to get to know Jesus better?
   b. Have I been praying to "change things" rather than to "change me"?

Before moving to the next section, ABCs, and *after prayer and reflection,* as God shows you, write a one-sentence conclusion about your spiritual life.

My Attitude, Behaviour, and Choices (ABCs)

In this section, you will get to the *heart* of your beliefs and practices. You act based on your beliefs. You choose based on your beliefs, your worldview. Again, each person should answer these personal questions:

1. What was my **A**ttitude toward money?
   a. Did I, do I, accept my stewardship responsibilities?
   b. Did I, do I understand I am Jesus' manager and should seek His guidance before I spend?
   c. Did I, do I understand I can't be God's manager unless I know Him intimately?

2. How did I **Behave** during the period?
    a. Did my **Behaviour** suggest I understand implications of God's ownership and my stewardship of money?
    b. Did I practice *keeping* or *tithing* (see chapter 9)?
    c. Did I use a budget or spending plan?
    d. Did I respond to advertising and easy credit terms?
    e. Did I spend for *needs* that could not wait? Did I practice these two essential words, *not now!*
    f. Did husband and wife agree to major buys?
    g. How did husband and wife solve money disputes that arose?
3. How did I **Choose** to spend?
    a. What decision procedure did I follow before spending?
    b. What were main *spending drivers?* What caused me to spend each time?
        i.   Did I spend for emotional relief?
        ii. Did I pray before spending?
        iii. Did I spend impulsively?

Before moving to the next section, finances, and after prayer and reflection, write a one-sentence conclusion about your ABCs.

Finances: Did I Have a GRIP on My (Our) Finances?

1. Did I work with **Goals**—a *life goal* and *material goals?*
    a. Do I have a life goal?
    b. Did I follow other goals?
    c. Were they from God?
2. **Review the past six months' spending;** where did funds go?
    a. If you don't have records such as bills, cheque stubs, credit card and bank statements, walk through the

house and list items bought recently. Use estimated prices if you don't have actuals.

   b. Where did I *get funds* to buy stuff during these
six months?

   c. Did I anticipate getting funds I didn't get?

3. Investigate features of all loans; what do they show?

   a. Do I know the annual percentage cost of each loan?

   b. Using present payment rates, do I know when I might
repay each loan? Sometimes paying minimum balances
on loans will never repay them.

   c. Do I realize a credit card is not a source of financing,
and I should use it only when funds are in the bank
and I can pay the full balance?

4. Do I have **Plans** in place to carry out God's goals?

   a. Did I work with a financial **plan**?

   b. Prepare a net worth statement; list items of value
you *own*—assets—less all your loans—liabilities. If
you need help to do this and the next item, see an
independent financial advisor.

   c. Prepare a debt repayment plan to erase loans, starting with the highest annual percentage cost loan. See
Appendix 5.

   d. Do I have assets I could sell to repay loans? Sell only
after prayer.

After prayer and reflection, write a one-sentence conclusion before moving on. So, did you have a GRIP on your finances?

What did you learn from working on this case? Do you
accept your findings? Again I beg you, don't rationalize why
you got here. You are here; work with God to move on. As the
Lord leads, *confess* misuse of funds; *repent—decide to change
your behaviour*—and ask God to give you a goal and plan to
become debt free in His time. Meanwhile, transfer the debt
burden to Christ as He requests in Matthew 11:28, "Come to
me, all you who are weary and heavy-laden, and I will give you
rest."

You might have to change your lifestyle as you bear the effects of poor choices. Prepare a budget and money map[15] to show lifestyle changes, such as less eating out. Assign responsibility for each budget category to relevant family members.

In the *Family Council*, get input from and discuss challenges, alternatives, budget, money map, and life style changes with family members. As well, go to Jesus and ask Him to show you how to change your life style, and the family's goals and plans to His. He will show you, but you need to be still and wait on Him.

After preparing and committing to a detailed loan repayment plan as in Appendix 5, as the Lord leads, ask creditors to lower interest rates. But do not consolidate or restructure loans[16] unless God shows you attitude and behavior changes you have made. Consolidation never works without these changes; indeed, without changed attitudes, it is the worst alternative because it gives you false hope.

Next, set up a spending decision procedure to avoid reentering the debt trap. Here is a suggested approach:

1. Never spend before praying.
   a. Use the Affordability Index in chapter 11 to help focus your prayers. As the name implies, it signals if you can afford an item before you spend. But even if you can afford to buy, consult Jesus before spending.
2. Decide to use cash to pay for all items except a home. And for a home, ensure you save a down payment that produces an affordable mortgage.
3. Couples should agree a joint spending approval path, and a dispute resolution procedure (see chapter 12)

You are ready to do it. Often folks need a specific action plan to get going. The best action plan comes from God, tailor-made for you. Ask Him to show you. Here is an example of an action plan you can mull over:

1. Surrender every area of your life to Christ. Accept

God's ownership and your stewardship of His funds. Ask Him to show you how to fund His work.

   a. Start lifestyle changes today.

   b. Identify vulnerable areas that might cause you to backslide and give them to Jesus—plug leaks.

2. Accept who you are, where you are, what you have, and what you need to do.
3. Covenant with Jesus not to buy stuff until you have funds.

   a. Cut up all credit cards, or put them in a plastic bag and then put the bag in the freezer.

4. Start to carry out PEACE Budgetary Control, discussed in Section II.
5. Set up accountability and reward procedures. Ask a trusted friend to hold you accountable to follow God's plan. Divide the plan in small steps to measure progress.
6. Depend on Jesus to fulfill your needs and to see you through this and other *crises*. He will.
7. Although listed last, this is important: You got in debt over a period; you will get out in time by God's grace. Be Patient! Remember nothing is impossible for God!

Summary

Because media advertising has been so effective, most people think it is acceptable to use their credit cards to buy goods and services they can't afford. I asked some high school students to define a credit card and this was their consensus: "A credit card is something you use to buy stuff when you don't have money." If you use your credit card only when you have matching funds in the bank, you will be treading the debt free living path.

Beware; borrowings' emotional cost can harm you and your family, and its financial cost transfers funds outside God's Kingdom. Let God do as He promised and guide your path His way and in His time. Seek Jesus rather than banks and financial institutions to provide your needs.

If you are in debt and worked on *The Case of the Vanishing Dollars,* I pray you gave God your *debt burden* and you have committed to live a radical debt free life under His guidance. You might look silly when you go against the world's view to fill your needs. I know; for over 10 years I have not owned a cell phone, don't have cable or satellite TV (I get over 20 channels with an outdoor antenna), rarely eat out; and don't buy stuff just because that's fashionable. Folks will think you are weird; but that's not the test. The test is this: Are you prepared to listen to God and do as He says, even if it's not popular?

Borrow only to buy a home. But ask God to show you His timing and to guide you to choose a down payment and mortgage that fits your household budget and doesn't take away funds He earmarked for His work.

Did you know you pay about $100,000 interest on a $100,000 mortgage @ 6% over 25 years? But if yearly on 31 December, you paid an extra $3,000, you would save $44,000 interest and you would repay the mortgage fully in 14 years, 11 years earlier.

God owns everything; has no debt, doesn't need debt. When He asks you to do a task, He will provide funds, so wait on His timing. If you don't get funds, maybe, it's not His best for you.

Think About This

As Missionaries of Charity, we are here to help the poorest of the poor in whatever form that takes, which is always Christ in His distressing disguise. We don't accept even one rupee for the work we do, as we do our work for Jesus. He looks after us. If He wants something done, He gives us the means. If He doesn't provide us with the means, then He doesn't want that work done.[17]

Chapter Notes:

1. Personal disposable income is personal income less income taxes and other mandatory deductions paid to government.
2. Peaking in 1982 in Canada at 20.2% and in the USA at 11.2%, personal savings rate (income less expenses and taxes) in 2005 was 1.2% in Canada, and -0.4% in USA.
3. Personal Debt, Statistics Canada, *Perspectives on Labour and Income*, January 2007.
4. Co-signing happens when a bank or other institution refuses to give you a loan and you ask some one to sign the loan agreement with you.
5. You become the borrower if the other party doesn't pay. You become the lender to that party, who will not be able to pay you.
6. Psalm 37:21
7. Job 1:20-22, Job 13:15, Job 42:5-6.
8. Romans 12:2.
9. Matthew 22:36-38.
10. Warren Wiersbe, *Be Series*: NT Volumes 1 & 2, Copyright © 1989 by SP Productions, Inc.
11. As a reminder, God's PhD is patience, humility, and dependence
12. James 1:1-6.
13. For couples, where these questions refer to *I*, read *we*.
14. Refer to Chapter 4
15. A money map is a budget for a trip or a short period.
16. If you have a loan with an interest rate of 10% and another with a cost of 15%, if possible, increase the 10% amount to reduce the 15% amount. Never do this unless God shows you attitude and behaviour changes you made, and you do not increase your total loans. At the end, your total loans must not increase; do it to reduce interest costs only.
17. Mother Teresa, *A Simple Path*, (New York: Random House, 1995), p. 64-65.

6

Money Value and Investing

This chapter is a tad technical, but if you don't know finance well, don't worry, *on your own* you won't have to know and apply the ideas discussed. Some you will grab quickly and start doing, others you won't think about until alone or with an advisor, you start looking deeply at giving, savings, and investing. I present these concepts and procedures so you *know about* them, not so you become expert using them. As you compare major spending alternatives, such as buying or leasing a car, retirement savings and investments, review each topic in this chapter and decide if you need to discuss them with a financial advisor, or if you are comfortable on your own. Though the topics might seem intimidating, I assure you, I have shown merely a smidgen of each, but most of all you do not need to use them on your own. I will discuss these:

- Inflation
- Time Value of Money
- Cash Flows

- Investing
- Tax Shield

Inflation

Does inflation affect the interest rate we get from banks and other financial institutions on our savings? Yes, it does. As well, inflation affects our spending and investing. Inflation is a general, continued rise in price levels in an economy. The most widely accepted inflation measure is the Consumer Price Index (CPI).

A CPI measures changes in retail prices of goods and services we buy. Governments calculate CPI movement over a specific period (one month), and for a precise *goods and services' basket.* If the government sets the CPI at 100 in year one and it rose to 150 in year 10, the goods and services basket prices' would have risen 50% over that period. Normally, governments keep the CPI for different regions and nationally.

Although inflation is under control in Canada and in the USA, still you must know its effects, because it can raise its ugly head anytime. If your savings or investments earn less than inflation, you lose spending power: If you got 5% on your bank deposits, and the inflation rate was 7%, you would be worse off because prices rose faster (7%) than your savings (5%).

Conversely, if you got 7% on savings and inflation was 5%, you would be better off; that's a *real return*—the difference between the interest and inflation rates is the *real interest rate.* The real interest rate is the relevant interest rate to assess savings and investment results. In our example it is negative 2% and positive 2% (5% - 7% = -2%, and 7% - 5% = +2%). When you discuss retirement, savings, investing, and your financial plan, you need to think about likely inflation effects.

Governments' Central Banks, such as the Bank of Canada, set inflation targets and use interest rate policies to try to *keep core inflation* in a *target zone*. Commercial banks link their key interest rates, such as deposit and mortgage interest rates, to the Central Bank's rate. When the Central Bank wants consumers to spend, it lowers the rate it offers to Commercial Banks, which lower their rates to customers for savings, loans and mortgages. Customers respond to lower rates and spend with loans. The reverse is true.

Outside this book's scope but a related and important issue to think about is the economy's growing dependency on consumer spending to keep it buoyant. Today it's about 55% of Gross Domestic Product (GDP),[1] and the government expects consumers to continue spending at current rates though that's feasible only by piling up more personal debt!

Time Value of Money

Because of inflation and interest on money that you will get or pay, normally $100 today is not worth the same as $100 you will get later. If today you deposited with a bank $100 at 5% interest, it would rise to $105 after one year ($100 + $5 interest). If you left it for another year, it would become $110.25 ($105 + $5.25 interest). Notice, in the second year, besides interest on $100 original deposit, you would get interest on the first year's interest of $5. This is *compound interest*—getting or paying interest on interest.

One dollar (or other amount) will double after 14, 10 and 8 years if the yearly interest rates are 5%, 7% and 9%. Table II shows how one dollar will grow (compound) when you reinvest interest earned; a ten-dollar deposit would produce ten times those numbers, twenty dollars twenty times, and so on.

Table II

Growth of $1 with Interest Reinvested

Years	Annual Rate of Return		
	5%	10%	15%
1	1.05	1.10	1.15
2	1.10	1.21	1.32
3	1.16	1.33	1.52
4	1.22	1.46	1.75
5	1.28	1.61	2.01
10	1.63	2.59	4.05
14	2.00	3.80	7.08
15	2.08	4.18	8.14
20	2.65	6.73	16.37
25	3.39	10.83	32.92

If you had to decide between getting $100 today and $110 in two years at 5% interest rate, you would be indifferent. Each has the same value today. Thus, the *present value (PV)* or today's value of $110 *(the future value - FV)* you would get in two years is $100. This present value idea will help you choose between spending or getting money today or later; use it for early loans and mortgages' repayments, comparing buying and leasing decisions, and investing.

Suppose you could choose to repay a $2000 loan. If repaid today you would get a 15% discount but if you repaid one year later, you would have to pay the full amount plus 5%. How do you evaluate these alternatives? Compare present values (today's values) of each as follows:

- The present value of $2000 payment today less 15% discount is $1,700, $2000 – (2000 x 15%)
- The present value of $2000 you will pay one year from today is $2000. If the interest rate is 5%, the future value (the value after one year) would be $2100 —$2000+(5% of $2000)

If you had the funds, you would repay this loan today and save $300 ($2000 - $1700).

In Table III, you see another and more powerful compound interest example. Here you save one dollar each *year-end* and accumulated interest. At the 10th year, the value would grow to $13.18 at a 6% yearly interest rate. If you saved $100 rather than $1, the value at year ten would be $1300.18 and so on. In Section II when I discuss the need to save, remember Tables II and III.

Table III

Growth from Saving $1 Every Year

Years	Annual Rate of Return		
	6%	10%	15%
1	1.00	1.00	1.00
2	2.06	2.10	2.15
3	3.18	3.31	3.47
4	4.37	4.64	4.99
5	5.64	6.10	6.74
10	13.18	15.94	20.30
15	23.27	31.77	47.58
20	36.78	57.27	102.44
25	54.86	98.34	212.77

I call compound interest the *multiplication principle* to show that interest on debt grows faster than interest on savings. In Table III, notice the difference in money growth at 6% and 15%. It's likely your savings might earn 6% or less, but you would pay more than 15% on unpaid credit card balances—take note!

Think about the multiplication principle when you consider your child's post secondary education. The Canadian Government encourages parents to save by giving incentives under two plans: Registered Education Savings Plan (RESP) and Canadian Education Savings Grant (CESG). If a parent sets aside $38.50 weekly and it earns 6% yearly, in 18 years with government *goodies* and compound interest, these savings would grow to almost $80,000. Still, many parents don't use these plans, but they let their children take student loans!

Parents, I pray that as you read about the *Capital Fund* in chapter 9 and the *Family Council* in chapter 12, the Lord will speak to you about saving for your children's post secondary education to avoid student loans. Mull over Apostle Paul's words in 2 Corinthians 12:14 to the Corinthian church about the parents responsibility to *save* for their children.

Cash Flows

Earlier we saw a *material worth statement* that I described as a *still* picture of what you owned (assets) and what you owed (liabilities). It changes when you get income, pay expenses, repay debts, buy or sell assets. To capture these changes, you need a *video camera* that we call a *cash flow statement.*

We divide this statement in two sections—*Inflows* and *Outflows*—as in Table IV. Inflows as the name implies show *cash coming in,* and *outflows, cash going out.* To prepare a cash flow statement for future expenses, you must know receipts and payments' timing.

Table IV

Cash Flow Statement

(Oct – Dec)

INFLOWS	Oct	Nov	Dec	Three Months
Gross Salaries	3150	3150	3150	9450
Interest income	11	11	11	33
Less: Giving to God ("Keeping")	(415)	(415)	(415)	(1245)
Less: Income taxes and other deductions	(885)	(885)	(885)	(2655)
Less: Capital Fund	(50)	(50)	(50)	(150)
Inflows	1811	1811	1811	5433
OUTFLOWS				
Rent	500	500	500	1500
Car Expenses – Loan repayment	300	300	300	900
Car Expenses – Gasoline	75	45	90	210
Car Expenses – Maintenance	0	0	90	90
Telephone	30	40	65	135
Entertainment and Recreation	125	160	200	485
Groceries	350	300	450	1100
Gifts	0	0	40	40
Outflows	1380	1345	1735	4460
Net Cash flow	431	466	76	973

You, not advisors, have the facts to prepare this statement. At first, preparing a cash flow statement might seem overwhelming to you, but the mystique goes when you realise it shows merely funds' flow timing: how much you plan to get, to spend, and the balance.

What conclusions can you draw from this cash flow statement? Do the net cash flow balances signal you will have surplus cash to spend or save? Probably; but you must review estimated spending over a longer period to know. Ensure you reserve funds that build up monthly to pay expenses that occur irregularly, such as car maintenance, Christmas gifts and so on. Don't spend cash that builds up during the year unless you use *PEACE Budgetary Control* and it shows a genuine cash surplus.

The cash flow statement is a key report to help prepare your budget. Ideally, you would build a cash flow statement for the twelve-month budget period to see timing of projected spending.

Investing

Investing is another spending form, and like all spending we must go to the Lord and understand His best and our motives. Before investing, first understand differences between, *saving, investing, speculating* and *gambling*. These are the *Concise Oxford Dictionary's* definitions:

- *Save:* Reserve, keep for future use, refrain from spending
- *Invest:* Apply or use for profit
- *Speculate:* Invest in stocks etc., in the hope of gain but with the possibility of loss
- *Gamble:* Take great risks in the hope of substantial gain, a risky undertaking or attempt

Note; invest, speculate and gamble include risks to different degrees. Savings do not. So, don't invest, speculate, or gamble with funds you earmark for savings. Even if not earmarked for savings don't use God's money to speculate or gamble. Investments can be safe, low risk with modest returns, or unsafe, risky, with possibly high returns. It depends on your goals and motives.

Spending is about your ABCs, so get advice to help you learn right attitudes for investing. Tell your investment advisor you don't gamble or speculate with God's money. Even so, the best approach is to stay close to the Lord, obey His commands, and remember:

1. Investing is about the future that only God knows.
2. The first and highest yielding investment is to *store treasures in heaven.*

Let me mention briefly a few investing matters. If you use an investment professional, I pray my comments will help you *oversee your investments.* If you don't, I pray they will complement your knowledge as you invest. These pointers come from over 15 years investing funds God entrusts to my wife and me.

The first question to answer about investing is this: Should a Christian invest? Why doesn't he give away funds he doesn't *need* in his household budget? The answer is simple: do what God says. God wants us to use time, talents and everything He gives us for His glory.[2] This could include investing under His direction, or giving away funds as He leads.

I have invested funds for years based on clear goals my wife and I believe God has shown us. Most important we do not invest for our account, but for His. We follow formal written guidelines. When He says give funds away, we say, "Yes sir; how much? Where? And we do it!

Chapter 11 of my *Managing God's Money: 7 Branches Workbook* shows *investment preconditions* I won't repeat here, except for these:

1. Ensure you are listening to God and funding the Great Commission as He shows you.
2. Pay off consumer debts, start a *Capital Fund,* repay your mortgage, and then you are ready to invest.

After you meet the preconditions and before you start investing, you need to know the *players, procedures, and principles.*

Players

Let's look at four important players:

1. You
2. Companies' managements
3. Security analysts
4. Investment Advisors

When you choose to invest, *you* will be the first and most important player and so you need to know and be comfortable with what you will be doing. Before you start investing, accept there will be risks and find out your and your spouse's risk tolerance.[3] Ask God how much risk He will accept. Agree these other matters with your spouse early:

1. Expected return on investments (stock markets rise and fall).
2. Investment period (when will you need funds invested).
3. How much funds will you set aside to invest?
4. How will funds set aside affect the family budget, including amounts to go to God's work?

Decide you will not borrow to invest even if your advisor shows numbers suggesting you could *make money* borrowing to invest. Understand your job is not to *make money.* Governments *make money* when they print it. Don't think of *making money*, think of earning investment income (including gains from non-speculative investment sales), or you might move away from investing to speculating, the essence of borrowing to invest. Called *financial leverage,* borrowing to invest could yield significant profits, but you could lose huge amounts if investments don't work out. Don't expose God's funds to speculating! When you follow the *earning income* mind-set rather than the *making money* mind-set, you will look at and accept more reasonable and attainable returns. Accept and surrender your greed nature to the Lord, if you don't, you will drift to the making money mind-set.

What can you expect from your investments? Expect interest, dividends, capital gains, and sometimes capital losses.[4] There is a direct correlation between expected return and risk, the higher the expected return, the greater the risk. Lower risk investments include government treasury bills and Canada Savings Bonds. High-risk investments you should avoid include *futures, foreign exchange trading, options trading.* Mutual funds' risks vary, so you need to know each fund's details. Most of all, ensure God is central to decisions.

The second player is companies' managements. Regularly, business leaders tell the public about their companies' expected earnings. Called *guidance,* Chief Executive Officers, CFO's and, or other executives look at the current and next period or periods, and based on their information, give their best earnings' estimate. Some leaders lied, created false accounts, and went to jail.

Notice in the following management forecast you need to decide if you agree with management's view that its earnings will grow in *double digits* over the next three years. As well, before you invest in this stock, you need to decide the likely effects on its results of outstanding lawsuits:

Reuters
Merck boosts 2007 earnings forecast; shares rise Wednesday February 28, 8:15 am ET CHICAGO (Reuters) - Drugmaker Merck & Co. Inc.
(NYSE: MRK - News) boosted its 2007 earnings forecast on Wednesday, based on early revenue indications from a range of products, sending its shares up nearly 3 percent in early electronic trading. The company

expects first-quarter earnings of between 63 cents and 67 cents a share, excluding restructuring charges related to site closures and job cuts. Analysts had on average expected earnings of 60 cents a share, according to Reuters Estimates.

Merck forecast 2007 earnings of $2.55 to $2.65 per share excluding special items, compared to Wall Street estimates of $2.63. The company expects net earnings of between $2.40 and $2.55 a share.

Merck said last month that it expected 2007 earnings of $2.51 to $2.59 a share, excluding restructuring charges, and it said it was on track to deliver double-digit compound annual earnings growth by 2010, excluding one-time items and restructuring charges. The company said the forecast does not include any reserves for litigation related to lawsuits over the withdrawn painkiller Vioxx. Merck's shares rose 2.9 percent to $44.45 in electronic trading before the market opened.

Third and probably most important, are folks who study businesses to predict their results. These *security analysts* specialize in industries and companies, provide research, company valuation reports, and recommend folks buy, sell, and hold stocks. Some analysts lied, cheated, and went to jail.

Here is an analyst's recommendation in February 2007 about Apple Inc.'s stock price:

Citigroup's Richard Gardner this morning upgraded his rating on Apple (NasdaqGS: AAPL) to Buy from Hold, while maintaining his $105 price target on the stock [the stock traded at $85 when I read this recommendation, $20 less than the target]. He also maintained his current EPS [Earnings per share] estimates of $3.46 a share for the September 2007 fiscal year and $3.88 for fiscal 2008.[5]

Fourth is the *investment advisor*. In chapter 18, I discuss how to choose a financial advisor, and at this section's end, I comment briefly on choosing an investment advisor. Meantime, I want to stress the difference between someone who *advises for a fee only* (an advisor), and someone who explains investment features while persuading you to buy investment products (a salesperson). Keep in mind this difference.

Don't let someone's title affect your view of his job, look at what he does. I will show a section of this Wall Street Journal piece that shows what happened to some titles over the years. Called, "How to Pick a Financial Planner," the article comments on the transition in financial salespersons titles' from salespeople to advisors or planners:

> "Nobody agrees on which way the stock market is headed these days, but everyone wants to tell you how to invest. Stockbrokers, insurance agents, bankers, certified public accountants and even some lawyers are vying to make money by advising where to put yours."

Why are these *players* important to you? A major influence on a company's stock[6] price is its future earnings. So, if a company's management, a security analyst, or an investment advisor misleads you about a company's future performance, the prospect of profit might lead you to buy those shares to resell them. Still, you might read in the press about this company's huge earnings growth forecast and like a sheep, follow others blindly to buy this stock. That's why it is important to buy stocks and bonds as investments rather than on hunches or other information, just to *make money*.

So how should you respond to information from business executives, security analysts, and investment advisors? Watch out; *be on guard for your greed nature to rise* to *let you accept* information that sounds good, but isn't true! Listen to these *players*, look at your goals, ask the questions I suggest later, and ask the Lord to lead you. But know; *if a statement or forecast is too good to be true, it isn't true!*

Procedures

Get to know differences between *stocks, bonds, mutual funds, savings certificates,* and other financial instruments. You *own* a share of the company when you own its stock; the company *might* pay dividends regularly.

You *lend* money to a company or government when you own a bond; the company or government *will* pay interest.

And you own a *piece* of a collection of investment instruments when you own a mutual fund; the mutual fund *might* pay dividends and, or interest.

Selling stocks and mutual funds could create *capital gains or capital losses.* If you keep bonds until they *mature,* companies and governments will repay you. Unlike stocks and bonds, professional managers manage mutual funds and charge fees that usually you do not see.

Another important matter to consider is securities' *liquidity.* Will you be able to sell or redeem your investments quickly at or higher than your cost? Savings in term deposits are *illiquid.* You can't withdraw money before the term's end without paying a significant penalty. Some mutual funds are liquid; others are not so liquid because they have fees if you sell before a set time.

Marketability is important when selecting investments. Publicly listed securities trade on *stock markets or stock exchanges* (in Toronto, the *TSX*). Like all markets, stock exchanges are places where buying and selling *listed* stocks and bonds happen. You can't buy or sell direct on the market, you need to go through a salesperson—titles vary, some suggesting a *salesperson* is an *investment advisor,* so always look behind the title to the role.

If you decided to buy 100 shares in ABC Company, if it's the first time ABC is selling its shares (called an *Initial Public Offering,* an IPO),[7] ABC would get the cash. After the first time, the seller of those 100 shares gets the cash, not ABC Company.

Full-service brokers buy and sell investment securities, charge large fees, will tell you about investment securities, and will give you other information to help you decide to buy and sell investments. They get commissions when they sell and when they buy for your account. Thus, you need to look out for your interest. They are in a *conflict of interest* when they *advise* you.

I use the significantly cheaper alternative, *discount brokers*. They buy and sell for you but give no information to persuade you to buy or sell; they merely transact your buy or sell requests for a much lower fee than full-service brokers charge. You need to know what you are doing to use a discount broker.

Principles

According to the 2006 Stock Trader's Almanac, $10,000 invested in the *Dow Jones Industrial Average* on *November 1* and sold on *April 30* yearly from 1950 would net ... nearly $490,000 for an average 7.9% return. Meanwhile, $10,000 invested and sold during the opposite period, *May 1* to *October 31,* would have lost the investor $502. This has nothing to do with stock or bond selection, or financial skills; it's buying and selling at different dates. I mention it to show that some folks buy and sell without looking at company fundamentals. I don't recommend you follow this or other practice that doesn't look at company fundamentals.

Investing can be as complex or simple as you decide. Still, it's about the future that only God knows. But if you follow a few procedures and get to know a few basic principles, you will be able to oversee your investments by *providing guidelines to your advisor.* The first principle to note is the need to write *clear goals and working guidelines* about your motives:

- Why are you investing? Are you investing to get *more* to invest?

- Are you investing for retirement? Or, are you planning to give away funds as the Lord leads?
- When would you buy or sell? Why would you sell?

To help answer these questions and to develop your guidelines, here are seven important principles to keep in mind:

1. *Seek God's* guidance to write clear goals.
2. *Own* the investment procedure; keep it *simple* because it can be simple.
3. *Invest*, don't gamble, or speculate; surrender your greed nature.
4. *Understand* stock valuation before *choosing* a stock.
5. *Understand* its makeup before investing in a *mutual fund*
6. *Choose* an investment *advisor*, not a salesperson.
7. *Be accountable* to follow God's guidelines

Seek God's Guidance

It's God's money so ensure you listen, hear, and respond to Him. Henry T. Blackaby and Richard Blackaby in *Experiencing God Day-By-Day*[8] say this:

Obedience to God's commands comes from the heart. When you begin struggling to obey, that is a clear indication that your heart has shifted away from Him.

Many folks lose their aim when they start investing and see possibilities to *make money*. As Jesus reminds us in Luke 12:15, *be on your guard against all greed.* That's why you need to ask God to show you His goals, and then write them. When they come from God, they will be clear. As well, ask Him to show you His plans, the steps to reach the goal. Husband and wife should be on the same page.

Own and Keep the Investment Procedure Simple

You are investing God's money and so He has the final decision. If you use an investment advisor, he works for you, so tell him your goals. His job is to help you reach them. Based on your age and years to retirement, he might tell you how your portfolio should look. Still, don't accept his view without prayer. He might use general *diversification rules* based on your age, such as 60% stocks, 20% bonds, 10% mutual funds, and 10% cash.

I believe in a portfolio with a few established, dividend-paying stocks, selected after research. Some utility stocks I treat like bonds. So my portfolio mix isn't typical for my age, it has mainly stocks. I listen to the Lord, and as He leads, I sell or donate securities. You are unique and God is in charge, so listen to God to decide your portfolio mix. He could tell you to place all funds in a low interest savings account!

Keep what you do simple even if you use an advisor. Don't invest in companies you don't understand broadly. For example if you plan to buy General Electric's stock, you need to understand it is diverse; it's in the entertainment industry (owning NBC), its products include commercial and military aircraft jet engines, medical diagnostic imaging systems, it has a finance arm, and much more. You do not need to know details of each business; just enough to appreciate you won't get a good feel for this huge conglomerate. Still, think like an owner and ask; if I owned this company, what would I want to know about it? Am I comfortable with its complexity?

Invest, Don't Gamble, or Speculate; Surrender Your Greed Nature

Your attitude decides if you invest, gamble, or speculate. You could study a company and decide to buy its shares because they fit your goals. Later, you would sell them if the long-term goals (from God) or other conditions you defined before buying, changed. That's investing. If you *heard* that same company was *doing well*, and bought those shares intending to sell shortly to *make some money*, you would be gambling and speculating.

To help you pray about investing and to invest wisely, use *facts*, not *tips* from friends, associates or others. Listen to God, ask questions, and don't follow the crowd. Most folks buy and sell for the wrong reasons and at the wrong times. They buy because the stock price is rising and sell when it is falling, rather than doing the opposite based on proper evaluation. MIT Professor Lester C. Thurow in a 17 April 2001 article in the Boston Globe titled, *Market Crashes Born of Greed,* highlights the greed that drives many people to "invest", and investors' *herd mentality:*

> "... Greed leads to stock market crashes. Go back to the first capitalist stock market crash—tulip mania in Holland in the 1600s. At the peak of the boom, four black tulip bulbs bought one of those nice row houses along the canals in Amsterdam. At the time, everyone knew it was crazy... there was a time when eight tulip bulbs bought a house.
>
> What was true in the 17th century is true in the 21st century. The high tech stock market crash now underway is not hard to explain. ... What has to be explained is not the fall in prices but how the stock market prices of companies with no revenues, no profits, and no business model could have been so high a year ago. And the answer is greed. We all knew that these stocks were overpriced, but we all wanted to get wealthy.
>
> ... If greed is the primary factor leading to stock market crashes, a secondary set of genetic characteristics makes crashes much bigger than what greed alone would do. This is the "herd" mentality. When a few of us start to run for the exits, we all start to run. And when we all run, prices don't return to normal. They crash right through normal... Stocks with good rev-

enues, profits, and business models crash right along with those that have none of these characteristics.

It is important you understand roughly, how people value businesses so you will be able to ask a few questions to spot overvalued stocks and flee from them. Still, the key is to accept and surrender your greed nature to the Lord.

Understanding Stock Valuation before Choosing a Stock

If it was simple to value businesses, most people would buy stocks at prices valued reasonably, and sell when they rose. Security analysts value stocks using different methods that sometimes give different answers. So even among experts, we might not get consensus about a stock's value.

You would expect companies you invest in to produce steady *value* increase for its shareholders. That means its earnings (sales less costs, reinvestments, taxes and dividends as a percent of capital used in the business) should be growing. In theory, the company's value is the Net Present Value (refer to the earlier time value of money discussion) of cash it will create over its lifetime—today's value of its future earnings' potential. To get to this number you must assume interest rates, inflation rates, company's products performances, future earnings growth, dividend pay out, and so on. The value will include many estimates.

Probably the most difficult to get and most influential to decide the stock price, is a *realistic earnings growth forecast*. Though subjective, you could check the other assumptions' reasonableness, but earnings growth might be the most subjective and difficult to check. Even so, before investing, it is important you *know about* the earnings growth forecast of the company whose stock you plan to buy. How can you know this? You could ask your advisor, or you could look on the Internet for reliable research reports. Still, as investment guru, Warren Buffet says, *you will know value when you see it.* I agree.

Usually, I select stocks first by choosing an industry. Then I identify a couple companies from it, and evaluate each. I might choose the financial services industry that I think should do well in the long-term. Then, I might pick a bank, say, Bank of Montreal. After that, I evaluate it as if I will become the *active owner.* Before deciding to invest, I would try to answer these two questions:

1. Over the long term, is this business likely to grow at a reasonable rate? Why?
2. What is its competitive advantage over its peers?

I wouldn't choose a business I couldn't understand *broadly* and whose products I would not buy, such as tobacco companies, junk food companies, casinos, and other gambling forms. After that, I would look at several areas *such as* earnings prospects and dividend yield:

Earnings prospects

To learn how solid its *earnings growth prospects* might be, I try to find out the business' (I will refer to this business as ABC) main products and services' sales growth forecast. If inflation is 2% yearly and ABC's sales forecast shows 60% yearly growth, I need to understand why that would be realistic. Sure, a company starting out can show high growth rates, but I need to understand how long ABC can continue such extraordinary growth rate.

What's ABC's *market position?* What's its competition doing? Is the overall market growing, declining, stable? How does ABC's *past growth* performance compare with growth rates for companies in the same industry. How do *projections* compare? Then I ask, what does my *gut* tell me? The real issue is this: Based on information I have, do I trust ABC's sales growth forecast?

Then I move on to look at ABC's financial position. I review its latest Balance Sheet (the *material worth statement* we discussed in chapter 4) focusing at first on its debt-to-equity ratio and its cash balance. Next, I try to find out about its plans to expand: how will it finance expansion; especially how might its debt, cash, and earnings change?

Important but not so obvious factors that could affect ABC's earnings growth are known risks. Does ABC offer a *defined benefits pension plan?* (See chapter 16 for this potentially costly and important matter). Has ABC funded fully its pension plans? Are there environmental risks? Are there major outstanding litigations? These matters could use cash that should be available to ABC's operations.

Then again, do one or a *few key people* control ABC? Is it likely to survive them and the present management team? This is important, especially for some high tech companies, and for companies where the founders play key roles today.

Next, I look at what the stock market thinks about ABC's earnings potential. I see this in the ratio of its stock price to its earnings per share[9] (P/E ratio). A high P/E suggests *investors expect* higher earnings growth in the future compared with companies with a lower P/E. But its P/E alone doesn't give the full picture. So I compare ABC's P/E ratio with other companies in the same industry, with the stock market in general, and against ABC's historical P/E. I would not compare the P/E of a technology company (high P/E) with the utility company (low P/E) as each industry has much different growth prospects.

Please understand there is a link between a company's stock price and its intrinsic value. Since its stock price captures today's future earnings value, unrealistically high growth forecasts for the company's products will yield unrealistically high stock prices that will tumble like *Humpty Dumpy!*

On the Internet, readily you can get most of the information you need to answer the questions I raised. That information will help you understand the growth forecasts' reasonableness. Often, common sense will tell you a business cannot keep its stock price growth because it can't keep its products' growth forecast. Recall what happened in the late 1990's and early 2000's: *Yahoo!* tumbled, on a stock price "split-adjusted basis"[10] from $180 per share to today's price of $30 per share. Its earnings growth forecast was unrealistic. Had it continued with the growth underlying its stock price valuation, by 2020, it alone would be 64% of the USA's economy! In addition, *Nortel's* price showed unrealistic growth rates, and as expected, tumbled.

Dividend Yield

I like dividend-paying stocks. The dividend yield is a ratio showing how much a company pays to its stockholders in yearly dividends compared to its share price. Dividends are like interest on bank deposits, except companies pay them at their discretion.

Yields vary and can range from less that 1% to over 10% for a few companies. High dividend yields can mean low capital growth. A yield of 3 to 5% is good enough for me at 1-2% inflation.

For companies you plan to invest in, ask your advisor about their recent and forecast dividend yields.

I don't expect most folks to do the analysis in this section, but if you plan to invest, I suggest you read this section and ask your advisor to answer the questions. If he can't answer them, probably you should find another advisor!

Understand the make up before Investing in Mutual Funds

If you plan to *invest in mutual funds,* understand the fund's makeup. Theoretically, mutual funds' professional management should do better than non-professional but knowledgeable persons who manage similar portfolios. Still, mutual funds managers are human, don't know the future, and might not do better than these folks. One big mutual funds' disadvantage is they pay managers even when funds perform poorly. Thus, your first goal is to know management fees, costs, and other payment arrangements.

Funds specialize, each with specific investment aims, so decide what you want, and then ask about each fund. Mutual funds will fall in one of four broad groups:

1. Money market funds
2. Fixed-income funds
3. Balanced funds
4. Equity funds

Money Market Funds

The *money market* consists of short-term debt instruments, mostly Treasury bills issued by governments. Because the *principal* is safe, here is where my wife and I keep our *Capital Fund.* And because of the risk to reward equation, the return is low, usually twice regular checking and savings accounts' returns, but less than *Guaranteed Investment Certificates'* (GICs). Money market funds are *liquid;* you can get money from this account when you need it without penalty, unlike GICs, which you need to keep for a set time.

Fixed Income Funds

In mutual fund jargon, *fixed-income, bond,* and *income* funds mean the same. These funds supply a steady income stream. They invest chiefly in government and corporate debt. You would not invest in these funds for capital growth, but for regular income. That's why they suit conservative investors, retirees, and others, who want secure incomes.

Bond funds are more risky than money market funds; likely, they will pay higher returns than GICs and money market investments. Bonds vary from safe government bonds to high risks, high yield, and unsafe junk bonds of struggling companies. You need to look inside the bond fund to understand its make up. Remember, the higher the return, the more risky.

Then again, interest rate changes can affect the bond funds' return. When interest rates go up the fund's value goes down. That's not a typo; I repeat, when interest rates go up, bond prices go down and when interest rates go down, bond prices go up—this refers to bonds previously issued that's trading on the open market; it does not refer to newly issued bonds.

Let's look at what happens *when interest rate goes up*. Assume you hold a bond issued for $10,000 for five years with a 5% interest rate, and interest rates rise to 6%. If you want to sell this bond, nobody will buy it because he or she can get 6% for a new bond. To get people to buy your bond, you would need to lower the price so the return (or yield) is 6% for the remaining life of your bond.

Balanced Funds

Balanced funds are safety blends of principal, income and capital growth. They are more risky than the two earlier funds because of the equity part. A typical balanced fund might carry 60% equity and 40% fixed income, but the fund could set different proportions.

Equity Funds

People call equity funds that invest in fast-growing companies, *growth funds*. They call equity funds investing only in companies in specific sectors or regions, *specialty funds*. Equity funds are the largest mutual funds' group. Their main purpose is long-term capital growth, but they will pay some income. Because there are many different types of equities, there are many different equity funds. Before investing, check the funds' make up.

Here are *some questions* you should try to answer before investing in income and equity funds:

1. What are the fund's goals and make up?
2. What's the risk profile?
3. What's the growth forecast of underlining assets?
4. What are the fees? When, and how paid?
5. What's management's performance record? What's the likely effect of a management change?

You can buy some mutual funds directly from mutual fund companies. Brokers, banks, financial planners, insurance agents, or others sell mutual funds for a fee. Get advice from an independent financial advisor before buying mutual funds. Before buying, review your goals, and understand your plans.

Choose an Investment Advisor not a Salesperson

Although I address how to choose a financial advisor in chapter 18, it is so important to this topic, I will repeat a few matters here. The issue you will need to deal with is the potential *conflict of interest* with which your advisor works. Probably, he *does not* recognize it, but if he sells products that he advises on, he is in conflict with your interests. He might offer to sell you products with high commissions, and not sell products he doesn't represent even though they suit you.

Before choosing your advisor, get satisfactory answers to these questions:

1. What's his fee make up for products he represents? This is essential, as you don't want him to steer you to his high commission products if they do not fit your needs.
2. If you think they fit your goals, will he offer products for companies he doesn't represent?
3. For mutual funds he plans to invest in your portfolio, what's the performance record and recent management changes?
   i. What are the fees, entry and exit conditions?
   ii. What are mutual fund types, and what are the associated risks?
4. For selected companies he plans to invest in your portfolio, what's their business model? Are they good and sustainable? Again, think like an owner and you judge answers you get.

Remember, you want to choose an *advisor* for advice, and a salesperson to sell and to buy.

Be Accountable to Follow God's Guidelines

Investing can bring out the worst in you. Already I cautioned about avoiding greed. Remember you are investing God's money, and you are His steward, accountable to Him. Take all decisions to Him, and know He must have the final say. If He says give it all away, do it! If He says give away some, do it!

As well, I suggest you get a trustworthy Christian brother (for men) or sister (for women) to hold you accountable to do the goals and plans God showed you. Give that person the right to ask how you are doing.

Tax Shield

The tax shield is the tax you recover from some expenses. If you earned $1667 monthly and your top or marginal income tax rate was 40%, your after-tax income would be $1000 (1667-(1667*40%)). So, to spend $100 for an item without a tax benefit, you must earn $167 and pay $67 taxes. Therefore, to pay a $100 car repair bill, you must earn $167, give the government $67, and then pay the garage $100.

For some outlays, you get a tax benefit. If you gave $100 to a registered charity in December, first you must earn $167 and pay taxes, say, $67 by payroll deduction. In the following March or April when you file your tax return, you would get a tax credit[11] of 45% of $100 or $45, your *tax shield.* Table V-1 shows the impact of giving $100 to an approved charitable organization and of spending $100 for car repairs.

Table V-1

Tax Effect of Spending $100 for Charitable Donation and $100 for Car Repairs

	$100 Payment For Car Repairs	$100 Charitable Donations	$100 Charitable Donations Restated
Income earned	$167	$167	$167
Tax @ 40%	67	67 →	(67-45) 22
Net Income after-tax	100	100	145
Payment for . . .			
Car Repairs	100		
Charitable donation		100	100
Cash available before filing tax return	0	0	
Tax refund	0	45	45

Tax Shield on Donated Stocks and other Securities

Starting 2006, if you owned publicly traded stocks, bonds or mutual funds and donated them to a registered charity, your tax shield would be greater than if you gave cash. The Federal Government removed capital gains tax on these gifts. Here is an example of the cost of giving stock compared with selling it and giving cash:

Assume you bought stock in the ABC Company years ago for $2,000 (the Adjusted Cost Base – ACB) and its current Fair Market Value (FMV) is $10,000. You decide to give this stock to a registered charity. If your combined federal and provincial charitable tax credit was 45%, you and the registered charity would be better off than if you gave cash. Your tax shied would be $4,500 compared with $2,700 if you donated cash.

Table V-2

Tax Effect of Donating Stock to a Registered Charity

Market value of donated stock $10,000

Capital gain (FMV-ACB) ($10,000 - $2,000 cost) ...$8,000

Taxable gain (0% x(50% x $8,000)) $0

Tax on gain (0% x $4,000) $0

Tax credit (tax shield, 45% x $10,000) $4,500

Net cost to you (10000 – 4,500) $5,500

Table V-3

Tax Effect of Selling Stock, and then Donating Cash to a Registered Charity

Market value of stock $10,000

Capital gain (FMV-ACB) ($10,000-$2,000 cost) $8,000

Taxable gain (50% x $8,000) $4,000

Tax on gain (45% x $4,000) $1,800

Tax credit (45% x $10,000) $4,500

Net tax credit (tax shield) (4,500 – 1800) $2,700

Net cost (10,000 – 2700) $7,300

The registered charity is better off by $1,800, getting your stock rather than cash. They benefit by the capital gains taxes you would pay by selling the stock and then donating the funds.

Donating stock and other securities could be relevant the year someone dies leaving an estate with these assets. If the deceased left funds to go to registered charities, to lower income taxes his executors would consider donating securities rather than cash (See chapter 18, *Estate Planning*).

Your combined federal and provincial tax rate will vary by province. Remember the tax shield idea when I discuss giving to God's work. The tax shield allows you to give to the Lord's work, more than you think.

Before you decide on important financial matters, get independent advice from a financial advisor.

Summary

You do not need to be a financial expert to handle God's money. But to help you decide on retirement planning, education funding, savings, investing and other matters, get to know about (not know in detail) inflation, compound interest, time value of money, tax effects of spending, and investment players, procedures, and principles. Know enough to refer to this book as you discuss these matters with your financial advisor.

Remember, you spend after-tax dollars so you spend more than you think. And if you don't repay your debts, interest on debt will grow rapidly, eroding funds available to God, and eroding your savings.

God alone knows the future; remember this when you read about companies' stocks price growth forecasts. Don't try to *make money;* ask God to show you how to invest His money. Don't gamble or speculate with His money. He will help you fulfill investment preconditions; if He wants you to invest, He will show you when, how, and where to invest. Be patient, watch out; be on guard against greed!

Think About This

Transformation in the world happens when people are healed and start investing in other people.[12]

Chapter Notes:

1. GDP represents the goods and services the economy produces.
2. Matthew 25:14-30.
3. The simplest way is to do the *sleep test.* If what you plan to do will cause you to worry and not sleep peacefully, don't do it; listen to God.
4. You earn a capital gain when you sell an investment for more than its cost. If you bought ABC's shares for $100 and sold it for $200, you earned $100 capital gain. The reverse is true for a capital loss.
5. http://biz.yahoo.com/seekingalpha/070212/26771_id.html?.v=1
6. I will use share, stock, and equity interchangeably to mean a unit of ownership in a company. When I refer to *securities*, I mean the group of investment instruments.
7. It is important you know where money from an IPO goes—direct to the company—compared with where it goes when you sell the company's shares that's issued already—to the person that owns the share. If you want to boycott a company, you hurt its cash flow directly not when you stop buying its shares (except for an IPO), buy when you stop using its services or stop buying its goods.
8. Henry T. Blackaby and Richard Blackaby, *Experiencing God DAY-BY-DAY* (Nashville: Broadman & Holman Publishers, 1998), p.42
9. This could be previous earnings or future earnings. It's best to look at current price divided by future earns per share. Still, you must work with what you have.
10. The stock price in 2000 was $360; but since then, for every one stock, it issued two to stockholders. So to compare with today's price, we must divide 360 by 2 for the split adjusted price of $180.
11. The tax credit is not the same in each province.
12. Michael W. Smith

Section II

PEACE Budgetary Control

By default, we manage wrong variables, which
cause us to spend more than we can afford.
PEACE helps us identify proper control
factors to measure and to manage.

7

PEACE Budgetary Control Overview

We finished touring Section I, *Money and Three Key Truths*, so we know where to look to recall three essential foundation principles to continue our trip:

1. *The Money Triangle* shows how we should approach spending; of the three Ms, *I* can control *me* only, not *money* or the *merchant*.
2. *ABCs* reinforce that I must know what I believe, my *attitude*, because that decides my *behaviour*, and my *choices*.
3. *The GAS Principle* gives the solid foundation: God owns everything, so I must accept what I have, and seek first His Kingdom and submit my requests to Him. Give Him control of my life.

The next stop on this money management journey is to look at *PEACE Budgetary Control (PEACE)*, an important planning and doing tool that builds on the solid foundation. Use it daily before you take on a job at home, in the office or at school. Simply, PEACE involves deciding what to do, estimating the cost in time talents and money, doing it, periodically checking how you are getting along, and if your reviews suggest you should, changing to stay on track. I use PEACE for simple tasks around the home and complex jobs in the office.

PEACE is a closed loop planning and implementation tool designed to help you stay focused on God's goals. It entails the following:

Plan for a specific period, to do precise **goals**.

Estimate and record the expenses needed to do those **goals**.

Act on the plan and record results as you do those **goals**.

Compare results **with plan** and with **estimated expenses** needed to do the **goals**.

Execute needed changes to do the **goals**.

As a reminder, here are key definitions to help you understand PEACE:

- A *Goal* is God's *destination:* where God wants you to go, or what He wants you to do.
  - A *Plan* is the journey to get to the destination: the steps to reach the goal.
    - An *Estimate* is the *likely cost* of the plan: the cost of the steps in the plan.
    - A *Budget* is a *record of your best estimate* of the cost of the plan.

PEACE Budgetary Control's main role is to help you do God's goals His way, in His time. Each step points you to the goal or goals you are working on. You start by developing a plan to do the pre-set goal or goals, and then you ensure your actions take you closer to the goal. I will develop this later but I would like you to keep it in mind.

Already you would have set your *life goal* to signal your primary life focus, and you might be working with *material goals*. Let's look at the other parts of PEACE that will help you reach identified goal or goals, on time and in budget.

Plan

Every goal needs a plan showing steps you need to take to get to the destination. So you need to decide and then record how you will go about doing the goal—how to get to the destination.

During my business career I learned two lessons about PEACE that influenced me. First, I must define what I need to control (*control factor[1]*) or I will try to control wrong items; I don't control money but I control the *spending decision*. Second, I need to measure and check regularly each *control factor*. That's why I must look at intermediary journey stages to allow me to watch each part of the journey. I can't wait until the journey's end; then it will be too late to adjust my behaviour to reach the goal on time and in budget.

If your destination is a return trip to Vancouver, leaving from Montreal, the planning part of PEACE would look at these matters for each leg of the journey:

1. How do you get to Vancouver from Montreal? By train, by car alone or sharing with a friend, or by plane?
2. Where do you stop along the way? Regina? Calgary? Other places?
3. Where will you stay overnight? How many nights?
4. What will you do, and where will you stay in Vancouver?
5. When will you return from Vancouver?

You would evaluate each alternative and choose one.

Estimate

Using the planning information, you would cost each of the journey's parts to produce the budget. Different alternatives would show different costs: expenses would differ if you stayed with friends or relatives compared with staying at a hotel. As well, choosing to go by air, or sharing a ride with a friend, would show different costs. Still, for the method you chose, you would list each item and calculate detailed costs for each leg of the Vancouver trip. You would include enough detail to allow you to *measure and check control factors*. You might identify and check these items:

1. Time away from home and work.
2. If you went by air, airline ticket's terms (non refundable airfare?) and costs.
3. If you went by car, gas, food, accommodation. If by train, fare, meals.
4. Accommodation in Vancouver, food, sight seeing, and so on, depending on why you are visiting.
5. When you do the estimate you must decide costs such as $5 daily gas consumption (if by car), $40 nightly hotel cost, and $15 daily food cost.

Think of the *plan* as your *road map,* and the *estimate* for the trip as your *money map*. With this mind-set, you will focus on the goal and likely you will spend no more than you need and you can afford.

Thinking about your trip's budget as a money map is so important I will mention briefly, similarities with a road map. To prepare a road map (the plan) and a money map (estimate), you need to know:

(1) Destination (your goal, trip to Vancouver)
(2) Origin (starting from Montreal)
(3) Signposts (where you might stop if you go by car)

	Roadmap	Money-map
Destination (Where you wish to go and in what time frame)	Address and appointed time	Fund The Great Commission (income per month sets the cap for spending)
Origin (Starting point that determines travel time)	Home, work or other place	Present financial picture (Assets, debts & expenses)
Key signposts (Indicates if you are on the right path)	Landmarks (Gas station, malls etc.)	ABC's (Attitude, behavior & choices)

We discussed destination already; your *goals*. Your *origin* is the starting point that influences travel time; you will travel from home in Montreal. For the road map, you must know if you will start from home, office, a restaurant, or elsewhere? This will decide when you start the journey. For the *money-map*, as you plan your trip, you must know your current financial picture: assets, items of value, such as your home, your debts, and your current and projected income and expenses. If you don't consider your current state, your planned spending might sink you deeper in debt. If you have no funds in the bank, how will you pay for your trip?

As you estimate the cost of each alternate plan, you need to decide expense categories (food, transport, sight seeing) you might need to *watch* during the trip, and assign values to each. So at this stage, based on the chosen plan, your money map will show available income and needed expenses by category to reach your goal.

For a regular monthly budget, you might need to record your spending for six to nine months before your money-map becomes reliable. But for a specific trip, like the Montreal to Vancouver journey, you use your best estimate.

Act

After you prepare the plan and the estimate, you are ready to *act;* to carry out the plan to reach the goal. As you set out from Montreal to Vancouver, if you are going by car, you would follow the road map, looking for key signposts along the way to tell you if you are on the right path. These signposts might be landmarks such as major shopping malls, universities, or other notable buildings.

To stay on track with your budget, your money-map, your ABC's are your key signposts. Recall, your attitude, decides your behaviour—why and how much you spend. So you would need to stay with planned Tim Horton and Starbucks' stops, planned motel stays, and other *actions* in line with the money map. Otherwise, you will overspend your budget.

As you carry out the plan, don't change the road map or money map unless God tells you. I have seen folks write goals, plans and estimates, put them aside, and then follow different paths; and they get lost!

Compare

When you use a road map to guide you to your friend's home, you check it so you don't get lost as you travel. In the same way, stick with plan (road map) and estimate (money map) like you would stick with directions to go to your friend's home. As you go, compare what you are doing with what you said you would have done and question deviations. As well, compare your costs as you go with the estimate, and question deviations. Daily, ask these questions:

1. Where am I, compared with where I should be according to the *road map?*

2. Where am I, compared with where I should be according to the *money map?* So far, what are my costs for food, gasoline and so on (spent and committed[2]) compared with the estimated cost up to the present stage?
3. How does today's estimated cost to finish the journey compare with the original estimated cost shown in the *money map?* This is important as it tells you if you are spending more than plan, and helps you with the next part, executing needed changes.

Execute

The comparing phase will tell you if you need to change your *behaviour* to stay with your estimated time and cost to get to your destination. Normally to finish the journey on time and in the estimated cost, you need to *change you*, not the goal or the plan. Remember, often your *behaviour is the control factor.*

Do you see Peace Budgetary Control's two major inter-connected parts? The *budgeting stage* that consists of the first and second steps, the *plan* and *estimate*, and the *control stage* that includes the final three steps: *act, compare* and *execute.*

PEACE is dynamic, it never stops! So, to be effective, the critical success factor for these inter-connected budgeting and control phases (from which I derive *budgetary control)* is to keep PEACE going. If circumstances change, adjust one or a combination of the following: your plan, your estimates or your actions (behaviour). But don't change the goal unless God tells you. You need to do each part of PEACE to reach your goal.

I repeat; PEACE starts with your life goal and specific material goals (trip to Vancouver). Use it daily to plan and do tasks at home, work, and church. It does not remove God from your actions. Rather, it should help you focus on His goals, His plans, and trust Him to provide time, talents and money in His time.

Figure 1

PEACE Budgetary Control

Summary

PEACE is a planning and doing tool you can use daily for all you do. Look at your plan as a *road map,* and its cost (the estimate) as a *money map.* We will expand on PEACE in the following four chapters.

Think About This

Planning without action is futile, action without planning is fatal.[3]

Chapter Notes:

1. A control factor is an item you isolate during the planning peri-
    od to monitor later on. If you planned to eat out five times at
    a cost of $15 each time for a total of $75, the control factor
    isn't $75, but your eating out decisions.
2. You must note your *commitments* such as your decision to
    overnight at a hotel where you have made a non-refundable
    deposit. If you consider items spent only, you will forget the
    amounts you committed to spend and you might reallocate pre-
    maturely these committed amounts.
3. Author unknown.

8

Budget Preparation

L et's look in detail at the budgeting part of *PEACE*. Budgets scare many folks. So sometimes, financial people refer to it as a *spending plan* or other name that excludes the word *budget*. Scared folks think the budget is a straitjacket that will control them. That's wrong; it's a tool, it frees you. You set it, you use, and you control it as part of stewarding God's funds. *It records merely how you think you will behave later.*

As you saw earlier, PEACE's budgeting part includes plans and estimates to support goals set in chapter 4. As a reminder, a goal is God's destination for you—what He wants you to do, or where He wants you to go, not what you want to do, or where you want to go. Each goal needs a plan to show steps needed to carry it out.

The Plan

The plan is part of the believer's holiness journey designed to draw him close to Jesus as he works God's goal. Separate the goal from the plan; God's goals are clear and do not change, but often there are several paths to the goal, several possible plans. Choosing His path, His plan, could be challenging, especially if you are not concentrating on Him. God told Moses to go to Egypt to free the Israelites and Moses obeyed (Exodus 3:10-12); that was God's goal. He told Moses the plan in Exodus 3: 19-20:

> "But I know that the king of Egypt will not permit you to go, except under compulsion. "So I will stretch out My hand and strike Egypt with all My miracles which I shall do in the midst of it; and after that he will let you go.

The plan was fuzzy to Moses, it challenged and frustrated him, but the goal never changed. Indeed, Moses was so frustrated when things got worse that he blamed God![1] God and His Word never changes, so don't expect His goals to change. Obstacles you meet when you carry out the plan are learning stations you overcome by trusting and obeying Jesus. Be patient; God might not act as we expect; His results might be different from what we expect!

Normally you must choose from several paths to reach God's goal. So, during the journey you need to stay close to Jesus and depend on Him to guide you as you select His path. In our flesh, sometimes we want the quick fix, so we select the short path and meet major blockages. Then again, we might select the comfortable path that has many obstacles too.

Like the goal, the plan must come from God. But unlike the goal, usually you do not get the plan to start the journey. As well, the plan might not be as clear as the goal and you have to lean on God to see it—God uses the plan to teach you to depend on Him. Still, sometimes, though God shows you His plan, you do not see it because your circumstances preoccupy you. Recall the widow in 2 Kings 4:1-7?

Each plan needs a budget to show the best estimate of time, talents, money and other units needed during a defined future period to reach specific goals. So the budget for a plan to go from Montreal to Vancouver will show transport and other costs to get there. But before you do the budget you would look at alternative plans to get there, and each might have different time and money costs. So you need to settle the plan with God before doing the budget. To plan for the Vancouver trip by car, before the trip you would review:

- Kilometres to drive daily
- Sights to visit along the way
- Places to overnight
- Estimated arrival time
- Money needed to spend
- Length of stay in Vancouver

After listing what you planned to do, where you planned to go, and so on, you would cost these items, adding extra funds for emergencies. To ensure you kept enough money, on the way, you would note spending and compare it with your estimate. Not enough funds might cause you to stop snacks, meals, sightseeing, telephone calls, and so on.

Planning, doing, and comparing what you do with your plan, is budgetary control, a handy tool to help you focus on you and your behaviour as a steward of God's money! It is a simple idea, but difficult to do consistently unless you think it is important.

Budgeting

Let's continue looking in detail at budgetary control's individual parts, starting with budgeting. First, you need to understand what a *budget* isn't. Remember, it isn't a straitjacket, or a *scheme* to show you what you can't do! *A budget is your best estimate of time, talents and money to reach specific material goals.* It can confuse you if you focus on money alone, rather than on your behaviour. Never is money the issue; your actions are. You decide to spend; you decide to travel! So keep your eyes on God and His chosen path to get to His goals. Without stressing *your behaviour and God's goals,* you will stumble along and advertisements will dictate how you spend time, talents and money.

To select the *best path* to the goal, and to identify potential *gaps and opportunities* that might arise, *budget before an event.* It's obvious but many folks don't do it. Either they don't budget or they budget after they start their journeys. Budgeting before the event allows you to depend on God to show you His path to handle *gaps and opportunities.* He might give you more funds and other supplies to fill gaps, or show you how to work with what you have, or, He might challenge you with excess funds!

Budgeting is putting the budget together—choosing the plan and methodically estimating and recording its cost to reach a specific goal or goals. It's writing the road map and money map, the *planning* and *estimating* phase of PEACE, the *counting the cost* before acting stage. Recall in chapter one I mentioned Luke 14:28 (RSV) where Jesus told His disciples about the cost of discipleship: "For which you of desiring to build a tower does not first sit down and *count the cost* whether he has enough to complete it?"

Budgeting is iterative. You need to go through a few cycles to prune projects, cut planned jobs and tasks to lower expenses to income. This is normal and the only way to stay debt free with a fixed income. As well, budgeting is useful to help you listen to God as you practice *keeping* that I discuss in the next chapter. Refer to Matthew chapter 6 before you trim projects and other budget categories to fit your income.

Budgeting helps you evaluate and narrow your alternatives before selecting the final plan, the road map.

Why Prepare a Budget

So far, it should be obvious why you should budget. Still, I will repeat it. You budget *before a planned event* to see if you will have enough funds to reach your goals. Back to the Vancouver trip, suppose you estimated it at $500 and you had $300 only. You would start only if you believed you could lower the cost to $300, or God showed you He would provide the extra $200 along the way. In all you do, be open to God and follow His lead. If you are short $200 and do not sense God telling you to travel with this shortfall, consider different alternatives such as:

- Taking the train
- Shortening the stay
- Inviting a friend to share expenses, or
- Other choices

A practical budget will lower your stress and will show the likely path to your goal. You don't know the future, which likely will change from your budget, still, ask God to help you with the budget. A budget does not remove dependence on God, merely helps you to focus your prayers to fill the budget shortfall or to share the surplus.

If you don't budget, you won't *count the cost,* before acting. And probably you won't give to God likely challenges and opportunities you might meet along the way. As well, you might reach your destination with much stress and at great cost. So, if you started your trip with $300 without God's guidance, the missing $200 could challenge you. Sadly, to finish the trip you might borrow funds at great cost, and great embarrassment.

Suppose you started the trip without a budget and you spent all your funds before the end. After you start your journey, you lose some available expense-lowering choices. During the journey, inadequate funds would force you to choose from current alternatives only. When you budget before you start your journey, you have more alternative solutions from which to choose.

Not budgeting and then spending all your funds midway would challenge you. Your stress would rise, and you and your spouse would argue. Besides, you would need to change the goal or plan:

1. Return home and not go to Vancouver.
2. Go to Vancouver stay fewer days, or stay at cheaper places, and or lower budgets for items such as food, sightseeing and so on.
3. You might finish the journey with borrowed[2] funds.

Often individuals say they prepare budgets but get no benefits. I am not surprised. A budget starts PEACE Budgetary Control; it's not the end, but a part of that procedure. When you budget, you get benefits only if you do the two parts of PEACE, *budgeting* and *control*.

Another question I hear often is this: *since God owns everything and we must seek His will, why should we plan or budget?* Planning and budgeting do not take away *control* from God. He is in charge, but He gives you a free will. Ensure you get His goals and plans; depend on Him to guide you as you do them and you will draw closer to Him. But you need to accept His sovereignty, your stewardship, commit to Him, and do your best with time, talents and money He gives you.

Second Chronicles 20 shows dependence on God to play His supernatural role while you follow Him and do your best. The Moabites and others were about to attack Jehoshaphat; verse 3 (NIV) says," Alarmed, Jehoshaphat resolved to inquire of the Lord, and he proclaimed a fast...." He agreed this was God's battle, not his. Then he sought God's direction. If God's goals look impossible, *resolve to inquire of the Lord and fast.*

Some folks say budgeting is simple, others complain it needs much discipline. Correct; it is simple and it needs discipline.

So what; you must do it as part of your stewardship role. And each *believer* can do it because he has the Holy Spirit as teacher and guide. He will give you the knowledge and discipline to do God's will; and it is God's will to *count the cost* before acting. When folks understand that discipline means *bringing under control by training,* sometimes they become more open to accepting God's directions.

Ask Jesus to help you be a good steward and to teach you to budget. When you learn, stress from finances will go (you might have to deal with other stresses), and couples will argue less about money.

If you spend money routinely, you should budget and track spending. Applying PEACE not only lowers worry and stress, but it reduces surprises. And you will get peace (pardon the pun!) knowing you have done your best forecasting your expenses. You might dislike the results but you will have enough information to know likely outcomes.

Another important question is this; *What if you can't predict your income accurately?* This happens often with farmers and self-employed folks. Answer three questions:

1. What's the best my income might be?
2. What's the worst?
3. What's most likely?

Use the most likely figure, but look at the worst case's effects to see how you might need to act if that happens. Still, ask the Lord to show you His plan and budget.

Specific Budget Goals

Besides your *life goal,* ask God to show you specific *material goals* for the budget period. You will need *material goals* to prepare your budget; they will help you develop specific budget goals. Review goals you are working on to see if you need to change them. Ask the Lord to show you His way. Here are two budget goals:

(a) No budget shortfall,[3] expenses must not exceed income.
(b) Fund the budget fully from your income; before you start, assign enough funds to finish the journey, or redo the budget, changing plans as needed.

Accept realistic budgets only. Still, as I said earlier, if God tells you to do His plans and He will provide funding as you go; go! Often folks delude themselves and use low budgets to *balance the budget* before they start their journeys. They might feel good doing this, but it sets them up for disappointment. Don't do it; show realistic amounts so you don't miss goals or spend more time and money doing goals. The following could be other budgeting goals that should match your *life* and *material goals*:

- Allowing God to direct all *spending* and *giving* to His work
- Taking your *dream vacation*
- *Saving* specific amounts for education or pensions
- *Lowering* your mortgage by a specific amount
- Erasing or *lowering* borrowings by a set amount
- Committing to spend only when you get funds

When to Prepare a Budget and How Far Ahead

When do you prepare the budget? Again, the answer is obvious; before the event, but many folks do their budgets during the trip. Strive always to do the budget before the trip because that's when you have all alternatives. I prepare my yearly budget in October and November for the following year.

How long should be the budgeting period? One year is normal for the household budget; but when you budget for other events, the period should cover the journey's duration. So, if you are at school, it should span the school year.

Another relevant question is this: How do I divide the expenses for the year? Probably you get a weekly or twice monthly salary; still, many folks assign amounts monthly, for one year ahead. Select the period and increment (weekly, twice monthly or monthly) with which you are comfortable. Remember, you need to understand and become comfortable with recording and checking your spending.

Essential Information to Prepare a Budget

Before you do your budget, remember you can't manage money (recall the money triangle in chapter one), you must manage *you*. So, the budget will show *your actions'* likely results. I will review quickly eight items you should look at before you start to prepare the budget:

1. Budget Principles
2. Budget Period
3. Budget Categories
4. Budget Spending Limit
5. Budget Tools
6. Other Budget Information Needed
7. Accountability
8. Quick Start Budget Kit

Budget Principles

Principles you follow as you prepare your budget will decide how you carry out your plans. Will you borrow to do what you want? Will you spend only when funds are available? Will you lean on God to fill gaps you see? Settle these matters early or your neighbours, friends, advertising, greed, available funding, will lead your spending away from your budget.

I think the most important principle is to agree the procedure you will follow before buying (especially upgrading) a house, a car, furniture, appliances, and *grown up toys* like cell phones, stereo, TVs.

Budget Period

Earlier I mentioned the one-year budget period. The budget period should be long enough to include the job or event's full cycle. These are other key dates my wife and I follow to do our annual household budget:

Month	Actions
September	Start praying about goals for next year's budget
October	Finish goals
November	Write a detailed budget that shows expenses below *income available to spend*. The Lord could tell you differently; obey Him.
December	Start doing the budget. Issue twelve (for each month in the following year) post-dated cheques to each charity God laid on our heart as we prayed about the budget. Remember, decisions in December will affect the following year: vacation, education, spring break plans, and so on.

Budget Categories

I mentioned many times you can't manage money because your behaviour creates expenses. You drive a car that creates expenses such as gasoline, repairs, insurance. As well, you rent a home that leads to different expenses than if you owned a home. Before you select the categories for your budget, understand these matters:

1. Your circumstances are unique so don't accept canned categories or your friend's categories.
2. Fit your categories to your lifestyle.
3. Don't let details bog you down; but don't choose general categories that prevent you from seeing where funds go.
4. Your budget is a tool to help you become and remain a good steward of God's money, you guide its preparation, not the reverse.

To give you an idea of broad spending categories, here are 11 categories representing 91% of the average Canadian household's spending of $66,860 in 2005 (see chart next page).

You are unique so these percents might not apply to your household. To get to your categories, analyse your spending for the past three months by looking through your chequebook, credit and debit card charges and then listing amounts spent. After, group these amounts by category and answer this question: what detail level do I need to know to help me control my spending? Rather than show *household operation* you might identify these items to track: rent or mortgage, insurance, heating, repairs, yard upkeep, and so on. It's your call.

Beware; don't let details blind you to important categories. As well, remember you can add, expand, delete categories as you go, so don't worry about getting it *right* to start.

Spending Category by Average Canadian Household in 2005	% Total Spending	Cumulative
Personal taxes	20.5%	20.5%
Shelter	19.0%	39.5%
Transportation	13.6%	53.1%
Food	10.6%	63.7%
Recreation	5.9%	69.6%
Insurance and RRSPs	5.9%	75.5%
Household operation	4.6%	80.1%
Clothing	3.9%	84.0%
Household furniture and equipment	2.9%	86.9%
Gifts of money and contributions	2.6%	89.5%
Education	1.8%	91.3%

Source: Statistics Canada, Survey of Household Spending, Average expenditure by household type, 2005

Budget Spending Limit

How much do you spend during the budget period? Budgeting is part of your walk with the Lord. Talk to Him often; listen to Him often. Let Him guide this decision. Don't let available funds drive you to spend wastefully. Equally, don't let funds' shortage turn you away from doing God's goals. He will give you what you need in His time.

In the next chapter when I calculate amount *available to spend,* you will see clearly how to get to your spending limit.

Budget Tools

Decide if you will use a *budgeting software* package or you will budget manually. Some folks don't like working with computers, and that's fine. Many budgeting software packages exist. If you are comfortable with computers, you will find them helpful to set up and work with your budget. As well, they will give good expense analyses, and with Internet banking,[4] you will spend less time on the budget.

Internet banking gives you great flexibility and allows you to stay on top of your finances. If you are comfortable with this arrangement, use it wisely. It can speed up reviewing your accounts and comparing results with plans and budgets. Before you use Internet banking, ensure you understand needed security precautions; never give out your password, and never reply electronically to requests for private information. Rest assured, these requests come from crooks posing as the bank.

Next, decide on your banking needs: cheques to write monthly and bank accounts needed. If you *budget manually* you might use two accounts, one for current payments such as groceries, the other for non-current payments such as specific savings for vacation, birthdays, Christmas, car licence. If you use a budgeting software package, and you prefer to use two accounts, that's fine.

After settling your banking needs, decide on your banking arrangements. What's the big deal with a bank account? No two bank accounts are alike. Have you reviewed different accounts that banks offer? Banks are aggressive with service fee charges. I have experienced a steady service decline and a rapid fee rise. Look at accounts banks offer, conditions attached to each, and then decide which account works best for you.

Before finishing your banking arrangements, shop around to assess different accounts. Select the right account, choosing consciously between an account with a bank or an account with a credit union.[5] Pick an account that fits your needs, at a reasonable cost. I have seen individuals pay over $30 monthly ATM fees to get money from their bank account; this wastes God's money that you could give to His work rather than to financial institutions.

Other Budget Information

Other information you might need to prepare your budget *include:*

- Income
  - Pay slips to guide you about income details
  - Pension and savings plans
  - Investment account reports
  - Tax return
- Expenses
  - Estimated cash flow for a typical month (if you can do it). No month might be typical, so look at the past three to six months
  - Agreed categories separating discretionary from non-discretionary
  - Grocery lists
  - Housing
    - Mortgage or rent details, property taxes, insurance documents
    - Heating and lighting bills
    - Needed repairs listing
  - Loans and other commitments
    - Bank and other financial statements
    - Credit card statements
  - Insurance policies: life, medical, dental
  - Special planned repairs or buys
  - Car

- Manual to estimate service needs
- Likely repairs or replacements – tire replacement
- Estimated travel during budget period
- Children
  - Clothing
  - Education expenses: fees, books, supplies, field trips
- Entertainment and recreation
- Vacation plans
- Family visits by you and by your family (coming in and going out)
- Eating out principle

Accountability

You will need encouragement and support to start and do PEACE Budgetary Control consistently. Ask the Lord to show you someone to hold you accountable to start and to follow PEACE. Successful businesses entrench accountability, answering to someone for their actions. So too should you and me for God's money. You won't contract formally with your accountability partner but his presence will remind you of your stewardship responsibility to Jesus. Discuss his role with him. Will he ask a few questions, weekly, monthly, or other period? Will you give him greater involvement? What do you need from this person to help you carry out your responsibility? You must answer that question before agreeing the accountability arrangement.

You don't need to involve your accountability partner with your financial details. He is there merely to remind you about your commitments, and to encourage you.

Usually Governments and individuals do not practice accountability; but as Christians we are accountable to:

- Jesus Christ for stewardship of time, talents, and other stuff He gives us (Matthew 25:14-30)

- Our brothers and sisters in Christ (Galatians 6:2) to encourage each other (Proverbs 27:17)

Choose someone trustworthy with whom you feel comfortable. You don't need to give him details of your affairs. Give him the right to ask a few simple questions such as this: *Have you been following PEACE?* Remember, your final accountability is to Jesus; it's His money you are spending.

Quick Start Budget Kit

This is a big challenge. Where do you start? You have read and heard so much; what's the first step. Here is a *Quick-Start Budget Kit.* Its main purpose is to allow you to get to *know your spending pattern:*

(1) Get seven 3X5 cards[6] and an envelope to carry them.

(2) On the front card's top right corner, write your *gross income* and this note: *This income belongs to God; He will tell me how much to keep in His Kingdom.* Pray and ask Him to show you this amount. Calculate the *amount to spend* by taking away from *gross income, giving (keeping)* to God, *taxes,* and *other deductions.* Write the amount available to spend in the centre of the card and circle it. In my example, $1600 is available to spend, and $400 will go to God.

(3) On each of the remaining six cards, write one of these categories: *Taxes and deductions, food, clothing, transport, shelter, and other.* On each of the last five cards (show your estimated taxes on the second), assign some of the *amount to spend* ($1,600) that you circled on card one. Use your best estimate to calculate each amount (my example shows food $400, clothing $100, transport $200, shelter $700, other $200).

Other $200

Shelter $700

Transport $200

Clothing $100

Food $400

Taxes and Deductions $1000

Gross Income $3000

God will tell me how much to "keep" in His
Kingdom: God $400. After tax spending must
not exceed $1600.

$1,600

Salary $3000
Less: to God $400
Less: Taxes $1000
Available to
    Spend $1600

(4) *Before spending*, use the *Affordability Index* and ask God to confirm if you should spend.

(5) *After spending*, record amounts on the relevant card and then subtract amount spent from the budget.

Food			$400
Date	Description	Amount	Balance
1 April	A Store	$35	$365
7 April	B Store	$50	$315

(6) At month end, note other categories you need, and start a card for each, without a budget.

(7) Review the procedure after six months. Settle the categories you think you need to watch to stay on top of your spending, and then reallocate budgeted amounts to all categories. But don't earmark more than the amount *available to spend from card one, $1600.* Choose a *personal allowance* category to allow you to buy small items for you; but don't spend more than the allotment.

(8) Remember, this is just a quick start to help you *get to know your spending pattern.* At this quick start stage, some folks prefer to exclude budgeted amounts from these cards; simply, they record spending, and reasons to spend to help them learn why they spend.

After six months, you should grasp your spending pattern. List categories you need and separate into discretionary[7] and non-discretionary. As well, review cash flows for the previous six to twelve months. Use knowledge gained from this review and the quick start procedure to calculate estimated income and expenses for the next twelve months.

Summary

Here is a chart summarizing key matters you should look at before you start budgeting.

Budget Preparation Outline

Principles	• Write goals for the budget period and longer term. • Agree your income sets the upper limit to spend. • You will not borrow to spend; you will depend on God to supply your needs. • Follow the GAS Principle, PEACE and the Affordability Index.
Budget Period	• Decide budget period—one year is normal for the household budget. • Annual budget timetable; I start in October for the following year.
Budget Categories	• Identify items you wish to track in right detail: Rather than food, you might choose *groceries, eating out, and snacks.* Instead of *shelter; heat, repairs, and rent.* And for *transport; gas, licence fees, repairs.* • Remember your *behaviour* will decide how to control each category, money is not the control factor.
Spending limit	• Settle *amount available to spend* with the Lord: Ask Him to tell you how much to allocate to Him, and then work out your spending limit. • You will see this more clearly, when we use the budgeting forms in the next chapter.
Tools	• How will you record spending: Bank accounts, budget software, review and reward procedures.

Needed budget information	• Look at documents such as pay slips, GICs and others to help you do the income budget. • After you agree the categories, look at documents that will give you information to help you decide next period's spending on your car, house, food, and so on. It would be good to get an accordion (expandable) file folder, and create a file for each main category heading.
Accountability	• You are a steward, accountable to Jesus. Ask a trusted same gender friend to hold you accountable to budget.
Start to Prepare the Budget	• Start by learning about your spending habits. This could take 6-9 months, rarely I have seen 3 months. • Record spending on six categories for one month; add one category monthly after. • In 6-9 months, start budgeting for all spending.

Probably your first budget will show estimated expenses around twice your income! Don't let this first result surprise you. As well, the size of your earlier spending could amaze you. Your goal at this stage is to learn about your spending pattern. You can't adjust your behaviour until you know, and the Lord convicts you, where you must change.

In the next chapter, I look in detail at calculating amounts available to spend, and assigning amounts to specific budget categories.

Think About This

One reason God's people miss hearing Him speak is their disorientation to His ways. Sometimes Christians expect God to do one thing, and when He does another they miss Him. The truth is, God is not our servant. He does not speak to us on demand. He communicates on His terms, in His timing, in His way.[8]

Chapter Notes:

1. Exodus 5:22.
2. You might not have to *borrow* from a third party. If you borrow from relatives, still you borrowed because you did not count the cost before travelling.
3. A shortfall comes from you spending more than you earn. Many Governments practice this with wasteful spending and poor accountability.
4. I have used Internet banking for years. It helps me record my spending, track it, and reconcile my spending records with the bank's records. I take many precautions to protect my privacy; the most important is, I never reply to e-mail requests for information from the "bank." Crooks are slick; posing as the "bank," they will ask you to go to their websites (these sites look like authentic bank sites) to give them (you will think it's your bank) needed information. Your bank won't do that. Second, try to control your greed; don't give out your information to "win" prizes.
5. A Credit Union is a financial institution in which the depositors own the institution.
6. I have suggested you use individual cards for each category to allow you to track each category's history in one convenient place—the main purpose of this quick start approach. Monthly, add the budget allowance to the existing balance. If needed, use the reverse side to write more data on each card.
7. You can choose to spend or not on discretionary items such as *entertainment* and *cable TV charges.*
8. Henry and Richard Blackaby, *Hearing God's Voice,* (Nashville, Tennessee: Broadman & Holman Publishers, 2002), p. 237.

9

Calculating Amount Available to Spend

How do you record the budget? How do you track spending? The *quick start budget kit* we looked at in chapter 8 is to help you get to know your spending habits; it is not permanent. Will you work manually or with a software package? This is the first matter to settle. Still, for this review it doesn't matter what you use because manual and computer budgeting use the same principles to prepare your budget and record and check spending.

As you budget, seek Jesus' will and be sensitive to His Spirit. You need your spending and income history, God's goals, plans, and either a budgeting software or specific paper form. Through the *Family Council* (chapter 12), involve each family member.

Separate budget preparation in two parts; first, calculate the *amount available to spend,* and then based on plans for the budget period, assign funds available to specific categories. In this chapter, I will look at the first part only and in the next chapter, I look at the second.

PEACE Budgetary Computation Forms (PBCFs)

I will discuss budget preparation using the PBCFs in Appendices 6. As you write up the PBCFs (6.1 and 6.2), use suitable frequencies (middle columns) for *income* and *expenses*. Your goal is to calculate monthly budget amounts for each category. If you get income weekly, enter amounts under the weekly section and then calculate the monthly budget:

1. Suppose $10 is the weekly amount (see Appendix 6-2, movies), divide $10 by seven days and multiply that result by 365 days to get $521 for the year.
2. Then divide $521 by 12 to get $43 for the month.

If you get a monthly income, or plan a monthly expense, enter those amounts direct under the *monthly budget* column. Or you could take the year's figure and divide by 12. Use the same procedure for *income* and *expenses*.

PEACE Budget Computation Income Form (PBCIF)

At the top of the PBCIF in Appendix 6-1, you see a *life goal* and three *material goals*. As we saw earlier, each budget category comes from a goal and a plan. Goals provide focus and remind us of what we are trying to do during the budget period. Separately, write goals for each *major* category using Appendix 3, Goal Statement Form.

Use the PBCIF to calculate *amount available to spend* for these categories :

1. Salary and other income
2. Giving
3. Taxes
4. Savings
5. Capital Fund

Salary and Other Income

You need pay slips, bank deposit slips, investment account reports and other financial information to help you calculate estimated income. I mentioned in the previous chapter how to get at your self-employed or other income that's difficult to predict. Do the best you can with what you have. Your main goal is to calculate a likely income number to help you plan your giving, savings and spending.

Be conservative; don't show income such as bonuses and other income that depend on uncertain future events. As well, don't borrow funds to spend for your household budget; learn to live on your income.

Appendix 6-1 shows $3,150 gross budgeted monthly income.

Giving

God owns everything; you own nothing. So, I prefer to call this "keeping": How much should God "keep" for His work from His funds that you got? This is such a huge matter I will discuss it in detail.

Teachings by many churches and Christian groups about giving to God continue to worry me. It's the same counsel I got over 20 years ago when I became a Christian, which confused me and led to me to stop giving temporarily.

Seasoned Christians told me to give God 10% of everything I got. I didn't question them; I did it. These folks said if I wanted to follow Jesus faithfully, I needed to tithe. "Why?" I asked. "The Bible says so." they replied, referring me to Malachi 3:10. They stressed that when I gave God 10%, He would give me more as part of His plan: "Give Him 10% and He will give you more," they assured me.

I thought this was a good deal for me; giving God less than a tip (in North America 15% is a standard tip), and keeping

90% for me, showed me that I controlled the money I got! Often I wondered how this fitted with God's ownership of 100%.

This tithing view with God as a *slot machine* (giving Him less than a tip and expecting Him to give me stuff in return), bothered me. But it got worse. Some folks confused me by telling me to give from my *gross* income, others from the *net*; still others said it didn't matter. These folks focused on the financial equation: give and then you will get. Another confusing item was where to give the tithe: do I give the church 10%, or do I give some to the church and some to other people and ministries? As before, the advice varied depending on the adviser!

Often I wondered about the difference between my income tax and my tithing tax. Except for the lower amount, what distinguished the tithe from income tax? To me, my income tax was clear, but the tithing rule depends on the preacher or ministry's views. But always, Church folks reminded me to "tithe because it was right."

Later I stopped tithing and giving because I didn't see the point. My giving was separate from my relationship with God; I was paying a tax to the church and others with unclear guidelines. Then the scandals came, including Jim and Tammy Baker who pressured folks flagrantly to give to fund their lavish lifestyles. This convinced me that anyone teaching *automatic* giving either was ignorant or preyed on others to build loyalty and dependence on his church and, or ministry.

The more I listened to pleas for money from Television evangelists, churches, and ministries, the more convinced I became about my decision to stop giving to these groups. My restricted Bible study showed me these people ought to depend on God, rather than on clever blatantly manipulative fund-raising schemes.

As I learned more, I invested more time reading the Bible, listening, and talking to God. I was uncomfortable not giving to God, but I was more uncomfortable listening to unbiblical teachings on giving. Frustrated, I did what I should have done at the start: *I started studying Bible teachings on tithing. Was I surprised at the results! You bet I was!*

Once I learned the truth, I started *Spirit-led* giving as part of my relationship with God, and found a freedom in Christ I never experienced before. Gone was the tithing bondage! Meanwhile, several pastors cautioned that church folks need a giving formula like tithing, or they would stop giving. I couldn't believe this counsel that I got consistently!

I will summarize the essence of what I learned about giving to God. I pray others in *bondage to tithing* as I was will go to the Bible, listen to the Lord and get out from under this mechanical giving.

Giving-Tithing

To understand tithing, first, you must understand God's plan for Israel when He introduced tithing.

The Levites were the only Tribe of Israel God didn't give a specific geographical area in the Promised Land. God said they would have no *inheritance;* He would be their inheritance. God chose them alone to work in the Tabernacle. As well, He chose from them, Aaron and his sons as priests. So all priests were Levites but not all Levites were priests.

To provide for the Levites, including the priests, the poor, widows, orphans, and to teach Israel to celebrate, commune with and revere Him, God introduced *three tithes*—a tithe is one tenth. The "Levitical" tithe in Numbers 18:21-32 called for all tribes except Levi to give one tenth of their *agricultural crops and livestock* to the Levites in return for the Levites' work in the *Tent of Meeting.* Levites had to tithe from their tenth. According to the Mosaic Law, the Levites ate some of the tithes they got.[1]

Though God did not give the Levites\a specific geographic area, from other tribes' geographic area allotments, God assigned them towns and pasturelands that they were not to sell.[2] Numbers 35:2-3 says:

Now the LORD spoke to Moses in the plains of Moab by the Jordan opposite Jericho, saying, "Command the sons of Israel that they give to the Levites from the inheritance of their possession cities to live in; and you shall give to the Levites pasture lands around the cities. "The cities shall be theirs to live in; and their pasture lands shall be for their cattle and for their herds and for all their beasts.

In the assigned towns, the Levites lived, farmed, stored most of the tithes they got, and helped other tribes worship God (Numbers 35). Not only did Levites work in the Tabernacle and on the land, but also they ran the "Government" (Deuteronomy 17:8-9, 21:5; 2 Chronicles 34:12-13).

We see another tithe, the "Festive" tithe of *agricultural produce and livestock* in Deuteronomy 14:23-27. Donors consumed it in God's presence to worship Him, to celebrate with Him and the community, and to learn to *fear* or *revere* Him.

The "Poor" tithe, recorded in Deuteronomy 14:28-29, *agricultural produce only,* once every three years (equal to 3.3% each year), went to feed the Levites, foreigners, widows, and orphans.

So these three tithes totalling 23.3% were specific to Israel and dealt with Israel's religious and social arrangements at the time. Eleven tribes of Israel were to offer them, each for a specific purpose, while the Levites also tithed from their tithe.

Before the Mosaic Law, Abraham (Genesis 14:17-24) and Jacob (Genesis 28:20-21) *tithed out of gratitude, not duty.* To be sure, Abraham gave away all the *spoils of victory.* As well, even before the Mosaic Law, tithing was an established taxation form that some Kings used to raise funds.

Did Israel carry out its tithing duty always? Like us, they were fallen people. And as fallen people, Scripture shows several instances when they didn't tithe:

1. Around 700 BC, King Hezekiah ordered payment of tithes (2 Chronicles 31:4-10).
2. About 430 BC, Nehemiah reprimanded officials for not tithing (Nehemiah 13:4-14).
3. About 455 BC, Malachi reminded Israel of the obedience-blessing relationship promised under the Mosaic Law (Malachi 3:1-10 and Deuteronomy 28: 1-14). Today, many folks use Malachi 3:10 wrongly as the basis to tithe. Look at the context.

Giving-Keeping

God set up the tithing law for Israel so eleven Tribes of Israel would provide food for the Levites, the poor, widows, foreigners, and orphans, and animals for animal sacrifices. As well, He introduced the Festive tithe to teach Israel to celebrate with Him, revere Him and commune with Him.

At the right time,[3] God sent His only Son, Jesus, to remove the need for animal sacrifices. So, Jesus' death and resurrection fulfilled the tithing law. Today, Jesus is the only High Priest (Hebrews 7:23-28), replacing the Aaronic priesthood. He is the High Priest according to the Order of Melchizedek.[4] In Hebrews 7:23-28, the writer of Hebrews tells us of Jesus' permanent priesthood, unlike the Aaronic priesthood:

> The *former* priests, on the one hand, existed in greater numbers because they were prevented by death from continuing, but Jesus, on the other hand, because He continues forever, holds His priesthood permanently. Therefore He is able also to save forever those who draw near to God through Him, since He always lives to make intercession for them. For it was fitting for us to have such a high priest, holy, innocent, unde-

filed, separated from sinners and exalted above the heavens; who does not need daily, like those high priests, to offer up sacrifices, first for His own sins and then for the *sins* of the people, because this He did once for all when He offered up Himself. For the Law appoints men as high priests who are weak, but the word of the oath, which came after the Law, *appoints* a Son, made perfect forever.

It is no longer necessary to appoint priests as our mediators with God. Believers, not Aaron's sons, are priests (1 Peter 2:5, 9). So, today we do not need to tithe *animals and crops*. Jesus' blood took our sins and gives those who accept Him as their Saviour, direct access to Him.

Today, Jesus wants each believer in a personal relationship with Him, to learn to revere Him, to commune with Him regularly in person and corporately. The early church and the apostles showed this pattern. As well, they set the grace-giving pattern. They didn't tithe, rather, they gave their hearts and then they presented everything they had to Jesus.

Since tithing does not apply today, how should we pay our pastors? Apostle Paul tells us to pay our pastors (1 Corinthians 9:1-19), not mechanically from a tithe, but from grateful hearts (2 Corinthians 9:7).

Believers to whom I speak individually or in a group, tell me they believe God owns 100% of everything and they are His steward. Yet, many believe they should tithe. They have not studied New Covenant teachings, and as with my earlier walk with the Lord, they hear the tithing teaching so often, especially when churches and ministries fund raise, they believe it. But the good news is this: *every person* I know who studies New Covenant teaching on giving understands tithing does not apply, simply because they do not see it taught or practiced by early believers.

Jesus wants us in personal relationships with Him where we place all money and belongings at His disposal and then follow His direction to use and share them. Still, many folks withhold parts of their lives and live in at least two silos. In one silo, they alone decide how to use God's 90%. And in the other, they give Him a tithe or less—in North America the average is much less. That's why I define tithing as *a guilt relieving way to spend God's 90% without His approval.*

It doesn't end there. Often, when folks give God this 10% or less mechanically, they ask for something in return—an attitude that reinforces the selfish lifestyle practiced in North America.

I call *grace giving* under the New Covenant, "keeping", because it accepts God's ownership of everything and my stewardship. Believers have nothing, so they can't give God anything but their hearts! *In the first account of Christian giving* after Pentecost, with the church new and unorganized, as needs arose, believers *shared* what they had directly with each other (Acts 2:44-45). They didn't tithe.

Shortly after, believers brought gifts to the apostles to share (Acts 4:35, 37; 5:2). They didn't tithe.

Later that practice changed and individuals started to fulfill their individual responsibilities toward God. They started to practice grace giving, *keeping*. We see the *keeping* lifestyle in these four Scripture passages:

1. The *selfless* giver - 2 Corinthians 8:2–7
2. The *hilarious* giver - 2 Corinthians 9:7-8
3. The *regular* giver – 1 Corinthians 16:2
4. The *sharing* and hospitable giver - Romans 12:13

Keeping aims to raise funds Jesus keeps for His work and lower amounts we use. We do it by:

1. Surrendering each part of our lives to Jesus
2. Obeying His directions
3. Applying His ownership and our stewardship to our possessions
4. Praying continually to seek Jesus' guidance to share funds

As the Spirit leads, ask Jesus to help you stop seeking stuff for you, stop focusing on your circumstances, and seek to get to know Him better to become more like Him. Then His *will might become your wish.*

Develop the mind-set that all funds you get go to *God's bank account.* Write "God" on the back of your credit and debit cards. Pray continually, ask Jesus to show you how to divide His possessions you manage. Don't wait until Sunday or when an organization asks for funds. Invest time with God regularly to learn His way to share His funds.

Each believer should use time, talents and funds God gives him, to further the Great Commission (Matthew 28:18-20). This includes giving to your Bible-believing church, selected Christ-centered Christian charities, and others, as the Lord leads. As well, it means giving funds to other people and, or groups God presents to you. Don't do this through a tithe or tax, but as the early believers did, present everything to God and let Him decide how much you should give to His Work. It means you must know about your local church's life, learn its needs and ask God to show you the right response.

Don't let pastors, leaders or others pressure you to fund building or programs God does not lay on your heart! When God wants buildings built and programs funded, He provides funding through *willing hearts* He gives to His people!

Many churches and Christian charities have been manipulating believers, preying on their naivety and greed. Do not give God's money to any group unless God tells you. Don't give *under compulsion.* These groups appeal to the tithing attitude; they suggest you give a bit to God and claim more. That's not biblical! You do not need these groups' intervention to access God; you need Jesus. Beware; don't give to a group when it tells you to give it funds so it can do something for you. Rather, ask God to show you where to give His funds.

Another growing practice Christian charities use is to ask you to give on credit cards. They do not teach you the proper use of a credit card, and so they don't tell you to pay your balance fully each month; rather they tell you to give them funds and then *believe for a financial miracle.* Yet, putting funds on credit cards give merchants a percent of those funds, wasting God's money. They ignore this! Then again, likely you will fall deeper in debt by giving on your credit card while the ministry gets more money. Stop; don't give unless God tells you!

I want to stress; I am *not saying* tithing is the start of giving, a minimum. No, you start with God owning 100% and you owning nothing. Then through your continuing relationship with Jesus, He shows you how much you should take from His 100% and how much He wants (He will keep) for His work; it's not about percentages, but about your heart. Study 2 Corinthians 8 to see the Macedonians' hearts.

After Jesus' resurrection, you won't find one instance in the New Testament where someone in the early church taught or practiced tithing. Like many folks I know who turned away from tithing to keeping, I pray you will study this topic, hear the truth from God, and stop giving under compulsion or giving to get something. I pray you will start to let God lead your giving. Folks who write, e-mail, and talk to me, testify to giving more to God when they practise keeping instead of tithing. Only, they become more discerning, and move away from ministries that manipulate and appeal to their greed nature. They say also, they draw closer to Jesus.

God will show you how much to leave in His Kingdom; stay close to Him. Learning to leave funds in His Kingdom is an important part of growing closer to Him.[5]

If after reading this section you want to continue tithing, I suggest you answer these questions:

1. What's the basis for your decision?
2. Which of the three tithes are you practising?
3. To whom do you tithe, and why?
4. Are you tithing 23.3%?
5. Do you give money, or stuff?

I repeat; the early believers did not tithe; the New Testament shows they presented 100% to God and then gave as He directed. Indeed, Apostle Paul states, each person should decide in his heart what he should give and God loves a cheerful giver.[6] Look around and notice how ministries fund raise; usually, they don't tell you to seek God's direction before you give. Rather they tell you to give and they or God will do something for you!

Though you shouldn't tithe, you need to listen to God and give as He directs. If you attend a Bible teaching church, as a part of that body, you are responsible to contributing to paying its legitimate bills including paying pastors fair salaries. Ask God to lead you to ministries and people to whom you should give His money. Give as He leads; you will notice you give more and with a grateful heart when you give as the Spirit leads, not through a tax.

Your responsibility doesn't stop with giving; believers must hold churches and charities accountable to manage God's money to further His Kingdom, to follow the GAS Principle, to obey and teach His Word, and to elect leaders according to the Word. Pray for church and charity leaders to look to Jesus to fulfill needs—turning away from borrowing and fund-raising.[7] Rather than borrow, churches and charities claiming to follow Christ should seek His direction. There is a clear pattern in the Bible: When God calls people to do His work, He gives them what they need. This applies to the church that is not a building, but a body.

If a church or charity is not getting enough funds *to do its plans,* that could be perfect for that organization! Perhaps it strayed from its call—following *growth, seeker-friendly* or other movements that take its focus from Jesus. God provides growth, our job is to be faithful to Him and His Word and not soften the Word to raise numbers.

Be like the Bereans in Acts 17:11 and look in the Bible to know what it teaches about giving. As well, mull over these seven conclusions on giving to God:

1. Jesus' death and resurrection fulfilled the tithing law.
2. Early believers did not tithe; in the 6th century, the church introduced tithing to pay its expenses, not as a part of worship.[8]
3. God owns everything so we have nothing to give Him but our hearts.
4. The tithing mind-set precludes presenting 100% of extra funds to God's work; tithing and offering implies we control a part of funds on our own.
5. God wants us to present everything to him cheerfully, not under compulsion.
6. As the Lord leads, each believer must do his part to fund the Great Commission.
7. Each believer must present 100% to God and let Him show him how much He will keep for His work and how much you can take for you.

Appendix 6-1 shows $415 giving. It's not an expense; act like you never got it because it went in God's bank account and stayed there!

Taxes

You don't control this item directly, but if self-employed or if you get gross income that later you must pay taxes on, you control that tax payment. How? Many folks who get untaxed income (profit, interest, dividends, and other income) do not estimate and set aside taxes payable. Rather, they spend the gross receipts, leave the taxes owing, and complain when the government rightly asks for its taxes. When they can't pay the taxes due, they incur penalties, *the avoidable amount* that diverts funds from God's work.

If your estimated income includes taxable amounts and the tax payable will not be deducted at source, set aside estimated taxes in the budget. Do the same when you get the funds. So, if you will get $500 income that you must show on your tax return, estimate taxes payable based on your marginal or top tax rate, say $200, and show that amount in the budget. When you get the $500, save $200 tax payable and pay it when you file your tax return.

Appendix 6-1 shows $600 deduction for taxes.

Savings

Savings is the third deduction item. Genesis 40 and 41 show an excellent biblical example of respect for God and saving for a future event. In a dream, God showed Pharaoh seven years of plenty followed by seven years of famine in Egypt. Because Joseph explained the dream, Pharaoh put him in charge of Egypt to carry out God's plan. For seven years, Joseph stored excess food systematically. The next seven years of drought, Egypt had enough food.

Think of savings as spending today for a future benefit. When you save, you set aside funds to spend later. So use the same procedures for saving, as for spending for today's use. Here is a modern day example of giving, saving and stewardship that we could copy.

"Oseola McCarty,[9] 87, did one thing all her life: laundry. Now she's famous for it—or at least for what she did with $150,000 of the $250,000 she saved by washing the dirty clothes of wealthy bankers and merchants in her hometown of Hattiesburg, Mississippi. For decades she earned 50 cents per load (a week's worth of one family's laundry). But when she finally laid down her old-fashioned washboard—which she always preferred over new-fangled electric washing machines —McCarty decided to ask her banker how much money she had stowed away.

The figure astounded her. Then it set her to thinking. "I had more than what I could use in the bank," she explained to Christian Reader, "and I can't carry anything away from here with me, so I thought it was best to give it to some child to get an education."

To the astonishment of school officials, the soft-spoken, never-married laundry woman from a not-so-posh part of town gave $150,000 to the nearby University of Southern Mississippi to help African-American young people attend college. The first recipient is 18-year-old Stephanie Bullock, a freshman at USM, who has already invited Miss McCarty to her 1999 graduation ceremony.

To date, McCarty has been interviewed by Barbara Walters, each of the major network news programs, CNN, People magazine ... and the list goes on. Though she had never traveled out of the South before, McCarty visited the White House, where President Clinton awarded her the Presidential Citizenship Award.

McCarty attends Friendship Baptist Church and reads her Bible every morning and prays on her knees every evening. Discounting the publicity, she says she is simply grateful for the chance to help others gain what she lost: in the sixth grade she was pulled out of school to care for an ailing family member and to help her mother with the laundry.

"It's more blessed to give than to receive," she tells reporters when they ask why she didn't use the money on herself. "I've tried it."

To be sure, Oseola McCarty was not amassing debt as she saved. Many folks save *nest eggs* but they gather large debts as they go. They don't realize that when they do this they are *going up the down escalator.* That's why I look at three savings types:

1. Debt repayment
2. Retirement savings (discussed in chapter 16)
3. Capital Fund

Savings - Debt Repayment

So far, I believe I have shown you are better off repaying expensive consumer debt than setting funds aside in *nest eggs* earning ten times less than interest on your debts. Your best savings is consumer debt repayment.

On the PBCIF under savings, show zero if you have consumer debt and include debt payment on Appendix 6-2, PBCEF. If you don't have consumer debt, focus on building a capital fund and then on your mortgage repayment.

Savings - Retirement

Retirement savings represent your retirement income supplement above your estimated pension income from your employer and Government's pension plans. I discuss this in chapter 16.

This person has debt and so normally, he would not save, but repay debt. But because of his company's generous savings plan, he is contributing his maximum of $150 monthly to get his company's matching amount, which he would *lose for the period* if he didn't *contribute in the period*.

Capital Fund

The capital fund represents regular savings geared to buying specific products or services at a certain or uncertain future date. As with God's plan for Egypt, ensure God controls all the capital fund's decisions.

Normally individuals don't plan to pay cash[10] for stuff such as cars, refrigerators, stoves, or heat pumps; they buy them as needed, on credit. As well, to repair or replace these objects, folks borrow or use funds from the household budget, which means they must forgo other stuff.

The capital fund is part of a debt free lifestyle to prevent erratic, stressful, expensive asset repair and replacement. It mimics *depreciation*, a practice well run businesses use to provide methodically for equipment replacement. Also, it is akin to "capital budgets" companies use to plan new plants, expansions, and asset replacements.

Simplistically, to replace an item costing $1000 with a ten-year life, companies would set aside $100 yearly for ten years. At year ten, they would replace the item and then repeat the procedure. Imagine the interest you would save if you paid cash for everything except a home, and you didn't buy a home until you saved a down payment that leads to an affordable mortgage!

Individuals and couples I have counseled, and who have attended my seminars, testify repeatedly that using a capital fund under God's guidance lowered significantly their family's stress level.

The capital fund is ideal for children: set aside at least 50% of funds you get for them from grandparents and others. As they grow older, encourage them when they get funds to continue saving for specific items after giving to the Lord. Don't lend them money. Encourage them to save to buy what they need. Be their example—follow this path. At a suitable age that will vary for each child, develop with each, his capital fund's purpose—paying cash for items such as these:

1. A Camera, bicycle, motorbike, video games, computer and other consumer items
2. Education expenses
   i. Remove the need for student loans. Assign capital fund amounts to Government-supported education savings plans

3. Engagement and wedding rings
4. Down payment on a home
5. A car and other items with a life span greater than two years

If you did not start a capital fund as a child, start when you repay all consumer debts. Adults, save to pay cash for items such as these:

1. Down payment on a home: get a down payment large enough to avoid mortgage loan insurance, and to produce an affordable mortgage and other home-owning expenses
2. A car, including major maintenance
3. Major spending for items such as, a fridge, stove, furniture, and major repairs on these and other expensive items
4. Emergencies expenses – three to six month's wages
5. Raise as high as allowable, "insurance deductibles"—this has major potential to lower insurance costs, but you must do it only if you understand the full implications. For example, you might consider raising "deductibles" on your car and house by building this section of the capital fund. Further, you could save in the capital fund to avoid buying *extended warranties*. But you must save regularly to have cash to pay needed repairs as they arise.

You won't know when you might need to draw down your capital fund to repair the car, replace the stove, or other emergency. So you should deposit your capital fund where it is secure and you can access it at short notice without penalty. These conditions mean the fund will earn little income. Invest these funds in the *money market;* don't put them in stocks and bonds, as these are longer-term and risky.

Since your consumer debts will bear high interest costs and your capital fund will earn little income, start your capital fund only after repaying all debts except your mortgage. The difference between interest income on a secured capital fund account and interest charges on consumer debt, could be over 20 percentage points. Your capital fund earnings might be 1-3% yearly before taxes, compared with 29% yearly after-taxes consumer debt interest charges. So, pay off your consumer debts before starting a capital fund.

The temptation to neglect the capital fund will be great. Urgent but nonessential items you believe you must buy will arise. Don't give in to slick, seductive advertising or cheap financing offers. Seek God's direction! Stay focused; save monthly according to God's guidance.

At your next salary raise, or when you get extra funds, ask the Lord to show you how to divide these extra funds; specifically how much you should put in the capital fund.

Most of all, decide not to buy items on credit. Use your credit card as a cheque. Even if you have funds available, before spending, use the *Affordability Index* as a guide. If you don't use this procedure, ensure you follow a similar practice before spending. Always ask God to confirm spending decisions.

Identify items to save for and fill in the Capital Fund Calculation Form in Table VI to decide how much to save each month. The amount to save should be your best estimate of today's price. So, $7,500 for the car would be your estimate of today's cost of the car you would like to buy in five years.

A rough guide to decide if you should save for an item in your capital fund is how often you might replace or repair it. I recommend you save for items with life cycles over two years, or other expenses that recur at least every two years. In other words, include in your capital fund, expenses you would not include in your yearly budget.

Another matter to think about is the minimum value of individual items to include in the capital fund. This varies; it will depend on monthly income and expenses. Each person must decide this amount; but understand many small amounts can pile up to big a problem. If you can't set aside enough to cover buying an item, save what you can; but save it regularly, and ask the Lord to guide you.

Review your capital fund yearly using the Capital Fund Calculation Form. Read Genesis Chapter 41:1-49 before the review, which should address questions such as these:

1. Should you add or delete items?
2. Should you stop saving for a specific item, either because you won't need the item, or you have saved enough.
3. Should you change future expenses' timing?
4. Should you change an item's "amount to save"?
    a. Earlier, did you use realistic prices to calculate the spending amount? Or, did the price change?
5. Are you listening to and depending on God or have you shifted your dependency to the capital fund?

Adjust monthly contributions only after thorough evaluation and prayer. These are three major challenges to starting and continuing a capital fund:

1. How do you get information and the drive to prepare the first list of items and amounts to save?
    a. Pray; focus on God. Understand the capital fund doesn't remove dependency on Him.
    b. Review your earlier spending and think about future needs.
2. Once you start, how do you keep the discipline to set aside funds monthly without exception?
    a. Ask God to give you insight and discipline to honour Him with handling His finances.
    b. Think about the interest cost you will save, if you buy the next car, or other major item for cash!
3. How do you keep track of amounts set aside and spent for each item?
    a. Track each item separately using the Capital Fund Tracking Form in Table VII.

b. Don't take from one item to spend on another. Yearly, adjust each balance in line with your current estimates. And I repeat, read Genesis 41:1-49.

If you decided to save to buy a car for cash, Table VI shows an example of the monthly capital fund calculation:

1. Estimated cost today of a specific car = $7,500
2. How long before you replace the car = 5 years
3. Amount to save yearly - $7,500÷5 = $1,500
4. Amount to save monthly - $1500÷12 = $125

Table VI

Capital Fund Calculation

Description	$ Amount to Save	# Years Funds Needed	$ To Save Yearly	$ To Save Monthly
Car	7,500	5	1,500	125
Down payment on home	20,000	4	5,000	417
Raise insurance deductible in all policies to $3,600	3,600	6	600	50

You would use this form to help your yearly review to see needed changes. This example does not show spending from the capital fund. But if you needed to spend, you would withdraw the specific amount for the item and lower its balance. For items like a car, when you buy it, you would continue to set aside funds routinely for the next one.

The Capital Fund does not remove dependency on God. Indeed, monthly before you set aside amounts, ask God if you ought to continue. As well, the Capital Fund should not lower funds God tells you to give to His Kingdom.

Table VII

Capital Fund Tracking Form

Activity	Down Payment on Home	Buy Car	Raise Insurance Deductible	Total
Goal	$20,000	$7,500	$3,600	$31,100
Balance 1 Jan	$10,000	$3,000	$1,500	$14,500
Contributions:				
Jan	417	125	50	592
Feb	417	125	50	592
March	417	125	50	592
Balance 31 March	11,251	3,375	1,650	16,276

Summary

So far, you listened to God and calculated the amount available to spend at $1,800:

Available to Spend

Salary and other income	$3,150
Less: Giving ("keeping")	($415)
Less: Taxes	($600)
Less: Savings	($185)
Less: Capital Fund	($150)
Amount available to spend	**1800**

You are ready to use Appendix 6-2, PEACE Budget Computation Expenses Form (PBCEF). The *amount available to spend* is the amount you will divide among your expense categories based on the budget period's goals and plans. Most folks don't prepare a budget by treating *giving* as income never received. But this approach fits the GAS Principle, I suggest you follow it. God owns everything and so, all funds you get go to His bank account. Thus, to calculate your budget, first you must set aside amounts to stay in God's Kingdom.

In the next chapter as you prepare the PBCEF you will use *control factors* to calculate each expense category's budget. You will notice budgeting is iterative, and so you might calculate *available to spend* a couple times before you finish the budget. Sometimes, to carry out some goals, you might cut or lower savings and, or capital fund.

Think About This

Since today is yesterday's tomorrow, putting off PEACE Budgetary Control to tomorrow is futile; start today!

Chapter Notes:

1. Numbers 18:31: 'You may eat it anywhere, you and your house-holds, for it is your compensation in return for your service in the tent of meeting.
2. Leviticus 25:34.
3. Galatians 4:4-5.
4. Hebrews 5:4-6.
5. To learn about hearing from God, read Henry and Richard Blackaby, *Hearing God's Voice,* (Broadman & Holman Publishers, Nashville, Tennessee, 2002)
6. 2 Corinthians 9:7
7. I believe church and Christian ministries' leaders should spend time seeking God's direction for their organizations. As God shows them, they should tell others about God's plans and invite them to seek God's direction about funding these plans. Selling raffle tickets, and other events that feed on our greed nature does not fit God's agenda. The Bible shows clearly, when God calls someone to do a task He gives him what he needs.
8. Catholic Encyclopedia, *tithes:* "...In the Christian Church, as those who serve the altar should live by the altar (1 Corinthians 9:13), provision of some kind had necessarily to be made for the sacred ministers. In the beginning, this was supplied by the spontaneous offerings of the faithful. In the course of time, however, as the Church expanded and various institutions arose, it became necessary to make laws which would insure the proper and permanent support of the clergy. The payment of tithes was adopted from the Old Law, and early writers speak of it as a divine ordinance and an obligation of conscience. The ear-liest positive legislation on the subject seems to be contained in the letter of the bishops assembled at Tours in 567 and the canons of the Council of Mâcon in 585...."
9. Kevin Dale Miller, *Christian Reader,* "Ordinary Heroes."
10. Reference to cash includes cheques, debit cards, electronic transfers and other payment means that do not put you in debt. It includes also, using a credit card and paying the balance in full monthly.

10

Allocating Amount Available to Spend and Recording Spending

If you used the *quick start budget kit* in chapter 8, you might be familiar with your expenses and ready to fill-in details on Appendix 6-2, PEACE Budget Computation Expenses Form. These are main points to consider as you work to finish your budget:

1. Remember your role as *God's steward;* He is available to help you.
2. *Amount available to spend* ($1800 in the previous chapter), sets the spending limit.
3. Your current *financial picture:* You might need to sacrifice basic items today to get out of debt. Remember, God is with you always, knows your condition, and wants you to grow out of it.
4. *Goals and plans:* Don't let advertising, greed, your neighbours, or other enticements take your eyes off God's goals and plans for you.
5. *Discretionary spending:* Ask God to help you understand the difference between *needs* and *wants.* Don't assign budgets to items you know you will need to borrow to do. If you don't have funds don't borrow.

6. *Vulnerable areas:* Identify areas that challenge *you.* If eating out is a test, ask God to give you a verse to help you deal with it. The issue isn't money but you! Write a goal, plan, and a budget for this item on a 5X7 card showing how you calculated the budget; refer to the card often, and stick with the budget.
7. Your *Capital Fund* is where you save to buy and repair major items; don't include these items in your household budget.

Appendix 6-2 is incomplete; it shows *sample* budget categories only. You need to show categories that will help you control *your behaviour* before you spend. Did you get that? You want to *control you,* not money!

To start assigning expense budgets, first, list categories you need. Next, divide them between discretionary and non-discretionary. To get budget costs, use *control factors* to calculate amounts you expect to spend. You could build and control your clothing budget by looking at individual clothing units such as, one shirt at $20, one pair shoes at $40 for a $60 budget. During the budget period, you would track the control factors at the budget price, rather than track dollars only. For groceries, you could look at a list including these items:

Budget Item	Control Factors	Unit price
Milk	Bags or boxes at a price.	My wife taught me to look at unit prices to help decide the right size to buy. For example, which would I choose: 6 lbs for $10 or 10 lbs for $13? The unit prices are (10/6) $1.7, and (13/10) $1.3. As well, my wife taught me to shop with a calculator to calculate unit prices!
Meats	Weight	
Cereal	Boxes or weight	
Vegetables	Weight or units	

Continuing your expenses budget preparation, look systematically at each non-discretionary category in enough detail that's right for you. Review each category's goal and plan, identify its control factor and estimated price. At this stage, for your first few budgets, you might find a worksheet such as this helpful; you would include your categories, goals, and so on:

Categories	Goal	Control Factor	Unit Price	Monthly Budget
Food	Eat healthy; more fruits and vegetables	You would do separate calculations for fruits and vegetables, as I did for meat, cereal, vegetables		
Clothing	Replace winter coat and winter boots	1 Winter coat 1 Winter boots	$150 $50	$150 $50
Car insurance	Raise deductible to $1000 that you saved in the Capital fund	Coverage value and deductible	$600 for the year	$50
Gifts	As the Lord leads, minimize gifts to family members; where feasible, do crafts. For Christmas, for each family member, give $25 to charity.	Craft supplies Donations	$10 monthly	$10

Continue until you finish assigning budgets to non-discretionary items, and then move to the discretionary items. As I mentioned in chapter 8, budgeting is iterative. In 32 years in business working with budgets, I have never seen a budget accepted as presented. As well in over 25 years doing the household budget I have not been happy with the budget on the first pass. So, don't panic when your first pass is over 50% greater than the amount available to spend. Go back over the procedure, but don't concentrate on money values, focus on control factors.

Probably you are thinking, "Is this guy for real? Does he expect me to do this? Get a life Michel! I am not going to spend so much time doing this!" I hear these comments often at my seminars and during counseling sessions. And I agree my suggestion is time-consuming if you haven't done it before, but that's not grounds to ignore it! Once you get the knack, financial stress will go because you will know where household spending goes! I promise you will see great benefits just by recording spending for one month. Try it!

To reach your goal to balance the budget, you might defer some items to the following year. Then again, if God tells you to accept the budget with a shortfall, go for it; assign under His guidance more than the amount to spend. *Always, God can override.*

Contingency

Do not confuse a contingency with the *Capital Fund.* You need the contingency until you know your spending pattern and become comfortable with budgeting. The contingency budget will provide funds for major-unplanned expenses, until you *establish* a Capital Fund.[1] As well, unintentionally, early budgets will exclude items such as insurance premiums, loan payments, hair care expenses, stove, lawn mower, fridge, roof, and other major items' repairs. Pay these items from the contingency budget.

The less your experience budgeting and recording spending, the larger should be the contingency. To start, earmark 10% of gross income until you become familiar with your spending pattern. Lower this percent to five percent and then to zero as you gain confidence.

Finishing the Budget

Don't be surprised when you finish assigning budgeted amounts that your expenses represent twice your available income; a common first budget result. That's when the fun starts as you start the unavoidable *cutting* exercise! But note, don't focus on dollars as you *cut*, look behind the dollars at *control factors*. So, cut eating out, buying one shirt, and so on, and calculate dollar effects, rather than cut assigned dollars not knowing what events, goods or services you won't do. You want realistic budgets that you won't get if you lower dollars without matching control factors. Before finishing the budget, go exploring! Review the following areas and you might find available funds:

- Cable, telephone, Internet charges
- Entertainment, eating out, coffee and snacks, daily lunch expenses, movies
- Bank charges, ATM fees, credit card interest
- Insurance premiums
- Car lease payments
- Gifts
- Groceries – junk food
- Vacation expenses

As you work to lower expenses, use the same review procedure you used for the budget. Divide categories between *wants* and *needs*, and understand some of today's needs didn't exist five to ten years earlier, so you can *cut* some. During the re-examination, remember this Benjamin Franklin quote: "Beware of little expenses: a small leak will sink a great ship."[2] As they explored, one couple found $150 monthly, another $400 in coffee and snacks alone.

Recording Your Spending:
The PEACE Budget Worksheet (PBW)

When you finish assigning expense categories, if you are working with a software package, it will transfer amounts to a worksheet to help you record spending against the budget. But again, because the principles are the same for manual and computer software budgeting, I will use the manual form in Appendix 6, PEACE Budget Worksheet (PBW) to explain how to track spending. I see many people use this form, but I see others use over twenty different forms. I include samples as Appendices 6.3-6.6.

If you are using a manual form, after you are comfortable with the budget procedure, look at a computer software package to see if it might work for you. Many are simple and "user friendly" with "menus" and manuals to guide you. Some sophisticated ones include several features you might not need, so keep looking until you find a simple one. Many will include these items you might need later:

- Allow you to work with many different currencies.
- You can use more than one budget. If your income is unpredictable, you might set a budget for the most likely and worst case. But you should use one only.
- Allow you to work with investments.

To continue our discussions, as I said earlier, I will comment on the PBW as the principles for manual and computer packages are similar.

Before spending, transfer monthly budgeted amounts from the PBCEF in Appendix 6-2 to the right section of the PBW. This PBW helps you calculate balances left in each budget category. After spending cash, cheque or credit card, enter on the PBW:

- Transaction date.
- Expense description and, or supplier's name.
- Dollar amount (if needed, note cash, cheque or credit card) in total and under the correct heading.
- Balance left for that budget category.

Many people say it is inconvenient to write up the PBW after each transaction. I agree, although with Internet banking, I find it simple to record and check my budget regularly. Still, I suggest you reserve two to three hours one day weekly to:

- Record and review expenses.
- Reconcile bank and credit card statements.
- Compare results with planned spending.
- Compare progress toward your goal or goals with the plan.
- Decide if you need to change plans to get to specific goals.
- Pay bills; postdate payment as needed.
- File important documents.

If you plan to stay with manual budgeting, rather than using the PBW, consider the system my mother used successfully for years; the tried and proved *Envelope System* that's simple and useful. Place cash in an envelope marked with the budget category's name and budget; spend cash from that envelope for that item only. When the envelope is empty, you finished that budget!

My wife, Doreen, varies the envelope system for the section of our family budget she looks after. On each envelope she writes the budget, spending details, and balance left. In the envelope she puts credit card receipts and other relevant bills for that budget category. She does not put cash in envelopes. This approach works for her, but not for me. For the budget categories I handle, I use a computer software package.

In our home we use one budget divided in two parts. Every budget item has an *owner*, Doreen or me. For each budget category, one of us is responsible to ensure *we* stay on track, or to signal early if he or she is spending the budget faster than plan for the same result. When we know early we can act. This is our *no surprises budget principle.* During our early married years life was simple, we had few expense categories and our spending seldom surprised us. As our finances became complex we adopted our no surprises principle that we follow by following the *compare* part of PEACE regularly.

I stress that my wife and I have one budget that we manage jointly by earmarking specific budget categories to each of us. We assign "ownership" of each category based on convenience. Still, together we prepare the budget and together we review it regularly. I record spending for my categories using a computer software package. For years

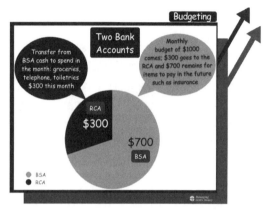

Doreen used the PBW manual form to record her spending details. Recently she switched to a simple computer budget software.

A few years ago, Doreen used two bank accounts. The Budget Smoothing Account (BSA)[3] where she deposited her monthly budget and kept funds for household expenses, car insurance, education, gifts, her clothing and other items she "controls" that she didn't pay out monthly. The next account, the Regular Chequing Account (RCA) got from the BSA the current month's estimated cash spending. Into the BSA, she deposited the monthly allocation. So if she got $1,000 in a month, she transferred $300 to the RCA to pay current month's expenses such as groceries. She kept $700 in the BSA. Monthly, the BSA would include $100 for car insurance (assuming the year's premium is $1200). When we got the insurance premium bill, she transferred $1200 from the BSA to the RCA to pay in the current month. She did the same for similar expenses.

Choose the method with which you are comfortable. Couples, decide how many bank accounts you need and who will record spending. It's confusing if each of you spends from the same account and don't communicate regularly. Think about using one budget as we do, but separate it physically so each person spends on categories assigned to him or her. One bank account can work if you speak to each other often.

Recording Progress toward Reaching Goals

Keep a dedicated notebook similar to Appendices 3 and 4 or computer file to record your goals and steps needed to reach them. Track progress toward your goals regularly. Don't neglect the longer term goals. Look at intermediate steps needed to reach long-term goals and ensure you follow them.

Implementing Three Spending Aids

You are ready to *Act!* Before committing major funds and before you decide to include a significant expense in your budget, apply these three spending aids. They are your prime tools in the control phase of PEACE:

- The GAS Principle
- The PLANE Spending Analysis
- The Affordability Index

I will expand on each in chapter 11. Before I move to the next PEACE Budgetary Control step, *comparing* what you did with what you planned to do, I want to mention again the *money map* I introduced briefly in chapter 8.

As a reminder, the money map resembles a road map. It is "a diagram" showing funds needed, by category for specific tasks,

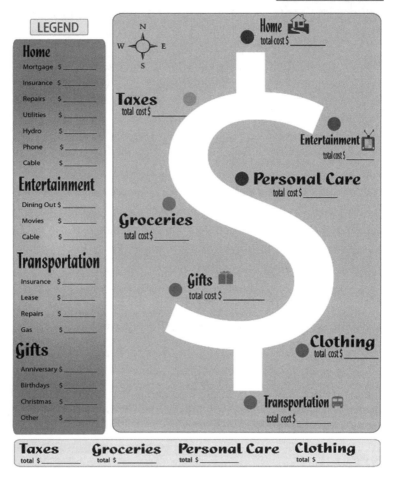

during a defined period. It is the budget for your specific spending trip or trips—part of the family budget. To carry out your week's plans, prepare a money map to guide you. As well, prepare a money map to go to the mall to buy specific items. The money map is part of your monthly budget with which you travel.

Notice the money map; each dot shows an expense item such as entertainment, groceries, and gifts, with their budgets.

The money map is a practical way to track spending against your budget. You do not need a diagram; a notebook listing spending categories works too. You need some tool that doesn't remove dependency on Jesus to help you track your spending. Try the money map.

Comparing What You Did With What You Planned To Do

You need to carry out each part of PEACE. You got God's goals and plans, estimated the plan's cost, calculated budgets, and started to carry out the plan. Now you need to know how you are doing. Where are you compared with the plan and budget? Often we neglect this comparing step. At first, folks complain it is cumbersome and time-consuming. I agree. Usually they reverse this view after doing it for a couple months and they see their stress levels plummeting.

To benefit from PEACE budgetary control, you need to compare results with plan. Your aim is *to signal early,* potential problems with reaching your goal so you can *act quickly* to avoid likely plan deviations. Let's look at these three matters:

- When to do the comparison
- How to do it
- Who should do it

When to Do the Comparison

For a monthly budget, I suggested earlier you set aside two to three hours weekly to do this comparison. Stick to a weekly routine or you will ignore this critical step. With occasional comparisons only, you lose some choices to correct deviations.

Try to use the same location each week. Ensure you have all the needed information at each session. Hang on to your chair! Don't laugh! This procedure could be fun! Yes, fun! Why not go on a weekly date after you and your spouse finish the exercise! As you will see in chapter 12, the *Family Council* is ideal for this review.

How to Do the Comparison

Already you recorded progress to reach your goals, noted spending against budget, so at this step, you need to answer two questions:

- How does your progress toward reaching your *goals* compare with your planned progress?
  - You provided most of the answers to this question in the earlier section dealing with *goals* only: "Recording Progress toward Reaching Goals."
- So far, how much did you *spend* to get progress compared with the matching budget?

If you didn't spend time at the budgeting stage identifying control factors, you will find this procedure cumbersome, time-consuming, and frustrating. In management we say, "If you can't measure it, you can't manage it!" This applies to our personal budgets too. If you do not identify in advance measurable interim targets you won't know how you are doing during your journey.

In your Vancouver trip example, if you decided to stop in Regina, the estimated cost up to Regina would be a measurement factor. When you reached Regina, you would compare your cost with the estimate.

For your monthly budget, dollar costs for each category would not be your control factor. Review planned measurement factors and compare with results. If you spent more on groceries than budget, don't look at the dollars spent compared with the dollars planned. You need to know unplanned items bought, and items you bought at prices different from plan. In the same way, if you overspent the clothing budget, look behind the dollars at the control factors.

Compare cumulative spending for the period. You might be within budget one month but over another. Further, at this comparison session look ahead to decide if you will have enough funds for the rest of the year or the rest of the journey.

Before ending the session, ensure you answered the two questions I mentioned above. Identify reasons for each deviation from plan. Here, computer software packages offer a great advantage: they provide flexibility for various analyses and comparisons quickly and easily.

Who should do the Comparison?

For couples, husband and wife should work together on this part as they did on the budget. Each must commit to PEACE and review performance to reach goals routinely. Reward yourself with a small treat each time you do this exercise.

Executing Changes to Remain on Course to Reach Your Plan

What happens if the budget comparison shows you are off target? First, review your goals to ensure they are still relevant. Next, decide what choices exist to get back on track, and then select one.

Except when you use the Affordability Index[4] to evaluate major spending, I do not support shifting funds in the budget to cover overspending on *discretionary items.* Don't transfer funds from one under-spent discretionary category (vacation expenses) to an over-spent discretionary category (entertainment). But, you could transfer amounts to cover an over-spent non-discretionary item (rent or mortgage).

Apply this guideline only after you end your budget gestation (no more than six months). In the early stages, do what you must to understand your spending pattern, shift budgets as needed.

What if in September you noticed that for the year you might overspend two non-discretionary items, rent and insurance? Look at your alternatives. You might find plenty funds in discretionary budgets of gifts, entertainment and meals. Reallocate funds from these categories to the two non-discretionary items (rent and insurance). But don't do the reverse; don't take funds from rent to entertainment!

For your monthly budget the journey ends only on 31 December. Then on 1 January it restarts. Executing changes doesn't end PEACE. If you are off-track, it could be the start!

Review all parts of PEACE Budgetary Control; remember it never stops! Change any part that is irrelevant or that needs changing. As a reminder, I will reproduce Figure 1 here.

Figure 1

PEACE Budgetary Control

Before closing this chapter, I would like to share three *budget truisms* that I confirm.

Budget Truisms

1. Usually, more money is not the answer to financial problems; changed *attitudes* and *behaviour* are the major steps.
2. Unless you control your *behaviour*, you will never have enough money.
3. Unless you control your *behaviour*, your expenses will rise as your income rises.

Summary

Dividing the amount available to spend, doing what you planned, and comparing your actions with plan, are difficult parts of PEACE. They are unnatural, and can be time consuming. But if you do them consistently, your financial stress will lift. As well, you will draw closer to the Lord and learn His plans for His money. Ask His Holy Spirit to give you the desire and discipline to stay on this path.

Think About This

But someone may *well* say, "You have faith and I have works; show me your faith without the works, and I will show you my faith by my works." You believe that God is one. You do well; the demons also believe, and shudder. But are you willing to recognize, you foolish fellow, that faith without works is useless?[5]

Chapter Notes:

1. A Capital Fund is "established" when you no longer need to use funds from your routine household budget for major purchases or repairs.
2. Bob Phillips, *Phillips' Book of Great Thoughts & Funny Sayings*, (Wheaton, IL: Tyndale House Publishers, Inc, 1993), p. 117.
3. Today, instead of two bank accounts, she replaced the BSA with a money market account. She continues with the RCA.
4. Refer to Chapter 10 for a full discussion of the Affordability Index.
5. James 2:18-20.

11

Three Spending Aids

The *GAS* **Principle**
The *PLANE* **Spending Analysis**
The Affordability Index

Before you spend God's money, use the three spending aids discussed in this chapter to remind you about your stewardship role. I developed them to help me before I spend, look for unusual, but helpful solutions; to remind me I mustn't borrow to spend; and to remind me not to spend just because cash is in the bank. They do not replace Jesus as my decision maker; the final decision is His always.

Factors to Consider Before Spending

Before committing to major discretionary spending[1]—each person must decide what's major—consider these matters:

1. What is the Need?
   i.   What do I need? You spend to fill a need or want. What is it? That's the question to answer.
   ii. The need is never to *upgrade or replace* an item. These reasons assume you *needed* the original item.
   iii. You might need transport that you *should not* define as a *car*. Or you might need to do graphic arts work, research on the Internet, or send and get e-mails that you *should not* assume means you need a new computer. The computer is one solution. These tasks could be rare so you could fill them by *sharing* a computer or in other ways.
2. How Do I Fill the Need?
   i.   After identifying the need, decide what will satisfy it. What's the best way to fill the transport need? Do you share a car, take public transport, use a combination, or buy a used car?
   ii. Until you look at alternative ways to fill the need, you won't know the solution. You might not need a car.
3. Can I Afford to Fill the Need?
   i.   How much will *the identified solution* cost in time, talents, and money?
   ii. Note, often money is one cost only.

After identifying the need, alternatives, cost, and selecting an item to fill the need, you are ready to apply these spending aids, first to see if the need is legitimate, and then to decide if you can afford to spend. These aids complement PEACE Budgetary Control (PEACE):

- The GAS Principle (GAS); use it to see if the *need is legitimate.*
- PLANE Spending Analysis (PLANE) and The Affordability Index[2] (Index); use them to see *if you can afford to spend.*

Refer to Chapter one for a refresher on GAS, chapter 7 for a refresher on PEACE, then answer these questions before you commit to spend.

Applying Key Truth #1: God Owns Everything

- If I buy the item, will I be in conflict directly or indirectly, with biblical teachings?
  - Buying these items would conflict with biblical teachings and support companies promoting antichristian values: Pornography, lottery tickets, renting movies with sexual immorality.
- Will spending dishonour Jesus?
  - What would Jesus say about this item?

I call these questions *external* drivers. They are the spending review's *moral* part. I am not suggesting you become paranoid tracing funds' final destinations; just reminding you it's God's money, not yours. So, knowingly don't spend funds that will dishonour Jesus directly or indirectly. Besides, your spending should show your beliefs as a Christian.

Applying Key Truth #2: Accept What You Have

- Am I being selfish?
- Am I being greedy?
- Am I trying to keep up with the neighbours?

These *internal* drivers focus on *you* and your spending *motives.* Even if the expected outlay honours Christ—more accurately, it does not dishonour Him, look at your heart to understand your spending motives. Answering these questions might help:

1. Why do I plan to spend? Why do I want more?
2. Does the need I identified earlier arise from advertising pressure, available cheap financing, or from peers?
3. Am I piling up stuff good to have but not needed?

Applying Key Truth #3: Seek First His Kingdom and Submit Your Requests to Him

- How is my walk with God?
- Have I been feeding on His Word?
- Have I sought Gods' will?

These *eternal* drivers focus on your *walk* with the Lord; answer these questions before spending:

1. Am I investing time with God, talking and listening to Him?
2. Am I practicing good stewardship?
3. Am I giving to His work as He leads me?

PLANE Spending Analysis

Why do I need more questions? The GAS review answered the questions mentioned earlier:

1. What is the need?
2. Is it Legitimate?
3. How do I fill it?

It focused on external, internal, and eternal drivers concerned with the decision's moral part, my motives to spend, and my walk with the Lord. If the GAS review is negative, I do not go to the PLANE analysis. *The PLANE doesn't fly without GAS!*

The PLANE analysis and the Affordability Index look at two extra areas, *cost* and *relevance*:

1. Cost
   i. Did I plan and budget the item?
   ii. How will I pay for it?
   iii. What will be the effect on my finances?
   iv. Is this the best way to spend funds today?
2. Purpose
   i. Is the item I plan to buy the best fit for the identified need?

These are the five PLANE questions:

✦ Did I **P**lan and include this expense in my budget?
✦ Will the expense raise my **L**oans?
✦ Are there realistic **A**lternatives to fulfill the identified need?
✦ Is the expense **N**ecessary to fulfill the identified need?
✦ Is this the most **E**ffective way to spend funds today, compared with my life, budget, and other goals?

The Affordability Index

I designed the Affordability Index after using the PLANE analysis for a couple years. PLANE's "subjective" results bothered me when I compared two or more spending decisions. So I decided to quantify the PLANE's result. Though still subjective, I find the Index more helpful. The only difference between these two reviews is the Index quantifies results, the PLANE analysis doesn't.

You benefit from this and earlier reviews with precise spending definitions. A clear, precise definition will allow you to look for creative, but effective solutions for the identified need.

Follow these ground rules when you use the Index:

✦ Define a need, ideally generically—not a *car*, but *transport*, not student loans, but *education funding*.
✦ Based on that need definition, in your earlier GAS review, you would have identified a solution to fill the need. If you have two similar solutions, use the Index for each.
✦ During this review, you expel "yeah-but". Answer each question *yes or no only;* do not explain or give reasons. Your loans will rise or they won't. PERIOD! It doesn't matter how you wish to explain it!

For this review, I will use the information below assuming it "passed" the GAS review—it doesn't dishonour God, my motives are fine, and I am not responding to slick advertising and I am not being *greedy*. If it didn't pass that review, I would not continue to the Index review.

✦ *The Need to fill:* Internet access, e-mail capability, word processing, and personal financial help.
✦ The *Item to fill the need* from the GAS review: A computer estimated at $1200.

Below are the questions to answer with comments to allow you to fill in the Index. Refer to Table VIII (page 231) as you read each heading.

Plan

In or will not cause overspending the year's budget (Can be accommodated)	0
Out—will cause overspending the year's budget (Cannot be accommodated)	2

The plan comes from PEACE we discussed in chapter 7. Recall it's based on the following:

Goals (destination - Vancouver) that translate into . . .
   Plans (journey – by plane) the cost you . . .
      Estimate (time and money needed) to become . . .
         Budgets (the trip's cost - $300 for transport, accommodation, meals...)

If you cancel the Vancouver trip (goal), automatically you cancel the related plan and budget. So, you would freeze the original budget amount ($300) and not spend it. I apply this principle to discretionary items, but not, nondiscretionary items like groceries, (not all groceries are nondiscretionary). For these, I carry forward unspent amounts.

Sometimes, for the Index analysis, you can use this "frozen" amount to buy an item that passed the GAS review. If you planned to buy a TV and included $1200 in the budget, this amount is available for this item only. If you are not going to buy it, you would "freeze" $1200—you changed your plans so you shouldn't spend these funds.

Later, if you want to buy a computer for $1200 but didn't plan and budget for it, you can "accommodate" it in the budget if it won't cause you to overspend the budget. So, if your total budget for the year was $20,000 and you estimate you will spend less than $18,800 ($20,000-$1200), you can allow $1200 to buy the computer—you can "accommodate" it in the budget. Otherwise, you cannot.

So these are the two questions to answer, yes or no, with no explanations:

1. Is $1200 in the plan for this computer? If yes, score zero[3] and move to *Loans*. If no, go to the question two.
2. Will you overspend the year's budget if you spent $1200 for this computer? If yes, score *two*, if no score *zero*.

Loans

	Unchanged	0
	Increase	6

Loans include all types, such as leasing, bank loans, department stores financing, and unpaid credit card balances.

The question is simple: *to buy this computer, will your loans increase?* Score six if they will, zero if they won't. I base this test on the change in total loans, including credit card balances. A credit card charge will score six unless you have enough funds in your bank account to cover the charge, and you plan to pay the balance in full when due.

PEACE teaches you to strive to be debt free. The Index captures this and penalizes all borrowing. I will discuss one exception later, buying a car that you need to earn your living.

Alternative

	None	0
	Yes	2

To fill the defined need—Internet access, e-mail, word processing, and personal financial help, identify realistic alternatives only. Focus on alternative ways to fulfill the need. Do not try to change the need. You would have looked at this before you started this review.

The key question to ask is this: *Is there a realistic alternative to fill the identified need?* In some countries, you can access a computer at the public library. As well, if you will not use the computer often, maybe you can share with family, relative, or trusted friend. If these or other alternatives could work, you have an alternative. You must decide if the identified alternative is realistic. Score *two* for a realistic alternative, *zero* if none.

If there is a realistic alternative, perform a separate Index analysis for that alternative then compare results. Probably the main difference will be the alternative's cost that could affect your loans.

Necessary

	Yes	0
	No	4

Don't go to extremes to define "necessary" to include or exclude most buys. You need an item if it satisfies the predefined need. Period! So you do not challenge the need to do graphics, word processing, and personal finances because you would have dealt with it when you "applied" Key Truth # 2. Recall, it "proved" the need for the item.

The only question to answer here is this: *Will the identified solution, the specific computer, satisfy the need?* Is it much more or much less than you need? Often, to lower costs, folks identify items less than their need. This could be shortsighted and turn out to be an expensive long-term solution. So this question's purpose is to get you to look at the need compared with the solution identified.

Nothing is wrong with consciously getting an item costing less or more than the need. Getting it without looking at likely future effects and costs can cause problems. Sometimes, compromising quality can be expensive.

There might be alternative ways to satisfy the need but that's irrelevant when you review "necessary". Stated simply, you want to know if the defined solution satisfies the need exactly. Why? To ensure you do not look for inferior alternatives that later might cost more.

If your answer is yes, the computer is necessary because it fits the need, score *zero*; and *four* if it doesn't. The solution could fit the need and you score zero even though there is an alternative. For example, buying the computer could fit the need exactly, although sharing your husband's computer would be convenient and would do the job. Don't confuse the alternative and the need; look at each separately.

Effective

	Yes	0
	No	6

Effectiveness is different from other questions. Here you look beyond the current need at your life and budget goals, to answer the question: *Is this the most effective way to use funds based on your present life, budget and other goals?*

If your most pressing budget goal is to pay off your loans this year, answer this question: *Will spending $1200 now prevent me from canceling my debt in this budget period?* If it will, score *six*; if it will not, score *zero*.

Effectiveness forces you to look closely at your priorities, and helps you to choose wisely.

TABLE VIII
The Affordability Index

Spending Decisions	University Course	"Vase"	Transport	Boat
Spending Objective (Identified Need)	Continuing Education	Specific Vacation	Work	Recreation
Plan				
In or will not cause overspending the year's budget	0	0	0	0
Out, will cause overspending year's budget	2	2	2	2
Loans				
Unchanged	0	0	0	0
Increase	6	6	6	6
Alternative				
None	0	0	0	0
Yes	2	2	2	2
Necessary				
Yes	0	0	0	0
No	4	4	4	4
Effective				
Yes	0	0	0	0
No	6	6	6	6
Total Score	4	8	8	20
© 1999-2005, Michel A. Bell	Affordable	Special case	Special case	Not Affordable

Affordability Index Scoring System

I designed the Index to give specific results. Except for two cases, you cannot "afford" an item:

- If you must borrow to buy the item (score 6).
- If spending to buy it is not the most effective way to use funds (score 6).
- If you did not plan the expense, the plan cannot house it (score 2), and it is not necessary (score 4).
- If there is and alternative (score 2) and it is not necessary (score 4).

Table VIII shows four different spending decisions each with a different result. The university course scored four (you get the total score by adding the five highlighted answers: 2+0+2+0+0 = 4). You did not plan it; it will not increase loans; there is a practical alternative—but note, you need this course or its alternative now—maybe for continuing education for your job—and this was the most effective funds' use. The boat scored the maximum 20.

You would use the index before you decide to spend, generally, not at budget time. Though, sometimes for major spending, we use it before we budget. Use it for discretionary items even if they are in the budget. Remember, even if the score shows you can afford an item; go to the Lord for His direction.

I encourage you to try this Index with specific examples. As I explained above, the scoring method is simple. Highlighted boxes show scores for proposed spending that are either zero or the specific numbers shown. Nothing else! Zero is the best (you can afford to spend) and twenty is the worst (you can't afford to spend).

I developed exceptions for two items scoring six to eight, spending on a Vase,[4] and under special circumstances, buying a car. I realize the Index is subjective, but I think you will find it useful to evaluate major buys. It helps to look for unusual solutions, to define needs from wants, to compare different studies' results, and to focus your prayers.

Table IX

The Affordability Index Scoring Regime

Scores	Results
0 - 5	You *can* afford the item
6 and above (except for a Vase and a car)	You can't afford the item
8 or less	• You can afford the item as a *Vase*. • You *can* buy a *car* under specific circumstances.

The Affordability Index and the Vase

Several years ago, my wife introduced this idea into our planning and budgeting. She believed we were too rigid, and insisted "we break a Vase" at times, and spend discretionary funds under specific conditions. She cited John 12: 3-7 as the basis for the Vase:

Mary took a pound of costly perfume made of pure nard, anointed Jesus' feet, and wiped them with her hair. The house was filled with the fragrance of the perfume. But Judas Iscariot, one of his disciples (the one who was about to betray him), said, "Why was this perfume not sold for three hundred denarii and the money given to the poor?" (He said this not because he cared about the poor, but because he was a thief; he kept the common purse and used to steal what was put into it.) Jesus said, "Leave her alone. She bought it so that she might keep it for the day of my burial...."

Mary's sacrifice is central to this story. She chose to use this expensive perfume to anoint Jesus' feet rather than using it for her. To include a Vase in your budget, you must be following strictly GAS, its supporting cast: PEACE, PLANE and the Index. And you must sacrifice!

To "break a Vase", you would have scored eight or less on the Index and:

- The plan and budget must include the item. "Out, will cause overspending year's budget", does not apply. *You must plan it at budget time; it's not for emergencies.*
- Your loans will *not increase.*
- There is an alternative; usually not doing it.
- The expense fulfills the identified *need.*
- It is not the most effective funds' use because you will use funds earmarked for a specific goal.
- Funds used must not reduce amounts God tells you to give to His work.

This is the only instance my wife and I consider buying an item knowing spending is not the most effective funds' use today. Usually, there lies the sacrifice; you forego achieving a goal to get discretionary spending.

We used the Vase for a special vacation we took. When we went to Israel in 1989, we knew we had to defer some specific goals. But equally, we knew we should not take funds earmarked for God's work. As well, the Vase recognizes Psalm 128:1-2 and these extra guidelines:

- We allow no more than one Vase each year (but we do not try to do one Vase every year).
- For a couple, each person must agree fully with the decision.
- We must seek God's direction.

The Affordability Index and Buying a Car

At first, I didn't think anyone should borrow to buy a car. But Doreen and others convinced me. After research, I added this exception. It's essential to identify the need accurately, such as "transport for work", rather than a car. I have seen this analysis convince someone he didn't need a car except on a few weekends each year. So he decided not to buy a car but to rent one the few occasions he needed it.

Scoring eight or less on the Index means you can buy a car under specific conditions:

- You need the car to earn your living,
- There is no alternative,
- Your loans will increase, but
- This is the most effective funds' use.

Look quickly at Jonah's circumstance. He graduated from university as an engineer. He cannot use public transport to go to work. Carpooling, weekday taxi rides, or taking the bus during the week, and renting a car if needed on weekends, would be cumbersome and expensive. As well, changing jobs wouldn't work. After prayer, his only choice was to borrow money to buy a secondhand car.

If you decide to buy a car with a loan, you should stick to these guidelines:

- Seek God's direction continually.

- Don't buy a new car—you are likely to get the greatest value from a one-or two-year-old car.
- Develop a plan to pay off the loan over a short period.
- Start following the GAS, PEACE, PLANE and Affordability Index.

Summary

These procedures do not remove the need to pray and do as God directs. Use them to help you define and identify needs, to help you to understand your condition, and to help you focus your prayers to seek God's best for you.

Do I expect you to follow the steps in this chapter before you spend? Yes, when you plan a major expense such as buying a computer, appliances, a car, or house. After all, in business, others and I must justify why we need to spend; so should you, as God's manager. Don't let the details confuse you. Try to remember your goal: *to find what pleases God and then to do it.*

Think About This

"You are the salt of the earth; but if the salt has become tasteless, how can it be made salty *again*? It is no longer good for anything, except to be thrown out and trampled under foot by men. "You are the light of the world. A city set on a hill cannot be hidden; "nor does *anyone* light a lamp and put it under a basket, but on the lampstand, and it gives light to all who are in the house. "Let your light shine before men in such a way that they may see your good works, and glorify your Father who is in heaven.[5]

Chapter Notes:

1. Discretionary expenses are expenses you could decide not to incur such as entertainment and vacation. The analyses refer to goods, services, and other intangibles
2. *The Affordability Index*, Copyright © May 1999, Michel A. Bell
3. Highlight the box on the *Affordability Index* with the correct score.
4. A Vase is a purchase that scores six to eight on the Affordability Index, for which you must make a sacrifice.
5. Matthew 5:13-16.

12

Family Finances

Money causes more disputes in marriages than other topics. Why? Money is the *means* to get what you want, the *bridge* between *merchants* and *me*. So, when *imperfect* man marries *imperfect* woman, even with Jesus at the helm, they quarrel and fight. In James 4:1, Apostle James gives us this insight, "what is the source of quarrels and conflicts among you? Is not the source your pleasures that wage war in your members?"

This conflict is even greater when parties do not know, and so do not practise, their God-given roles. Therefore, when the unavoidable arguments happen, husband and wife do not follow God's procedure to settle disputes. Besides, couples do not realize they need to manage God's finances *as one flesh* under His directions.

To get to the heart of family finances, we must look closely at God's plan for the family, so in this chapter I cover these family matters:

- God's goals for marriage
- Dispute resolution procedure
- Family Council
- Special marriage matters
- Children

God's Goal for Marriage

Hurry-sickness[1] leads to shortcuts to doing everything. Merchants oblige us with products like the *HCSB Light Speed Study Bible* that one advertising claims, "...you can read and comprehend every word of the Bible in 24 hours!" Can you imagine? I surrendered my life to Christ over 21 years, I study the Bible often, yet the more I study, the more I realize I don't know!

No wonder many folks don't know, do, or teach God's word to their children. So Governments, liberal media, and liberal politicians fill the truth-void with politically correct and loose morals. These groups redefine the family, confuse our kids, and try to convince us about their right to teach our children liberal values.[2]

How do we learn and teach our children to become like Jesus? How do we develop strong family values? Bible Teacher and Dallas Theological Seminary Chancellor, Chuck Swindoll says it correctly: "A family is a place where principles are hammered and honed on the anvil of everyday living." That's Moses' message to the children of Israel in Deuteronomy 6:4-9[3] that we must heed to understand God's best for our families.

Pause, listen for God's voice, and then respond to the Holy Spirit's call to *study*, *do*, and *teach* His Word to your family. Besides personal study, the *Family Council (Council)* is the forum to learn, model and teach God's Word. To understand the *Council*, first, husbands and wives must *know God's plan for marriage*.

Man sinned, the first family lost its utopian existence, still, God's design for marriage is permanent, between one man and one woman, and as the family's[4] foundation. It's a partnership; still, successful partnerships need the parties' agreement on at least three fundamentals: goals, values, and a dispute resolution procedure.

In my 32-year business career, I negotiated partnerships and joint venture agreements in different countries involving hundreds of millions of dollars. In each agreement, my company and the other party or parties needed to agree the same three key essentials:

1. *Goals:* Explained clearly, so partners knew the partnership's purpose.
2. *Values:* So partners knew acceptable methods to do its goals—key approaches about employee benefits, environment, health, safety, financial, and the like.
3. *Dispute Resolution Procedure:* So partners knew the procedure or procedures to follow if they couldn't agree. Binding arbitration by a third party was one approach we used.

God's marriage design, laid out clearly in His Word, shows the same essentials. Genesis 2:18 and 25 remind us about God's permanent marriage covenant: the man leaves his parents, cleaves to his wife, and they become inseparable, one flesh.

Today, feminism, self-centeredness, ignorance, arrogance, and other reasons lead to no-fault divorce, and other means that rip apart the family. Those who take this course do not count the huge direct and indirect spiritual, social, emotional, and financial costs that result from divorce. Nor do they understand God's best for the family. Look at Jesus' reply to the Pharisees in Matthew 19:4-6:

> And He answered and said, "Have you not read that He who created *them* from the beginning MADE THEM MALE AND FEMALE, and said, 'FOR THIS REASON A MAN SHALL LEAVE HIS FATHER AND MOTHER AND BE JOINED TO HIS WIFE, AND THE TWO SHALL BECOME ONE FLESH'? "So they are no longer two, but one flesh. What therefore God has joined together, let no man separate."

When you interpret this passage with God's words in Malachi 2:16, "I hate divorce," His original plan for marriage becomes even clearer: *God designed a permanent marriage between one man and one woman.* We should enter marriage accepting its permanence and realize God's grace is enough to solve all challenges.

Man's Role in the Marriage

The Bible gives believers their *values.* In 2 Corinthians 6:14-15, we see God's underlying marriage *value* for believers: *a believer should not marry an unbeliever.* And in 1 Corinthians 7:12-13, we read about God's plan when only one person in the marriage is a believer—the believer must not leave the marriage. On this foundation, God laid out the man and woman's role in marriage.

God created man to be His representative in the marriage. In Ephesians 5:23, Apostle Paul wrote: For the husband is the head of the wife, as Christ also is the head of the church, He Himself *being* the Savior of the body.

The man should set the tone in the marriage by his godly leadership, and must provide for his family.[5] Men must exude values such as selflessness, love, caring, kindness, patience, mercy, grace, justice, tenderness, and the like. When men grasp God's marriage values, by God's grace, we will accept and do the servant leadership[6] role needed in every marriage. Besides, we will keep our focus on Jesus, away from circumstances, lawyers, and bad counsel. And our wives will see Jesus in us.

Apostle Peter's comments in 1 Peter 3:7 must grab every husband's attention:

> You husbands in the same way, live with *your wives* in an understanding way, as with someone weaker, since she is a woman; and show her honor as a fellow heir of the grace of life, so that your prayers will not be hindered.

Obeying this instruction removes one hindrance to answered prayers. But the man's responsibility doesn't stop there. He must love his wife the way Christ loves the church, ready to die for her.[7] What's more, husbands would do well to pay attention to these two admonitions:

- Husbands, love your wives and do not be harsh with them (Colossians 3:19).
- "...husbands ought to love their wives as their own bodies. He who loves his wife loves himself. After all, no one ever hated his own body, but he feeds and cares for it, just as Christ does the church (Ephesians 5:28-29).

I don't need to mention the wife's role, do I? Let's remember Ephesians 5:21 calls for mutual submission "out of fear" (reverence) for Christ! Did you get that?When men surrender to Jesus and do our role, our wives will have no problem with their role. Feminists and politically correct folks in society tell us man's servant leadership no longer applies, so too, God's plan for the wife to be the husband's helpmate doesn't apply. But the Bible doesn't support this view—God and His Word remain unchanged!

Husband and wife need to surrender their lives to Christ and covenant with Him to do their God ordained roles. Still, as fallen people husband and wife will argue and fight. That's why we need a dispute resolution procedure.

Dispute Resolution Procedure

How do you solve disputes in your marriage? Without the Holy Spirit, and a procedure to resort to when disputes arise,[8] he or she who is strongest will *win* the *fight!* That's why a big challenge in a marriage is to get a mutually acceptable, working, dispute resolution procedure.

I am not talking about preset solutions to preset problems. I am talking about a preset procedure to *discuss disputes;* a procedure rooted in individual relationships with Jesus. A procedure the parties accept with its imperfections. And most of all, a procedure they have enough confidence in, to accept its results!

What does the Bible tell us? It says in 1 Corinthians 6:1, "When any of you has a grievance against another, do you dare to take it to court before the unrighteous, instead of taking it before the saints?" This passage sums it up well. Believers, we need to settle our conflicts using Bible guidelines, under God's direction, not with lawyers or courts.

As well, husbands and wives, *calm down,* heed the wisdom in these verses:

1. He who is slow to *anger* has great understanding, But he who is quick-tempered exalts folly (Proverbs 14:29).
2. A hot-tempered man stirs up strife, But the slow to *anger* calms a dispute (Proverbs 15:18).
3. This you know, my beloved brethren. But everyone must be quick to hear, slow to speak and slow to *anger* (James 1:19).

Before deciding on a dispute resolution procedure, husband and wife should affirm these significant marriage fundamentals:

1. *First,* accept God's goal for marriage—its permanence.
2. *Second,* accept the role God gave each of you: the man is the servant leader—the wife his helpmate who accepts His leadership except if he asks her to commit sin.
3. *Third,* agree you can solve problems under God's directions.
4. *Fourth,* have realistic expectations; know disputes will arise.
5. *Fifth,* when you argue and fight, agree you won't behave unhealthy, calling names and shutting down communication.

After, ask God to show you a dispute resolution procedure. Meanwhile, husband and wife, mull over these points I think each dispute resolution procedure should contain:

1. Accept Jesus as head of your life and marriage.
2. Agree to solve disputes under God's direction only. Alone or with trusted Christian help, talk about what needs fixing, and try to fix it under His direction and timing.
3. If you can't agree, remember, sometimes one of you must decide. And no decision is a decision.
   - Suppose your automobile needs changing; you (the wife) agree you need an automobile; but your husband wants to borrow to upgrade the car and the wife doesn't. You know you can sell the current automobile and buy a similar one without borrowing. How do you decide? Borrowing will strain the marriage because you, the wife, disagree. Not borrowing will strain the marriage because your husband disagrees. But husband and wife agree you need to decide! The husband as the head of the household should listen, hear, and *feel,* his wife's comments. He should look to see if his approach goes against Bible teachings. Husband and wife should pray and fast to seek God's direction. Each circumstance is different, but each should look to the Bible for solutions. Sometimes a

trusted third party can show the couple the Bible's counsel on the matter. Still, try not to decide by doing nothing and stash away emotional hurts that will explode later.[9] After the decision, give it to the Lord and try not to pout but accept the results. If one party doesn't like it, agree she has two choices:

    i. Ask God to show her truth, if she thinks the husband is wrong, or

    ii. Ask God to show him truth, so if biased, he can see the truth.

4. Set aside time to deal with disputes and time to have fun; they don't mix – this can be hard for guys like me who are *fixers!*

Could a procedure with those points work for you? It could, but if it doesn't, it might get you talking and not shouting at each other. Each couple needs to ask God to guide him and her to His procedure and solution for him and her.

I have seen these other ways to settle disputes: Parties agree to see a named Christian counselor, a trusted mature Christian couple, or their pastor or another pastor. Still, I repeat, every marriage needs a pre-agreed dispute resolution procedure that's rooted in Jesus. Disputes will arise, and without a pre agreed procedure, you will deal with them the *natural* ways— *fighting, withdrawing,* or other unhealthy way; why not choose God's path? In every case, the procedure needs love, patience, gentleness, grace, mercy, humility, respect, and each party's willingness to let go of his or her *rights while clinging to Jesus!*

Special Marriage Matters

Here are some issues couples should discuss and agree before marrying, and as they arise during marriage:

1. How to set goals, plans and budgets
   a. If husband and wife don't work with similar family goals and spending plans they will have difficulty understanding wants from needs—they will argue about money.
2. How to treat assets that each brings into the marriage
   a. Will they own these assets jointly? Or, will husband and wife keep his or her assets separate?
      i. Pool two incomes. If tax reasons suggest you shouldn't, though not physically pooled, work with them like pooled. My-money-your-money ignores that it is God's money!
   b. How will they treat loans and other liabilities?
      i. Treat like assets, pool.
3. How to title property they get after marriage
   a. Again, treat as owned equally.
4. Procedures to follow to decide on major buys
   a. Commit to starting and keeping a Capital Fund for major buys including down-payment on a home.
   b. Buy everything for cash; borrow only to buy your main home.
   c. Set a dollar value above which husband and wife must agree to buy items
5. Children's post secondary and your individual education expenses
   a. Save in the Capital Fund and seek God's guidance. Look for scholarships and grants; they are available. Study and react to 2 Corinthians 12:14.
6. How to identify and plug potential leakages
   a. Develop a common view about entertaining, eating out, vacations, insurance, spending habits, and *grown-up* toys.
7. How will they show God's ownership of everything in their giving?
   a. God loves a hilarious giver (2 Corinthians 9:7), follow the GAS Principle.

Your source for answers to living the Christ-centered life is the Bible. Still, get Christian pre-marital counselling that includes handling finances and dispute resolution.

As you start the marriage, if you plan to start a family save 100% of the wife's income. Her income will stop if she takes time off to raise children, if dad will be a stay-at-home dad, save 100% of his income instead. Learn to live on one salary early if either husband or wife is likely to stay home to raise the kids. This approach assumes you will pool incomes. Save unspent income in the Capital Fund, unless God tells you to the contrary.

Even if married for several years and one spouse will not stay-at-home, as the Lord leads, try to use one income only in the family budget while saving the other. It is never too late to try to live on one income and save the other, but it will be more difficult the later you start.

To work with PEACE, husband or wife should decide some key matters:

- One should record spending[10] though together they develop the budget
- Agree spending limit, beyond which they use the Affordability Index
- Commit to PEACE's control phase (ACT, Compare, and Execute), particularly executing changes to reach goals

Family Council: What and Why

Rejoice if you use a dispute resolution procedure that gets you talking about issues under God's direction! The *Council* is the ideal place for couples to discuss disputes, but not in front of the children. The *Council* is Home Inc's (your household) board of directors with Jesus as its foundation and Head. It's the family's learning, teaching, and discussion centre. The family learns—parents learn and train each other—and teach each other and the children to become like Jesus. It's here parents do as Moses taught in Deuteronomy 6:4-9.

Jesus chooses the *Council's* members—husband, wife and children. The sooner parents involve children, the better.

Besides, in the *Council*, parents should carry out the duty of older folks to younger folks—a duty to model. To "... be an example of good deeds...to speak the things which are fitting for sound doctrine...."[11]   In the Council, parents, "train up a child in the way he should go, even when he is old he will not depart from it."[12] Does this mean you will produce perfect children if you follow this path? No, but that shouldn't be the parent's goal. Parents train your children in God's ways and He looks after the result.

So, like Apostle Paul with his young pastor protégé, Timothy, teach your children about accuracy and permanence of God's word so they can withstand onslaughts they will face outside the home.[13] Further, teach them to test what they hear from others, including pastors, Bible teachers, and you.[14] Parental training responsibility is part of your responsibility to be Jesus' disciples and to *go* and *make disciples*. It starts at home and never stops!

The *Council's* workings could challenge you. What if only one parent is a Christian and the children are not Christians? Work with what you have. Pray; seek God's guidance. If mom is the believer and dad isn't, or if he withdraws, mom should seek God's guidance. The same applies in the reverse.

Moms, dads, understand that nagging, pressuring, guilt tripping and other subtle and not-so-subtle *enticements* won't convince one spouse to do his role. In my early Christian life, my wife tried some of these tactics and they pushed me away. The tactic that worked was when she gave me to God and allowed Him to change me. He continues to work on me!

Family Council's Leadership

A healthy *Council* needs good leadership. And God gave dad the *Council's* servant leadership role. Recall Ephesians 5:23, "for the husband is the head of the wife as Christ is the head of the church, his body, of which he is the Saviour." Dad needs to take responsibility to lead. He is Home Inc.'s Chief Executive Officer (CEO). Dad needs to know, as CEO, he is Christ's representative in Home Inc., the servant leader, and so he must set the tone at home.

If dad is unwilling or unable to lead the *Council*, this critical role falls to mom. Already she might have much to do, but by God's grace, she will be able to cope. In a one-parent home, that parent-believer who has the perfect spouse, Jesus, leads.

Besides setting the tone at home, the servant leader's primary responsibility is to arrange regular sessions, special training sessions, suggest discussion topics, and help during each session. But, he or she must guard against acting dictatorially, and must understand servant leadership means surrendering to Christ.

Parents might rotate leadership to train family members. Still, it is dad's role.

How the Family Council Might Work

Council sessions should include Bible study not for family members to become theologians, but so they might draw closer to Christ. Sessions must stress spiritual, attitude, and behaviour matters that affect life in a secular society. Don't isolate your family from the world, equip them with God's Word to live in but not conform to the world. These are some *Council* goals:

1. **Spiritual**
   a. Introduce family members to Christ. The Holy Spirit prepares hearts to surrender to Christ; we plant seeds. The *Council's* role includes modeling God-ordained

parental roles: Parents showing each other and their children how to grow to become like Jesus—exuding love, kindness, patience, grace, mercy, justice to one another.

b. Systematic Bible study and formal and informal discipleship training

2. Attitude, Behaviour and Choices (ABCs)

a. Each family member to learn from the Bible, to teach, and practice his and her God-ordained roles, and biblical attitudes needed to handle time, talents, and money.

b. Develop healthy family traditions, such as family dates and fun periods.

c. Encourage and hold one another accountable to do his and her role and to carry out goals, plans and budgets.

3. Financial

a. Learn, model, teach financial practices to build on God-centered ABCs: goal setting, budgeting, and money mapping.

b. Share experiences, learn from mistakes, and build on successes.

To work well, each *Council* should have at least seven basics:

1. Listening: The key word is listening. Each person must listen when another person speaks. The *Council* should adopt this *chain link method.*

a. Place a key ring (or other object) in the middle of the group.

b. To speak, each person needs it.

c. The *Council* convener, usually dad, must let each person with the key ring speaks until he finishes, no interruptions.

d. When a person stops speaking, the next speaker must build on or respond to the topic unless the former speaker says he does not need more comments.

e. Introduce a new topic only when the last speaker says he is happy everyone understands what he said. Folks do not have to agree but they should try to understand. If the speaker asks someone to paraphrase what he said, that person should do so.

2. **Meeting time and place:** Regular (weekly) meetings; same time, same place, followed by a family fun time

3. **Meeting duration:** Work for *time* not for *task*. Set a start time and end time, stick to them. Start slowly, at first, keep *Council* meetings short; don't overwhelm your family with this *new idea!*

4. **Meeting Topics:** Use an agenda; divide it in topics, each with a start and end time:

a. Agenda items could be ... (1) brief devotional—rotate who brings the devotional (2) discussion on specific family matters (3) disputes for resolution affecting the family; exclude one-on-one disputes, discuss these separately (4) household finances: spending plans, capital fund, and vacation.

5. **Convener:** Dad should arrange meetings and be the meeting helper. Dad must listen, understand and encourage others to follow the key chain listening method.

6. **Participation:** As relevant, encourage the children to join in discussions. Most of all, dad should encourage the *shy* children to speak; don't let those who like to talk monopolize meetings.

7. **Transparency:** Be transparent, but respect each person's confidentiality.

The Family Council and Single Parents

It's an understatement to say a single parent's task is difficult. After all, this isn't God's design! Usually, besides mom's[15] full-time challenging home management job, mom works full-time at another job. Likely mom alone will handle home and children events, so her greatest challenge might be learning to set priorities and to practice *selective neglect.*[16] She must learn to choose what to do and what not to do daily. Most of all, she must provide the emotional security the children need, and model biblical attitudes and behaviour to the children. When moms say they can't *neglect* specific matters, I ask this question: Suppose you died, who would do those urgent tasks?

The children's cooperation could be another big challenge. Depending on the cause of single parenting, special issues could exist with the children. What's their emotional state? Do they visit dad? When? How often? How are they adjusting to the forced parental separation? What's the state of sibling rivalry? How much energy does mom need to spend after a full day at the office to gain peace at home?

These and other reasons will affect how smoothly a *Council* works in a one parent home. Still, mom needs to start a *Council* and provide its leadership. For a lone parent, the *Council* could meet even more often to help communicate family matters and to hear about school and children's non-personal social life (school outings, birthday parties, baby-sitting). As with the two-parent family, don't use the *Council* to discuss personal matters affecting a child. Set aside one-on-one-time with each child.

Mom can train children to assume greater home responsibility and to participate in the *Council*. It's important for older children to understand they need to contribute to household management. As well, to help mom handle the children's needs and wants, mom should give the children allowances and budgets early. Children should know at suitable ages, the state of household finances as it affects their needs and selective wants. For example, your teenager who had plans to attend a specific university should know early if the new family arrangement could support that dream.

Mom should follow the same guidelines to work the *Council*, except, she might shorten the agenda and the time for each session. To the main goals I mentioned earlier, here is another goal: *to talk about and set spending plans for discretionary spending* on events and stuff like, school field trips, birthday parties, movies, video games, and other kids peer-driven spending.[17] As soon as feasible, mom should let each child control his and her spending plans. Mom should explain to younger children how their behaviour could affect the household budget. The same should happen in a two-parent family, but I stress it here because it causes greater friction in one-parent families.

Mom should ask a trusted Christian female friend to hold her accountable to hold regular Council meetings.

Children

Though the *Council* is the ideal training centre, the best way to teach your children biblical truths is to model them in everything you do, daily. When the store clerk gives you too much change, remember your child is watching. When the car swerves in front of you, know your child will see your body language and hear your remarks.

I got a wake up call when my 12-year-old daughter designed a special card titled "To: Father". Below the title on the front, she drew Confucius. Dressed in a blue robe, arms crossed in front, he wore a traditional Chinese hat. She, my wife and son signed the card and gave me. Inside was a quotation they claimed was from (. . . You guessed, Confucius!), "The nobler man first practiceth what he preacheth and afterwards preacheth according to his practice." What a powerful message! I got it then and I am aware of it continually. I must ensure I walk my talk. I hang this card in my study where I see it daily. I thank God for the openness and love of my family that led to this wake up call. Still, they give me reminders.

Allowances

An allowance is a great teaching tool. Around age six or seven (or earlier, if fitting) when they start to appreciate that you need money to buy stuff for them, give each of your children an allowance, no matter how small. To earn the allowance, give them chores to develop responsible attitudes toward work. From this allowance, teach them to give, to save, and to work with spending plans, but keep it simple.

Teach them to set realistic goals and to work diligently to do these goals. Don't lend them money. Teach them to save to buy stuff in a Capital Fund. Model this practice.

As your children mature, change their chores and allowances. Before Shabbir left home for university in British Columbia, he and I signed annual snow removal contracts with my responsibilities and his. I supplied a snow blower in good working condition. When it snowed, he had to clear the driveway before seven a.m. In return, I paid him the going market rate but he had to perform. The contract included a penalty clause for non-performance to an agreed standard, and an incentive clause for performance beyond that standard. Happily, poor performance never delayed me! Most years he earned a bonus.

As well, in their teens, my children managed budgets while at University and Bible College. Each studied in a different Province from where we were living at the time. We developed budgets with each of them and held each responsible to do his and her budgets. Monthly, to get repayment for amounts spent, each sent us a spreadsheet showing spending compared with budgets and receipts for expenses.

Guidelines to Teach Children Good Money Habits

Parents, your attitude to your children's accountability will decide how much they will learn. Here are some guidelines to help you teach your children to work with the budget and to become good stewards of God's money:

1. Let them see you living as God's steward, accepting what you have, and saving to buy stuff.
2. Do what you say; be consistent, fair and gracious.
3. Parents, pray about the *right age* to give them dollars to spend to do their budgets. This could be as young as age five. After you agree the path (goal, plan and budget) with the children, stick to it.
   i. Children will play one parent against another.
   ii. If the child has an issue with the agreed goal, plan or budget, teach her to go to God first, for His guidance.
4. Don't accept excuses from your children when they follow *their goals,* rather than the agreed goal. Be merciful, but teach them they must bear effects of poor judgement and disobedience.
5. Don't give more funds than agreed, unless after prayer you see a need to fill.
6. Teach them patience, to save to buy items. As well, teach them that God supplies our needs in His time and His way. Let them see you practise this.
7. Listen, hear, understand your children; pray for them daily: it doesn't matter that what they are doing is different from what you did at their ages.

Parents, if you don't follow these or similar guidelines, you will cause your children to stumble. They won't learn a key lesson: How to work with what they have and depend on God to see them through difficulties.

Accountability

Dad, ask the Lord to lead you to a Godly Christian man to hold you accountable to do your role in the marriage and in the *Council.* Mom, ask a trusted female friend to do the same.

Dad and Mom, hold your children accountable to agreed budgets and to get to agreed goals and plans. The budget's size is important. Each child is different. So, with each child, work out his or her needs, and add a few *wants* in his or her budget. Ensure your child understands his goals and the likely effects of not reaching them. Hold your children accountable for these items that their budgets should include:

- **Giving**: They should know God owns everything. Teach them to ask God to show them how to give.
- **Capital Fund**: Encourage them to save regularly for specific buys.
  - The Capital Fund is the basis for children to be debt free as adults. Pray about encouraging them to save 50% of all their income, especially income family members give as birthday gifts.
  - Use their Capital Fund only for capital items (stuff that will last over two years) such as a car, skateboard, bicycle, wedding expenses, university education expenses, down payment on a home, buy and repair appliances, and the like.
  - Your children's Capital Fund is for the same purposes as yours.
- **Clothing**: Buy all their clothes from their yearly budget.
- **Entertainment**: This item is essential. The main purpose is for them to value the cost of eating out, going to the movies, video rentals, and so on. Eating out can become expensive even at fast-food restaurants.

As well, hold your children accountable to do *contracted* work. Teach them to develop spending habits that honour God. As proper, let them decide, let them stumble, but teach them to learn from their mistakes. It's tough, but allow this freedom and be ready to rescue them from harm. Praise and encourage them. Most important, let them know, with Jesus living in them, they can do everything God wants done. Love them unconditionally, as Jesus loves each of us.

Summary

The family is society's foundation. As the family goes, so goes society! Churches, schools and other places teach our children values. Unless we provide a solid biblical base in the *Council* or equivalent, our children will drift to the world's values. We are not responsible for the results, just for teaching, modelling, and encouraging, continually.

Parents, answer two questions. First, do you accept your God ordained roles? Second, are you prepared to *sacrifice* to teach your children as Moses commanded the children of Israel and God demands of you today? This might mean a smaller home, one car, fewer vacations, delaying the wife's career, and so on!

As early as feasible, give your children allowances and work with them to develop their character through a budget, a Capital Fund, and a spending decision procedure with Jesus at the centre.

Think About This

Children are not casual guests in our home. They have been loaned to us temporarily for the purpose of loving them and instilling a foundation of values on which their future lives will be built.[18]

A child who is allowed to be disrespectful to his parents will not have true respect for anyone. [19]

Chapter Notes:

1. I define hurry-sickness as rushing about doing urgent stuff while complaining continually about busyness. We forget busy is normal, a blessing. It means *occupied with the mind concentrated.*

2. Former USA Vice President, Al Gore, told the 1996 Democratic National Convention this: "I believe that Government has the right to be involved in the growth and progress of our children."

3. Deuteronomy 6:4-9: "Hear, O Israel! The LORD is our God, the LORD is one! "You shall love the LORD your God with all your heart and with all your soul and with all your might. "These words, which I am commanding you today, shall be on your heart. You shall teach them diligently to your sons and shall talk of them when you sit in your house and when you walk by the way and when you lie down and when you rise up. "You shall bind them as a sign on your hand and they shall be as frontals on your forehead. "You shall write them on the doorposts of your house and on your gates.

4. Genesis 2:18, 20-21, 24-25: The LORD God said, "It is not good for the man to be alone. I will make a helper suitable for him." ... for Adam no suitable helper was found. So the LORD God caused the man to fall into a deep sleep; ... Then the LORD God made a woman from the rib he had taken out of the man, and he brought her ... For this reason a man shall leave his father and his mother, and be joined to his wife; and they shall become one flesh. And the man and his wife were both naked and were not ashamed.

5. 1 Timothy 5:8.

6. Luke 22:26-27.

7. Ephesians 5:25.

8. Disputes will range from stereotypical "in-laws," to money, eating out, shopping, vacation and the like.

9. Remember also, when you don't decide, the car deteriorates, and later might cause you more to fix or replace.

10. Refer to chapter 9 for discussion on recording spending on the PEACE Budget Worksheet.

11. Titus 2:1-8.

12. Proverbs 22:6.

13. 2 Timothy 3:16.

14. Acts 17:11.

15. As in the rest of this book, I use gender interchangeably, so references to mom apply equally to dad.

16. I coined Selective Neglect in my book *Managing God's Time* (page 94). It's accepting you can't do everything you and others would

like you to do each 24 hours. So, daily decide what you won't do and whom you will neglect as you re-order priorities continually.

17. In a two-parent family, dad would discuss these items also. But in a one-parent family with less available funds, it's more important to identify early, children-related expenses that could cause leakage in the family budget, and look at ways to handle them. That's why it is essential to share with the children, the state of family's finances as it affects the family's ability to fund some of these expenses.

18. James Dobson.

19. Billy Graham.

Section III

Selected Spending Decisions

The More Time Spent in His Word,
the Clearer His "Voice",
And The More Automatic
Your Dependence on Him

13

Insurance

Many folks don't realize how much money they spend on insurance premiums, so they don't calculate potential savings. Then again, some don't know enough to know when they need insurance, or when they should self-insure—do without.

Insurance is risk assessment and coverage. It entails paying a premium to an *insurer* who will pay a predetermined sum—the *insured amount*—to a named person—the *beneficiary*—if a risk develops. It does not remove risks. Rather, it provides income or equivalent if the firm or uncertain future event happens.

Insurance deals with the future, so like all decisions about future events, we need to go to Jesus for guidance—only He knows the future. Prophet Isaiah reminds us in Isaiah 26:4 to "Trust in the LORD forever, For in GOD the LORD, *we have* an everlasting Rock."

Does trusting God mean we should have no insurance? No, it means we should understand we can't secure our future; Jesus is our security and He might tell us to go without insurance coverage!

The same principles apply to decisions about all insurance forms. Whether life, disability, or car insurance, when you consider insurance, answer two questions:

Insurance Questions

1. Is there a risk I must cover?
2. How much coverage do I need?

In this chapter, I will look at a couple, Joshua and Rebecca, and daughter Sara, as I discuss briefly, six insurance types. Joshua works outside the home; Rebecca manages the home and looks after five-year-old Sara, and does not get an income:

1. Life
2. Mortgage Life
3. Mortgage Loan
4. Homeowner's
5. Disability
6. Equipment and appliances (otherwise referred to as extended warranties)

Why Life Insurance

Life insurance provides money to your dependents (family and others) when you die. Income loss on Joshua's death is the risk to cover. Joshua and Rebecca must settle this risk question before moving to the next question: how much coverage they need. Simply, on Joshua's death, the *insured amount* should be enough to replace his income and pay funeral and other expenses that might arise, such as costs to care for Sara. This insured amount might be lacking for Rebecca and Sara because Joshua might be a part-time student, working to improve his earning potential. So to decide life insurance coverage, Joshua and Rebecca need to look at a *realistic* future living standard for Rebecca and Sara. Most important, as they decide the insured amount, Joshua and Rebecca need to depend on Jesus for their security, confident He alone knows the future, and nothing they do will secure it.

You could buy life insurance for another reason. A way to fund the Great Commission on your death is to name your church or other charity to get life insurance funds. Even if your family depends on your income, ask the Lord if you should take out extra term life insurance with your church or charity as beneficiary. I urge you not to do this unless the Lord directs you.

Who Should Take Out Life Insurance

Life insurance replaces, and sometimes replaces and supplements, someone who dies' income. So get life insurance coverage on the income provider's life. In our example, Joshua, is the income provider, so on his death he needs enough life insurance to provide Rebecca with income for her and Sara. Sometimes insurance agents will sell newlyweds insurance on husband and wife's lives. Rebecca has no income so normally she doesn't need life insurance. But if they agree that if she died, Joshua might need to *supplement* his income to cover child care and other household expenses, they might buy insurance on Rebecca's life enough to pay these amounts. As well, Joshua might buy life insurance on Rebecca's life to pay her funeral expenses.

As Joshua and Rebecca's material worth and investment income rise, they would review their financial affairs to decide if on the next renewal they should lower their life insurance coverage.

Who Should Not Take Out Life Insurance

Anyone who has no dependents and who has enough savings to pay all expenses on death does not need insurance. As I said earlier, there are exceptions. Individuals might buy life insurance to leave funds to their favourite charities or others when they die.

How Much Life Insurance Do You Need

Assume Table I in chapter 4 and Appendices 6-1 and 6-2 show Joshua and Rebecca's material worth ($38,500) and monthly salaries ($3,150). On either Joshua or Rebecca's death, how much insurance would they need to be no worse off? Excluding inflation and future salary rises, on Joshua's death, Rebecca would need to replace Joshua's $38,500 annual income, and about $6000 funeral and related expenses. To decide the insured amount, Joshua and Rebecca would consider future matters such as these: Rebecca's likely earnings, child care costs, Sara's education costs, inflation, interest rates, life expectancy.

After applying these assumptions, Joshua and Rebecca might decide $50,000 yearly would be a more fitting income for Rebecca on his death, and would calculate insurance coverage based on this amount. After this decision, they would choose the life insurance type they need and then get quotes.

The insurance company would calculate its premium to replace $50,000 yearly income and $6000 funeral expenses using several ingredients such as interest rate, age, smoking habit, and life expectancy. Rebecca would receive a lump sum, which she could invest or convert to an annual $50,000 payment. Each person's life insurance premium quote would be unique, showing his circumstance.

Different Life Insurance Types

After deciding insurance coverage and amount, with an independent advisor's help, if needed, Joshua and Rebecca must settle how to get coverage. I group life insurance coverage into two classes, *renting* or *buying*—temporary or permanent.

The insurance industry calls the *renting* class *term insurance*. It is basic; there for a time and then you must renew it. You pay a premium to cover a fixed amount for a time. Joshua might pay $250 yearly for $250,000 for 10 years insurance coverage. And if he died within 10 years, the Redemption Insurance Company would pay Rebecca $250,000. If he lived beyond the tenth year, he will have to renew his insurance coverage or go without. So, with God's guidance, Joshua and Rebecca would look at their family circumstance at year 10 to see how much insurance they needed. Their condition might have changed; they might have investments and other income-producing assets that would allow them to lower or in some circumstances, go without insurance coverage.

If they decided they needed to continue term insurance coverage, by then it will be more expensive say, $400 yearly for the same $250,000 coverage: the older you are the more expensive the coverage. But, the older you are the more savings and investments you are likely to amass and so lowering your insurance needs.

The *buying* class includes term insurance coverage and something else, such as savings or health coverage. So Joshua would pay premiums for more than his basic life insurance coverage need. Whole Life, Universal Life, or others that build cash reserves are examples in this class. You must understand this insurance class so you can decide if this is the best form to get the extras beyond your term insurance coverage.

For the same $250,000 coverage, Joshua would pay, say $350 yearly—$100 representing excess premium over term insurance. Simplistically, the company would invest this excess and keep some investment income as profit and assign the rest to you, the insured. This is how *cash builds up* and becomes available for you to borrow, or use to lower future premiums.

If you borrowed against this cash build, the interest rate would be lower than you might pay at a bank, but higher than your regular savings would earn. If you are a good steward of God's funds, *why allow an insurance company to amass your savings to lend you at a rate higher than your savings could earn?* To me, this isn't sensible. You would be much better off using the excess premium (the difference in premium between whole life and term) to invest in a mutual fund[1] or other investment form. This way, the insurance company does not benefit from your savings. But if you sense this is the way the Lord is leading you, go for it.

Each person and family's condition is special so consult an independent financial advisor before buying life insurance. Don't let insurance salespeople prescribe your insurance needs. Ensure you understand all choices including term, whole life, and mixtures. If you choose whole life or other similar policies that build up cash reserves, understand your reasons. And know the insurance company will reap some benefits.

Mortgage Life Insurance

The risk for mortgage life insurance is the same as for normal life insurance. But, Joshua would buy mortgage life insurance from the financial institution for the mortgage loan's value and not for his annual income. And the financial institution would be the beneficiary. Joshua and Rebecca would not look at this insurance alone but would look at their full life insurance needs.

Let's look at how mortgage life insurance might arise. If Joshua borrowed $50,000 from a bank to buy a house, the bank would *write* its name on the property's title, and so become *co-owner* up to the loan's value. This is the typical mortgage. If Joshua died before he paid off the mortgage, the bank would have two choices. It might sell the house and then give Rebecca the difference between the amount they got on sale and the outstanding loan. Or, it could allow Rebecca to take over the mortgage loan and repay it. To do the second, the bank would need to be comfortable with Rebecca's finances after Joshua's death. The bank might accept this alternative if Joshua's life insurance and other assets provided enough income to pay the mortgage and give Rebecca and Sara an acceptable income to live on.

To prevent these events, when he gets a mortgage, Joshua could insure his life for the mortgage's full value. This would supplement his regular life insurance coverage. But is this a sound financial decision? I do not think so. Why? If Joshua and Rebecca ran the numbers and looked at their flexibility, they would agree it isn't a sound choice.

Joshua would be better off with extra term insurance with an insurance company. He would own the policy, the financial institution wouldn't, Rebecca would be the beneficiary, not the bank, and Rebecca would have the choice to take over the mortgage, if that alternative fitted her finances then.

Though mortgage life insurance through the bank is inexpensive, it has other disadvantages. First, the insured amount falls as the mortgage balance drops over the mortgage's life, but the premium does not fall. Second, unlike a term life policy, the bank has the right to hike premiums. Third, it isn't portable. So, if you switch your mortgage, you need to reapply for life insurance with your new bank. Like all financial decisions, listen, hear and understand your alternatives and let the Lord guide your decision.

Mortgage Loan Insurance

Besides *mortgage life insurance,* in Canada, borrowers who pay less than 25% down payment to buy their primary home must buy *mortgage loan insurance* to cover the borrower's potential inability to repay the loan. The Canadian Mortgage and Housing Corporation (CMHC), a Government agency, insures mortgages for borrowers with less than 25% down payment. CMHC's Mortgage Loan Insurance covers lenders' financial loss risks that might occur if a homeowner defaults on his mortgage loan. CMHC charges a premium varying between 0.5% and 3.10% of the loan depending on the price financed. Don't confuse this *mortgage loan insurance* with *mortgage life insurance* that is a guarantee to pay your mortgage outstanding when you die.

The lender, the financial institution, is the beneficiary. I discuss mortgage loan insurance in chapter 14, buying a home.

Homeowner's Insurance

So far we looked at insuring against income loss risks or mortgage default. There is another insurance class, *homeowners insurance*.

Homeowners insurance is a package policy covering damage to your property and damage caused by many disasters. There are exceptions, so you must read the policy, as boring as you think it might be. This insurance excludes maintenance-related problems; that's the homeowners' responsibility. As well, coverage includes liability insurance for accidents that might happen at your home.

Insure your home for the replacement cost, the estimated rebuilding cost. Normally, the insurance policy will include your personal belongings' coverage at 40 to 60% of the home's coverage. In some policies, you can separate insurance on personal belongings. So if the insurance company's value is too much, list your personal property and value major items at its replacement cost. Pray about this value. Do you want to replace the stuff you amassed? Do you want to pay a high premium to insure your personal belongings? You can't replace some belongings, others you wouldn't want to replace. This can be an emotional decision. Don't pay large premiums for stuff you wouldn't replace if stolen or lost!

For *valuables* such as jewellery, you should review the policy coverage to see if you accept the limits or you wish to raise them. Be alert; the *small* extra cost to lift your insurance could trap you into buying insurance you don't need!

Sometimes with the homeowner's insurance package is up to almost half million dollars personal liability coverage for accidents in the home. For a small increase in premium, you could raise this coverage to one million dollars. Prayerfully review your affairs before deciding how much coverage you need.

Yearly, I notice my insurance company adding small amounts for coverage I don't need, so before I decide my coverage, I ask them to remove these items. Don't accept blindly renewal notices from your broker or insurance company, review the policy and delete unneeded items to lower your premiums.

If you rent a home, you can buy inexpensive insurance to cover your belongings' value. You must decide if you will insure for replacement cost or cash value—the difference in the two is the deprecation reduction in the second. As I mentioned earlier, you might not want to replace many items if you lost them or someone stole them, so you might not wish to include their value to decide the premium.

Disability Insurance

Often we overlook this area. Life insurance protects against the income loss at death. Disability insurance protects against the income loss if you become disabled, and your income stopped. Some companies subsidise disability premiums. During my 32-year business career, mostly as a senior executive, I bought disability insurance, even though I did not work in a factory or other job that had an obvious risk of becoming physically disabled.

Decide where risks exist and how much insurance you need using the same principles as for life insurance. Some professions have obvious risks, others don't. Your insurance salesperson might show you a table with disability risks at different ages; it could startle you. Still, ask the Lord to lead you.

Equipment and Appliances Insurance

When you buy a TV, DVD player, fridge, stove, or other item, the salesperson will ask you, casually, to spend an extra $50, $100 or other amount to buy *extended warranty* coverage for the item. What are the risks your equipment and appliances will break before the extended warranty expires, and repair costs will be more than the extended warranty's cost? Different research shows, for most consumer goods the risk is low, and when the item breaks, likely you will spend less than the extended warranty's cost.

Providing extended warranty is big business in the consumer product industry. Some companies' profits come almost fully from this source!

I don't take this coverage and I have never regretted those decisions. I do not think it is a needed expense. Appliances will last for years before you need to repair them. Usually, if there are problems they will arise in the early period when the equipment is under warranty. It is unusual for them to need repairs during the early years. And when problems arise, the repair cost is likely to be less than the extended warranty's cost. Still, as I discussed in chapter 9, I provide systematically for equipment repairs and replacements in the *Capital Fund*—I self-insure.

Beware; salespeople will pressure you to buy extended warranties and tell you about the small extra cost compared to the product cost. For consumer items, the cost is around 30% of the price, but that's not the point; you don't need it. Don't buy extended warranty without prayer and reflection. Start a capital fund by putting aside a small amount each month to cover future equipment and appliances' repairs and replacement. Then you will not need these extended warranties.

Insurance Deductible

As I mentioned in chapter 9, a way to lower premiums on some insurance policies, is to raise the deductible, the amount you would pay on a claim. So, if you insured your car and agreed to pay the first $250 if you claimed, your deductible would be $250. Over many years, I raised deductibles for my car and home insurances to the value I saved in my capital fund. Gradually, I hiked the deductible and put saved premiums in my capital fund. These days, the insurance deductible part of my capital fund represents 100% premium savings. Currently, my car deductible is at the maximum allowed by the insurance company, $2,500.

Summary

The same principles apply to decisions about all insurance forms. Whether life, disability, or car insurance, when you consider insurance, answer two questions:

1. Is there a risk I must cover?
2. How much coverage do I need?

Before buying insurance, consult an independent financial advisor and explain your condition. Do not rely on an insurance agent's advice. He might be a friend and trustworthy, but he will benefit from selling you insurance, so unwittingly, his advice might not be objective.

Think About This

How much insurance do you need? Jesus Christ
What is the risk you need to cover? Separation
from Jesus

Chapter Notes:

1. As a reminder, a Mutual Fund is an organisation that invests
    many depositors' pooled funds. Usually a professional manager
    manages it. Mutual Funds specialise, each with a different
    investment objective. Examples of different funds are as fol-
    lows: money market (typically government bonds), *income, balanced,
    Latin America, USA growth,* and so on.

14

Buying a Home and Choosing a Mortgage

What Buying Your Home Entails

In the 1960s through the early 1980s, except for few brief periods, when you bought your home, you would have set the base for the most predictable major, tax-free capital gains in your lifetime. Today or later when you sell that home, you would expect to get a tax-free gain substantially larger than the inflation rate; that was for houses bought then. These days, the results of selling your home bought after mid-1980s will vary based on when you bought it and where you live.

In the early 1980s, North Americans went on a spending spree; spending money they didn't have. The greed mentioned in chapter two was rampant, and like many areas in the economy, housing prices soured. Canadian real estate markets in

Vancouver and Toronto sizzled until the mid-1980s when prices fell. The slump lasted almost 10 years.

No longer can you assume housing prices will climb at a rate significantly greater than inflation, or even at the inflation rate. Look at Table X; it shows selected housing prices in the Toronto and Montreal areas for 1989, 1998, and 2005. The 1998 prices are between five and fifteen percent lower than the 1989 prices. Though the 2005 prices are up significantly over 1998 prices, in Oakville, prices *fell* between 2004 and 2005.

Am I suggesting you should not own your home? No, I am cautioning you to pray about the *timing* to buy a home. Most of all, do not buy to get a capital gain. Your home is not—should never have been—a speculative investment. Use the same procedures and spending aids to buy a home as you apply to all major spending decisions—*GAS, PEACE, PLANE* and *Affordability Index.*

Table X

Housing Prices[1] (Detached Bungalow) in Selected Areas
($000)

Detached Bungalow	1989	1998	2005
Toronto Area			
Markham	285	232	425 (375 at end 2004)
Oakville	210	200	295 (310 at end 2004)
Montreal Area			
Beaconsfield	130	118	240
Dorval	114	104	210

In recent years as mortgage rates and other interest rates fell, monthly mortgage payments dropped below monthly rentals for similar homes, and many people bought the houses or apartments they were renting. Several didn't grasp that owning a home entailed more than a mortgage payment. And some couldn't meet monthly housing costs and so sold their homes at significant emotional costs, and sometimes at a financial loss. Still others took large mortgages, bought large homes to rent parts to reduce their mortgages. This worked well until problems started with tenants, and, or they had no tenant for a few months.

Before you buy a home, understand home ownership's full effects. Owning a home involves these annual expenses:

- Mortgage payment that can rise or fall (I recall 12-15% mortgage interest rates in the mid-1980s compared with 4 and 5% recently, and 6-8 % today)
- Property insurance
- Repairs and upkeep
- Property taxes, and school tax
- Heat and lighting costs
- Transfer taxes in some Provinces—paid once
- Other expenses including one-off legal fees and several small charges for mortgage and property title

Normally, when you own your home, you build equity in it as you lower your mortgage loan, but your property could lose value if the housing market falls. Still, if you didn't buy to resell, this shouldn't be an issue.

Renting a Home

Renting a home, on the other hand, includes a monthly payment with responsibility to upkeep the grounds and often, responsibility for heating and lighting. You have no other expenses, but your monthly rent does not build equity in the house, and falling property values isn't your risk.

For many properties, monthly rental rates change in a narrow range. Moreover, sometimes for some properties, Governments regulate rents to keep them in this narrow range. In contrast to owning, depending on your mortgage term (see Composition of a Mortgage Payment below), mortgage rates, and so your mortgage payment, might vary significantly over the mortgage's life.

Today, folks rush to own their home and plunge deep in debt as their housing costs consume a significant share of their monthly budgets. Be patient, rent until you can afford to buy. Then you will build a solid financial base and lower financial stress.

Issues to Consider for the Rent or Buy Decision

Before evaluating the renting or buying a home decision, review the three essential money management steps discussed in chapter four. Next, ensure compatibility among your *material goals*, budget goals, and your goal to own your home.

Intuitively, you might think always, owning will be better than renting. After all, owning builds equity; but owning could cause you to defer or cancel *other goals*. So, with your *material goals* and the *GAS Principle* as focal points, evaluate the rent and buy choices only after considering the following matters:

1. Your *Capital Fund* balance: What's the status of your capital fund? Have you been saving a housing down payment?
2. *Mortgage:* Do you have 25% down payment for a *conventional mortgage* or will you need an expensive *high ratio mortgage?*[2] Without *adequate*[3] down payment, you cannot afford to buy the house.
3. Your preliminary *budgets* to rent and to buy the house: Will you be able to allow in your household budget, extra

expenses resulting from buying? What will you sacrifice to do so? How realistic is this?

4. Your *family*: How much space will you need? Are you and your wife planning a child shortly?

5. Current and projected *economic conditions*: What is the state of the economy and housing market? Booming, flat, or declining?

6. Available *financial benefits* for first time homebuyers: Some provinces offer incentives to first time homebuyers. As well, first time buyers can withdraw tax-free up to $20,000 from their RRSP account, as a loan to them for the down payment on their homes.[4]

7. Your *job* circumstance: Are you likely to remain at your current employer in the next year or so? Is your employer likely to transfer you to a different location? What is the company's policy if they move you and you lose by selling your home? In my thirty-two year career, we moved nine times and we dealt with these matters.

Buying a house likely will be your most expensive lifetime outlay. Pray, look at the issues systematically but do not procrastinate. Remember, you must face decisions you put off today, so tackle them today. Understand that your expenses to rent or to own a home will differ.

You can do the rent or buy analysis with help from several sources including the Internet. Some books and financial advisors might tell you to calculate two net present values (NPVs),[5] one for the annual renting costs and another for annual owning costs. For this analysis, you will need a key estimate: your home's future selling price. Nobody will know this price but you might estimate it by looking at past, current, and expected trends. Still, it's your best guess that will influence the calculations.

Do not rely on this NPV analysis alone. Your home is not an investment property. Do not buy your home just to resell it, though you can consider its resale in the future. If you believe you might need to sell the property shortly after buying it, rent rather than buy. If you are uncomfortable with high housing prices, ask God if you should wait until prices fall. Set up your price range based on your buying standard, your budget, and buy when your preferred conditions exist; otherwise rent.

This rent or buy decision is important and will affect your household budget. So look at its full effects, tangible and intangible. Consider your financial condition and sift it through the GAS Principle. Let *Key Truth # 3: Seek First His Kingdom and submit your requests to Him*, guide your decision.

Buying the Home

If you decided to buy rather than rent a home, try the form in appendix 7 that my wife and I used successfully to help us buy homes during our nine job-related transfers. We would buy a house within three days of visiting a location because we prepared extensively before our visit. If you move in the same geographic area, the approach will be much simpler as visiting the location might not be an issue. Our moves usually were outside Quebec (our home province for many years) or outside Canada.

In our many moves, my wife and I tried to resolve most buying issues before visiting the new location to house-shop. With the Internet and other available means, today it is much easier to research the physical location where you plan to buy a house, and so shorten your physical presence at that location. Remember, buying a home will affect your household budget significantly. Here are some matters to consider as you decide where to live:

- Services you need in the new area.
- You and your family's transport needs—this will settle commuting to work and its time and money costs. When

we moved to Tokyo, Japan, we decided I would commute by train, so we needed to live close to a train station.
- Recreational services for each season.
- Security
- Available schools
- Property tax rates
- Nearness to a library
- Closeness to shopping, medical and other services
- Closeness to parks—helpful with young children

Each item will affect your decision differently. Identify and rank the top three. Before you go shopping for a home, prepare a budget with an upper limit. Agree with your spouse key goals and guidelines for the home you wish to buy— size, bedrooms, finished or unfinished basement, kitchen style, and so on.

Ensure you get a down payment you can afford (that fits your budget). Arrange your mortgage, interview and then select a Real Estate Agent (agent). Ask about his experience and ask him to refer you to two people whose homes he helped buy, not sell. Check these references.

The seller pays the agent who takes his commission from the selling price. The two agents—yours and the sellers'—get their commissions from the selling price. So do not expect your agent to look after your interest only. Your agent works for you although you do not pay him to help you buy the house (the seller does).

Unless you have some basis to trust your agent, do not disclose to him your final price. Tell him a listing-price[6] range, services you need (such as closeness to a train station), and other guidelines to help him select houses to show you.

Learn the sale procedure in detail. Ask your agent and others as many questions as needed until you understand fully the nuances. Prepare, prepare, prepare! Nothing beats preparation. When you visit the location, ask the agent to schedule several appointments in sequence.

During your house-shopping trip, don't become overtly attached to one house or you will buy it at an "emotional" price. Use Appendix 7 as you visit each house. You and your spouse should write separate notes about each house. Each evening, compare notes and list the top three houses you have seen so far; rank them based on previously agreed goals and guidelines. Repeat the procedure daily, changing the top three if relevant. When you decide to stop visiting houses, revisit the top three for a more thorough inspection to clarify issues you noted during previous visits.

Later, put an offer[7] on your number one choice knowing you would be happy with your two other selections, and so you would be ready to walk away from this house if the price isn't right. Do your best to get your number one choice, but don't exceed your original maximum price, unless you and your spouse agree. If you and your spouse believe you must raise your maximum price, look at your goals, budget and other areas you looked at to set the price. Pray; answer this question: *what has changed that motivates you to pay a price higher than you prayed about and agreed?* Have you and your spouse changed the goals with which you were working? Have you or your spouse become emotionally attached to the house? Are you responding to coercion or pressure from your agent?

After selecting one house, sign the sale and purchase agreement subject to satisfactory (to you) building inspection. Get an independent, professional building inspector to give you a report on the property. It would be normal for him to identify around $10,000 urgent repairs you did not notice. Negotiate a lower price for the house to offset needed repairs that the housing inspection showed.

According to the 2001 Canadian Census, 65.8% of Canadians owned their homes, up from 64% in the 1996 Census. Booming real estate markets pushed this number to 67% by 2006. Normally, folks build equity when they own their home, but I want to caution you about two mortgage types to avoid; they can lead to financial disaster, and equity loss:

- No down payment and low down payment
- Interest only

No down Payment and low down Payment

For a conventional mortgage, you need 25% of the purchase price (or appraised value) of the home as a down payment. As housing prices soared, *to help individuals own their home,* financial institutions lowered and later some eliminated down payments to buy a house. In Canada, the Canadian Mortgage and Housing Corporation (CMHC), a Government agency, promotes buying homes this way.

The CMHC insures mortgages for borrowers with less than 25% down payment. CMHC's Mortgage Loan Insurance covers lenders' financial loss risks that might occur if a homeowner defaults on his mortgage loan. CMHC charges a premium varying between 0.5% and 3.10% of the loan depending on the price financed. Don't confuse this *mortgage loan insurance* with *mortgage life insurance* that is a guarantee to pay your mortgage outstanding when you die.

So, if you borrowed $200,000 from a bank with no down payment, you would pay an extra 3.10% or $6,200 for mortgage loan insurance, spread over the mortgage's life. If your mortgage term was 25 years, without extra payment, this would cost $10,000 at 5.2% interest rate.

What is no, or low down payment effect on families? To be sure, owning a home can build equity, but without a down payment, or with a small down payment, home ownership will strain your family budget and strain family relations. If you don't have a down payment, you can't afford to own a home, wait; renting is the better alternative.

It gets worse! Recently, financial companies introduced a new mortgage type. Interest-only mortgages.

Interest-Only Mortgages

An Interest-Only Mortgage gives *qualified homebuyers* the option to pay interest only for the first 5 or 10 years of their mortgage. Following the interest-only period, the lender will adjust payments to allow for principal and interest payments. Still, homebuyers must qualify for a mortgage based on the *ability to support monthly principal and interest payments amortized over up to 25 years.*

The monthly payment for a traditional five-year $175,000 fixed mortgage at 5.30% is about $1,050. With an Interest-Only Mortgage, the payment would be $765, a $285 monthly or $3,420 yearly difference.

I thought no down payment mortgages was a bad idea that created financial hardships on people already struggling financially, but this interest only idea is ridiculous! Society needs to encourage folks to save to buy stuff, and to wait until they can afford to spend. An item is affordable if it fits in your budget, does not expose you to undue risks, and does not cause emotional and financial stress. Affordable does not mean removing down payments or paying interests only to buy a house you can't upkeep, and whose normal operating costs you can't pay regularly.

Look again at owning compared with renting a home. Without a down payment, probably you won't be able to find regular cash flow to pay regular housing and other costs.

Please understand when you take on an interest only mortgage, you could get the worst of all worlds! You take on home ownership's costs and risks but you cannot *afford* to buy a home. Wait! If you plan to get an interest only mortgage, think again, you cannot afford to buy a home now. What happens when during the 10-year interest-only period housing prices fall, and you need to sell your home for an unforeseen reason?

Before you take on a no down payment or interest only mortgage, pray, seek God's direction. I cannot see a circumstance when this is a good idea.

Composition of a Mortgage Payment

As we saw earlier, your mortgage is the loan the bank or other institution will advance to you using your house as security. If you cannot repay this loan, the institution will sell your house, and from cash they get, they will take the amount you owe and give you the excess above their loan balance.

How does the financial institution calculate your mortgage payment? Table XI shows a simplistic annual mortgage payment analysis, highlighting the principal and interest parts.

Note how the interest part falls and the principal part rises with each payment. Therefore, a one-off principal payment, with regular mortgage payment, ensures a more rapid principal decline. View your mortgage payment as your monthly rental with a rising savings part![8]

Table XI

Simplistic Mortgage Amortisation Schedule (Assuming Annual Payment)

Year	Start Balance	Payment	10% Interest	Principal
1	1000	263.80	100.00	163.80
2	836.2	263.80	83.62	180.18
3	656.0	263.80	65.60	198.20
4	457.8	263.80	45.78	218.02
5	239.8	263.80	23.98	239.82

Normally your mortgage is more complex, but the principle is similar. In Table XI, I assumed the mortgage term and the amortisation period were the same, but usually they are not. The mortgage term represents the life of the agreement with the financial institution—six months, one year, five years and so on. Your monthly payment will be the same during the term; when it ends, you can re-negotiate the mortgage. Ask your financial institution about available mortgage terms. Understand differences between open and closed, and fixed and variable rate mortgages.[9]

How do you decide what *term* to select? Look at goals you are working with God. What can you glean from them? Ask the Lord to help you see His plans. Look at your financial plan, your budget, the economy, interest rates, and inflation rate. In the early 1980's with high and rising interest and inflation rates, you would be prudent to arrange a *term* with a fixed rate for about one year, so you would know your cost at least one year ahead. You would not set the term for 10 years. Today with interest rates and the inflation rate low, you might choose to fix the *term* (and rate) for five, ten or more years, depending on your budget, risk tolerance, and view of the economy.

If you believed interest rates were trending down, you could choose an interim position: an *open* six-month mortgage. After six months, you would review the term again. If rates went down, you might fix the rate for five, ten or more years. This is not a science. Beware; seek guidance and ensure you understand available alternatives. Remember, your mortgage will affect your budget and could cause emotional instability in your family; don't gamble with interest rates!

Besides the mortgage term, you must decide over what period to repay your mortgage; this is the *amortisation period—* 20, 25, 30 years. The longer the amortisation period, the longer to repay the principal and the more interest you will pay. Table XII shows examples of amortisation periods of 20 and 25 years, and monthly and twice-monthly (26 yearly) payments. Notice the differences in interest paid over the mortgages' lives, and the interest amounts. As well, notice your mortgage loan (principal) hardly changes after five years even though you paid the set monthly amount; most early years' payments go to interest.

In Canada, mortgage interest on your principal residence is not a tax-deductible expense, so if your marginal or top tax rate is 40% you must earn $100[10] to pay $60 of mortgage.

Table XII

Repayment of $100,000 Mortgage With Different Assumptions

	Monthly Payment	Twice-Monthly Payment	Monthly Payment	Twice-Monthly Payment
Mortgage amount	$100,000	$100,000	$100,000	$100,000
Interest Rate	10 %	10%	10%	10%
Mortgage Term	5 years	5 years	5 years	5 years
Amortisation Period	20 years	20 years	25 years	25 years
Payment	$952	$438	$894	$412
Interest Paid Over The Loan's Life	$128,402	$127,898	$168,343	$167,751
End of Term Balance	$89,588	$89,587	$93,992	$93,991
Principal Paid at the end of term (5 years)	$10,412	$10,413	$6,008	$6,009

Mortgage Refinancing

Sometimes falling interest rates might prompt you to consider renegotiating your mortgage. In other words, you might believe repaying[11] your mortgage and getting a new one at a lower interest rate, will save money. Before I review an example, I should remind you that when your mortgage term expires you would be able to renegotiate your mortgage, penalty free. So, if you are thinking about renegotiating your mortgage, first find out how long before your mortgage term expires. If it is short, wait.

If you bought your home at what you thought was a great interest rate, and interest rates fell, how would you approach refinancing or renegotiating your mortgage rate? Here are some principles to consider:

- Look at the full picture using a net present value (NPV) analysis. Do not look at only the original mortgage payment at the *old rate* and the new payment at the *new rate*.
- The bank or financial institution (Institution) will not be out-of-pocket by refinancing or renegotiating. Why would they allow you to break a contract so they become worse off and you become better off? They won't! They will recover the NPV of the interest rate differential (that is, the difference between the existing 9% rate and the new 7%) rate for the unexpired mortgage term. So, when you renegotiate at 7%, the Institution will calculate the NPV of interest they will lose (2%) and charge this to you as a penalty, so they are no worse off.
- You won't know if you will benefit from renegotiating your mortgage because you would need to guess if interest rates would rise in the future. You could benefit, but I emphasize, you would be gambling with interest rates, if these conditions were to exist:

  (a) You renegotiate an extended mortgage term (say, from five to seven years) *and,*
  (b) During the extension, interest rates rise about your negotiated rate (say, from seven percent to ten percent; but you won't know this in advance) *and,*

(c) The NPV of this interest rate hike during the extension exceeds the NPV of the penalty paid.

You will never know before you renegotiate if interest rates will rise during the extension period. So, pray and seek God's guidance as you do the calculations. Each case is different with two influencing causes:

1. The percentage drop in the mortgage interest rate
2. The unexpired mortgage term

Depending on these two reasons, the Institution might propose a blended[12] rate to cushion the penalty's impact. Before you renegotiate, perform the following calculations:

Assume you bought your home several years ago and your outstanding mortgage is $90,000 at 9% interest. The unexpired term is five years, and the amortization period is 20 years. Today mortgage rates have fallen to 7%. Should you refinance? These are the facts based on semi-annual compounding:

○ Your current annual mortgage payment at 9% is $9600 (one twelfth paid monthly).
○ The annual payment at 7% (excluding refinancing penalties) would be $8304 (one twelfth paid monthly)
○ Annual savings (excluding penalties) will be $1296 ($9600-$8304) over five years.
○ Rough estimate of the Institution's penalty charge is $7000 (representing the NPV of the 2% interest rate differential over five years - the unexpired term).

Base your decision solely on the lower of the NPV of your projected annual savings of $1296 over the unexpired mortgage term, compared with the NPV of the Institution's penalty charge. The NPV at 7% of annual savings of $1296 (computed monthly) over five years is about $5,500. So if you had to pay the penalty of $7000 either up-front or over the unexpired term only, it would be more expensive to refinance.

The Institution may offer a blended rate *to spread the $7000 over the new mortgage term of say seven years.* So, it might add, say, $110 monthly to the proposed monthly payment referred to above[13] to recover $7000 over seven years (if this was the new term). Even so, the bottom line is this: the Institution will not lose but will recover its penalty either as a lump sum or over the new mortgage term.

See an independent financial advisor to help you understand this matter.

Selling the Home

To sell your home, prepare as I discussed for buying your home. First, identify your goals. Next, apply rigorously the planning and estimating parts of PEACE Budgetary Control. Then select an agent to whom you outline your objectives. The reason you are selling will be critical to the *acting* or doing stage. The more time-flexibility available, the longer you can wait for your target price.

Research the market with the agent and set a realistic final price. Remember, the time value of money (refer to chapter six). It may be better to accept a lower price sooner rather than a higher price much later.

Often you might think you should spend money to repair your house before you sell. Don't do this automatically; rarely will you increase the sale price by your outlay.

Summary

I believe at the right time and with God's blessing, home ownership is good. Equally, at the wrong time it can push you deep in debt.

Low interest rates sparked a buying frenzy in Canada and the USA. It will fizzle. Don't panic believing you need to buy a home today. Be patient. Some folks bought without *counting the cost*. It's not too late to review what you did and if needed correct it. Before you buy a home, prepare a budget to see if you can afford to buy. Seek God's timing, and remember you might be better off to rent for a while until you save a down payment that fits your budget. As well, ensure home ownership costs do not rob God of amounts He wants for His work.

Flee from Interest-Only, and low, and no down payment arrangements to buy a home. They will *bind* you and your family.

Think About This

Patience is the companion of wisdom.[14]

Chapter Notes:

1. Royal LePage: *Survey of Canadian House Prices, Historical Data–Quebec-July 1989; Quebec-Jan 1998; Ontario–July 1989; Ontario 1998.* Royal LePage, *Survey of Canadian House Price,* Fourth Quarter 2005, Issue 34.
2. Larger down payments give smaller mortgages, and lower interest payments. If your down payment is less than 25% you can get a high ratio mortgage but you will need mortgage loan insurance from CMHC.
3. What is adequate for you? After answering these questions, you should decide. For me, less than 25% down payment is inadequate. So your first home needs to be small and in a location with modest prices!

4. See Chapter 16, Retirement Planning. I discourage borrowing from your RRSP (pensions). Start a Capital Fund and use amounts from this source as your down payment.
5. Net Present Value: As a reminder, the present value (today's value) of future cash flows, discounted (the process of finding today's value of a series of future cash flows) at a specific interest rate (your average cost of borrowing), minus an initial outlay, where relevant.
6. This is the advertised price. Typically, you will buy the house for less. Research the current pattern in the area. What percent of listing prices have been final selling prices? This is an important input to help you decide your final price.
7. This is a formal process where you stipulate the price and conditions under which you are prepared to buy the house. Understand it before you start house shopping.
8. Table XI shows the split of your mortgage payment between interest and principal. The savings component in each payment is the amount allocated to principal. If housing prices fall below your cost you will save less.
9. With an open mortgage, you can repay the principal anytime without a penalty. For a closed mortgage, you pay a penalty if you repay before the term expires. There are also Variable Rate Mortgages and Fixed Rate Mortgages: A Variable Rate Mortgage is a mortgage with fixed payments, which allows for fluctuation in interest rates due to changing market conditions. Changes in the interest rate will determine how much of each payment will go towards the principal. Thus if the mortgage interest rate increases, the allocation to principal as in Table XI will decrease, and the reverse. A Fixed Rate Mortgage is a mortgage with fixed payments and the interest rate does not change during the mortgage term. Table XI shows the impact of a Fixed Rate Mortgage.
10. Income of $100 at a 40% tax rate is equal to taxes of $40 and disposable income of $60.
11. You might not repay the mortgage, rather, the bank might redo the terms with the same results.
12. Blending merely apportions the penalty over the new term (over seven years in our example) so that your monthly payment will be lower than the current level. Still you pay the penalty.
13. This extra payment will result in a blended rate greater than 7%.
14. St Augustine.

15

Leasing Compared with Buying an Automobile

L easing an automobile for private use is popular with individuals because it creates an *affordability illusion*. Folks use the monthly payment to decide if they can afford the automobile; often they can't. To understand leasing an automobile's effects, I will comment broadly on leasing.

Before the 1950s, we related leasing with real estate (land and buildings). Today you can lease almost every asset because leasing has become a proved and acceptable borrowing form. Let's look briefly at these leasing types:

1. Sale and leaseback
2. Service leases
3. Financial leases

Sale and Leaseback

Under this arrangement, a company needs cash and decides to *sell* an asset to a finance company. The company needs to use the asset in its business, and so it contracts with the finance company to use the asset for a fee. So, it sells the asset for, say, $100,000, and immediately *leases it back* for, say, $12,000 yearly. Here, the cash-need drives the company's decision.

After signing this lease, nothing changes but the asset's ownership. The company will continue to use the asset as if it owned it. Before the lease, the company deducted a *deprecation charge* that allowed it to write-off the asset's value over its useful life. After the lease, instead of depreciation, it will deduct the annual lease charge from its annual revenues.

The main reason the company would do this transaction is for the favourable cash flow effect.

Service (or Operating) Leases

IBM pioneered this lease type. The *lessor*, the company that owns the asset and offers the lease, allows a *lessee* to use the asset for his or her purposes. Often the lessor is responsible to up-keep the asset. In many offices, companies lease computers, office plants and other items. These are this lease's unique features:

1. The lessor allows the lessee to replace the asset, usually with a later version.
2. Often the lease is short-term and cancelable any time.
3. Unlike the sale and leaseback, lease payments do not cover each asset's full cost.
4. Usually the lease period is less than the asset's life.
5. The lessor can lease the same asset sequentially to others (the plants that I return today, he can lease to you tomorrow).

Why would a company choose this lease? Unlike the sale and lease back, a *financing arrangement*, this is a *convenience arrangement*. Often, companies use it for assets with short lives and assets not connected with its main business, and so the company doesn't want to use its staff to upkeep this asset. As well, it might choose to change this asset often, so it doesn't want to own it; houseplants are good examples.

Financial Leases

Individuals use this lease rather than the others. Sadly, it is a convenient way for many folks to contract to buy assets they can't afford. These folks do not separate the asset buying decision in its two essential parts: the need—do I need it; the affordability—how do I pay for it? In the *sale and lease back*, first, companies decide if they need the assets before deciding how to finance them. When companies use *financial leases*, again, first they decide if they need assets before looking at the best and most tax effective way to pay for them.

That's not what many individuals do. For private use, many people do not apply the *GAS Principle*, *PLANE Spending Analysis* and *Affordability Index* to see if they need an item. Rather, they look at the payment, a *low* monthly payment, and use that as the main decision input. Often they do not realize their actions' effects—they agree to buy an asset based solely on the monthly lease payments.

As I mentioned often, before committing to buy an item, like companies, use a spending decision procedure to help you decide if you need the item. And don't borrow except under special conditions that I discuss in chapters 5 and 11 to buy a home or to buy an automobile for work.

Today you can lease almost every asset. Still, the automobile is the most popular asset that individuals lease. As automobile prices soared, manufacturers came up with a clever strategy to get people to drive cars they can't afford, and be happy! By stressing a *modest* monthly payment, manufacturers create the illusion that leasing an automobile is a great deal.

Leasing is complex and many people don't understand its effects fully. Most folks do not *count* their spending decisions' cost, and so they do not understand their responsibilities in agreements they sign—folks lease automobiles and many don't realize their financial responsibilities under the lease agreement.

Leasing an Automobile

What does leasing an automobile entail? A person who decides to get an automobile might select it from the manufacturer (Ford), who arranges with its finance company to buy the automobile. For you to use and upkeep the automobile to a specific standard, the finance company (the lessor) signs an agreement (a lease) with you. In this agreement, you agree to pay a monthly amount (lease payment) for a period. After the period, either you pay a lump sum to buy the automobile based on terms in the lease, or you return the automobile to the lessor and take another automobile for the second lease, and the cycle resumes.

This is a financial lease in which the lessee keeps the automobile to an agreed standard, like he owned it. The lessee will benefit from repairs covered by warranty like an owner. Besides, there is a high but loose upkeep standard the lessee must uphold throughout the lease period to ensure he returns the automobile to the lessor in good condition. Here are this lease's other features:

- The lessee cannot end the lease; it is for a fixed term. Essentially, the lessee commits to pay the full lease cost spread over the lease period.
- The finance company, the lessor, pays the manufacturer the automobile's full price, including a profit.
- In the lease charge, the finance company, the lessor, gets its full cost, and a profit.

When the lease ends, if you return the automobile and restart the cycle (without buying the automobile after the lease), leasing is more expensive than outright buying. It's like renting a home. Your payment gives you no *equity*.

Table XIII
Leasing compared with Buying an Automobile

	Input from the Lessor	Lease	Buy
A	Buy Price including taxes	$18700	$21527
B	Residual value to buy after 4 years	$7025	0
C	Financing – Interest rate	2.0%	2.8%
D	Lease Period, and Loan Period –months	48	60
E	Kilometres allowed each year	20k	Unlimited
F	Down payment	0	0
G	Refundable deposit	$325	0
H	Monthly rate	$305	$385
	Payment Calculations		
I	Annual payments (H x 12)	$3660	$4620
J	Payments for 4 years excl. residual (I x 4)	$14640	$18480
K	Payments[1] incl. Residual (B+J)	$21665	$18480
L	Payments for 5 years (K+I)		$23100
	Net Present Value (NPV) Calculation[2]		
M	NPV of lease payments over four years and NPV of residual payment in B to buy the automobile (NPV of individual parts of items in row K)	$17568[3]	
N	NPV of payments over five years under buy alternative (NPV of individual payments in L)		$18692
O	NPV if automobile turned in at year 4 and an identical new lease entered for another four years	$21540	

Table XIII shows a Canadian lease example including taxes, with several important numbers. You get the figures in the shaded area "A" to "H" from the lessor. The final three rows, "M" to "O", show the key numbers that will affect your decisions: Row "M" shows the NPV of $17,568 to lease and then buy the automobile after the lease term (4 years). This is the least expensive alternative; it's about $ 1100 less than the second choice of outright buying in the "Buy" column.

If you returned the automobile after the lease and took another lease under the same terms, the NPV of $21,540 in row "N" is the highest of the three choices. So, if you planned to use the automobile beyond the first lease's end, you would be better off to lease with the idea to buy the automobile after the lease. Refer to chapter 11 where I discussed the *Affordability Index* and buying an automobile.

Summary

Before you decide to lease an automobile or other asset for private use, try to understand your responsibilities under the lease agreement. Look at the numbers and ask a trusted capable person to help you understand your commitment. Pray; seek God's direction. Realize you can't end the lease, and so, in essence, when you sign the agreement, you commit to buy the automobile or other asset.

If you plan to use the automobile or other asset for a short time, a week, a month, three months, rent it. But if you plan to use it regularly, you might be better off owning (including leasing then exercising the buy alternative) rather than leasing and then returning it when the lease ends.

As with all comments in this book, these comments apply to an automobile or other asset for personal use.

Think About This

Preparing a spending plan will not solve your problems but it will identify in advance your choices to reach your goals. Then you might decide if and how you aim to live in your means.

Chapter Notes:

1. This figure includes the "residual" because you decided to buy the car. Otherwise lease payments would be $21665- $7025 = $ 14640 from row J.
2. I will remind you of the concept of Net Present Value: It is today's value of a series of expenses in the future discounted at a specific interest rate.
3. This NPV excludes two potential expenses: Cost of mileage in excess of 20,000 kilometres per year, and expenses after the lease that is necessary to return the car in an acceptable state of repair.

Section IV

Looking Beyond the Sunset

List your Many Blessings and then
Tell Someone Today
about the Wonderful God We Serve,
Jesus Christ

16

Retirement Planning

What a wonderful *retirement* gift Jesus prepared for His children! He assures the *believer* that He has arranged a place in heaven for him. But what about retirement while on earth? First, you need to understand what retirement means to you. According to some dictionaries, it's "withdrawal from one's occupation or business." But I found a definition that intrigued me: retirement is, "withdrawal from office, business or active life." Withdrawal from active life; isn't that death ... almost!

The only reference to retirement in the Bible is in Numbers, referring to Levites who worked in the *Tent of Meeting*. Numbers 8:24-25 says:

> "This is what *applies* to the Levites: from twenty-five years old and upward they shall enter to perform service in the work of the tent of meeting. "But at

the age of fifty years they shall retire from service in the work and not work any more.

The Levites were the group God chose as exclusive workers in the *Tent of Meeting* while the Israelites sojourned in the wilderness (Exodus 25-30). *Retired* Levites though not primary workers, helped their younger colleagues in the *Tent of Meeting* (Numbers 8:26). You will recall that in return for working in the *Tent of Meeting,* Levites got a tithe from the remaining eleven Tribes of Israel (Numbers 18:24).

Retirement Isn't Biblical

Except during this temporary period when Levites worked in the *Tent of Meeting*, the Bible does not mention retirement. The retirement provision for Levites ended when Solomon's temple (1 Kings 8) replaced the *Tent of Meeting*.

Modern day retirement means leaving a job or career for a recreational lifestyle. For many people it means the end of a 9-to-5 schedule and the start of a self-directed lifestyle—doing what you want, when you want. Still, for others, it means a new career or extending the current career.

Freedom 55 is the utopia some commercials promise. As they promote it, retirement is selfish, impossible, and contrary to regular living patterns. Normally, people don't sit on beaches doing nothing every day! Although, when they are *busy* at work, this lifestyle *looks* attractive. But if it's their life's aim, it is unhealthy for mind, body, and soul. Besides, that pattern is against God's Word.

According to a 2005 Statistics Canada survey (Survey),[1] of 7.4 million people aged 55 and older:

1. 63.0% had retired at least once
2. 24.4% intended to retire

3. 9.7% do not intend to retire
4. 2.4% had never worked for pay

The Survey found these top four reasons to retire:

1. 24% personal or family responsibilities
2. 23% personal health
3. 20% completed required years of service
4. 17% sufficient financial security

Although people buy insurance policies to get freedom at 55, that's not driving their retirement decisions. As well, the Survey found around 17% of folks who retired returned to work, at least part time. Main reasons to return to work were financial (48%) and for interesting work (39%).

Today, God's people need to be alert to His call and do what He asks always, regardless of age, or other condition. To do His tasks, He will provide what we need.

Succession Planning

So, should a Christian retire? Although there are no biblical bases for retirement, the Bible shows folks who moved from their main jobs and careers to other tasks God prepared for them. The Bible shows also that sometimes God tells us to prepare others to replace us to do His call. This *succession planning* is integral to retirement planning and recognizes two essential ingredients. First, although you might not retire at a set age, later you must leave some jobs because of physical or other demands. Second, before you move on, often you need to get ready for the later task God prepared for you, which might entail preparatory full-time or part-time study.

We see God's hand in succession planning in Joshua replacing Moses (Numbers 27:18-23; Deuteronomy 31:7-23; Joshua

1:1-9), and Solomon succeeding David. As well, we see Apostle Paul mentoring Timothy in Titus 2:1-8. Paul highlights the need for older folks to show proper traits to younger folks so the younger ones might mimic and pass on right attitudes.

Note how God replaced Moses. Although Moses did not retire to today's promised utopian life on earth, he knew God was preparing him to move on and he needed to bless his successor, Joshua, under God's direction; and he did. These are some messages for us from God's succession planning He worked with Moses:

- As he did the job God gave him, Moses trained his successor, Joshua.
- Moses supported Joshua, and accepted God's decisions when God told him to pass leadership to Joshua.
- God provided everything Moses and Joshua needed, including timing the leadership change.

Rely on God to tell you when to move on to something else He prepared for you. This might be hard to accept, especially when you know you are good at your job. I know; I have been there! The key is to get to know God's will by staying in His Word continually, talking, listening to Him, and being sensitive to His Spirit.

God's call on your life is not age dependent. Look at Abraham and Sarah (Genesis 18:1-18). God might want you to give up a well-paid career at a tender age. According to the world's standard, this is when you are in your prime. Will you be willing then to do God's job that seems unattractive to the world? At age 55, with significant assured earnings ahead, the Lord showed me clearly, to leave my 32-year business career to work full-time for Him for no pay. After wrestling with this for over a year, leaving was one of my most peaceful and joyous moments.

I faced these three tough questions as I wrestled with the leaving decision:

1. How much is enough money to save for this change in occupation?
2. If God is in charge, knows the future, and involved in succession plans, why should I save?
3. Why shouldn't I spend all current income feeding the poor?

To answer these questions, I had to fall back on God's Word. Jesus is in control, but He has given me a free will to choose. He wants me to be prudent and wise with everything He entrusts to me. He describes this attitude in the parables in Matthew chapter 25. He wants me to obey Him always. So, if He says to change career or jobs, I must *go for it!*

Saving for Retirement

So, should a Christian save for retirement? Nothing is wrong with saving for retirement if God directs it. But don't become dependent on those savings; that's the wrong reason to save. Another wrong reason is to save to amass wealth to *guarantee* your *security* or to show your importance and value.

According to God's Word, saving with the correct motive is valid. Proverbs 19:21 (NIV) tells us that only God's plans will prevail: "Many are the plans in a man's heart, but it is the Lord's purpose that prevails." And in Proverbs 6:6-8 (NIV) we see an excellent example of the need to save for predicable events: "Go to the ant, you sluggard; consider its ways and be wise! It has no commander, no overseer or ruler, yet it stores its provisions in summer and gathers its food at harvest."

Although there are no biblical bases for retirement, God might want you to change from a full-time paid, stable job, to unpaid work. So be sensitive and responsive to His direction as He might ask you to save during your prime career years to provide funds in later years when you will have no income.

Like everything you have, savings belong to God so place them at His disposal always. If the Holy Spirit prompts you to give away savings, do it! But don't do it if while fund raising, a TV evangelist or other Christian worker tells you to do so.

In Luke 19:1-10, after Zaccheus' conversion, his heart changed. He decided to give away 50% of his wealth, and repay four times the value to those whom he defrauded; for this four-fold repayment, Zaccheus used the principle of restitution called for under the Law (Exodus 22:1; Proverbs 6:31). Notice Jesus didn't criticize him for holding onto 50%. Jesus knew Zaccheus' heart had changed and he was no longer in bondage to wealth!

Continuing in Luke 19: 12-27, Jesus tells us He will reward good stewards; he will give them *more* to manage for His glory, and to further His Kingdom. Bad stewards, on the other hand, will manage nothing for His Kingdom. Isn't this how we would treat our children? Here again in these verses we see savings with the right motives confirmed.

So, if God tells you about a season when He wants you to change occupation, ask Him if you should save for those *winter* years; like the ant! But never place your self-esteem or security in those savings; Jesus must be your only security.

Regrettably, the consumerism craze has grabbed many folks. They borrow money and pay interest that robs God of His due. They don't listen to His voice as they spend His funds to satisfy their wants: a pattern that's approaching epidemic proportions even with *churched* folks. As their debts pile up, mortgages remain unpaid at age 60 and older, and they complain they can't retire. But they haven't listened to God and followed His lead about, spending, saving, and making disciples.

Where are you in your career? Where are you in your Christian journey? Are you thinking about changing to a lifestyle with Jesus as your focus? Is God central to your planning? How are you balancing your daily wants and needs compared with God's directions about spending and savings?

If you sense God telling you to save for your retirement, ask Him to help you be a good steward of time, talents, and money. Ask Him to help you live in a budget that honours Him. As well, ask Him to help you identify the retirement budget gap[2]—the difference between your estimated retirement income and your estimated retirement expenses—and then prepare a financial plan (see chapter 19).

Th Statistic Canada Survey I mentioned earlier found interesting differences in net worth (material worth), debt, and income for folks who didn't intend to retire, and those intending to retire:

Median[3] Values $'000

	Debt	Net Worth	Income
Intend to retire	43	407	54
Do not intend to retire	56	227	33

Before I look at specific retirement-related questions that you need to answer to prepare this plan, let's look at one important retirement income source, your pension plan.

Pension Plans

Normally companies offer one of two pension plans: either a *defined benefit plan* or a *defined contribution plan*.

A *defined benefit plan* promises the participant a specific monthly benefit at retirement. It might state this as a dollar amount or as a formula, which considers a participant's salary, age and service. In private funds, some participants might not have to contribute, but most public sector funds call for employee contributions. Defined benefit plans can be expensive for companies because companies promise pensions to participants independent of the funds' ability to pay. That's why many companies are moving away from this plan to the other.

A *defined contribution plan* provides *an individual account* for each participant. Benefits come from contributions, income, expenses, and gains net of losses. Defined contribution plans include *Registered Retirement Savings Plans* (RRSPs, in Canada), which I comment on in detail later, and 401(K) plans (in USA), employee stock ownership plans and profit sharing plans. Employees drive defined contribution plans. Because of the move from the first plan, defined contribution plans are becoming increasingly popular. Often in these plans, companies match or give a percent of participants' contributions.

There are significant differences between these two plans such as these:

Defined Benefits	Defined Contribution
1. Guaranteed retirement income for employees a. Not dependent on the participant's ability to save b. At the company's discretion, can include cost of living adjustments to pensions	1. Not guaranteed income a. Participants choose how much to save. They can save through payroll deductions
2. No investment risk to participants	2. Participants bear investment risks and can benefit from good investment results
3. Not portable (an employee cannot take his account with employer *A* to employer *B*), and so this is not favorable to employees who leave before retirement	3. Portable; employees can continue to contribute in their individual account if they go to a new job. But it can be difficult to build a fund for those who start an account late in life
4. Can be difficult for participants to understand	4. More easily understood by participants, but can be difficult to do a. Participants are responsible to choose investments and, or investment advisers

Subject to prescribed limits, employees' contribution to both plans, and companies' matching contributions (where relevant) are tax deferred. When participants retire and get pensions, the Government taxes that income.

If faced with an early retirement decision, understand your pension arrangement and choices available. If you have a *defined benefits plan*, your age, service, and concession your company plans to offer to "encourage" you to retire will decide your pension. Seek advice because as you saw in the comparison table, defined benefits plans are not transportable. As well, probably you would not be following a *retirement savings* routine, which you need for a *defined contribution plan*.

About 71% of family units in the Statistics Canada Survey had pension assets in 2005. Those approaching retirement or recently retired had median pension assets of $242,500, compared with the median for all family units of $68,000.

Questions to Answer to Calculate Your Retirement Budget Gap

You are ready to look at your *retirement budget gap* after you understand your pension arrangement. Here is a quick checklist to help you develop your retirement income and retirement expenses budget to give you the retirement budget gap, your retirement savings' goal.

Timing
- Has the Lord shown you when you will retire? This timing will help you calculate your likely retirement income.
- When will need to draw your retirement income? This will help decide investments you select today—the closer to retirement, the more conservative your investments.

Pension Plan
- Do you belong to a company pension plan?
  - Is it a defined benefit plan or defined contribution plan? Are you taking full advantage of your company's matching contributions? If no, why not?
  - Do you have an estimate of your retirement income?

Housing Needs
- Where do you plan to live when you retire?
  - Do you have a budget for today's housing costs and likely housing cost at retirement?
  - Do you have a mortgage?
  - At current rates, when will you repay your mortgage?
  - Do you plan major repairs or renovations to your home?
- Will you lower your housing needs? Will this free equity to go to retirement income, how much?
- Will you rent or own your home, and, or a vacation home?
- Will you spend time in warmer climates, how long?
- Do you plan to move to a retirement community? Do you know the estimated cost?

Lifestyle
- Will you support or help to support family members?
- Will you do volunteer work, work part-time while retired; travel often?
- Do you plan to take up hobbies, join golf or other clubs? What's the likely cost?
- What other lifestyle choices could affect your retirement budget?
- Do you plan to spend your investments and other assets over your lifetime? Or, do you plan to leave an estate? This is important; it will affect how you spend.

Retirement Budget (Part of your Financial Plan)

- After answering the earlier questions, and as you work on your financial plan, estimate your retirement income and your retirement expenses.
- Estimate years to retirement, yearly inflation, and yearly return on investment.
- Prepare a budget for estimated living costs and estimated retirement income; the difference between retirement income and retirement expenses is your retirement income gap.
- Ask the Lord to show you His plan; adjust yours as needed.
- Save in your RRSP or equivalent, an amount that will grow to fill the retirement budget gap.

Yearly, review this list, update the budget, and adjust amount to save, if needed. But most of all let the Lord guide this procedure.

Registered Retirement Savings Plans (RRSPs)

An RRSP is an example of a popular *defined contribution pension plan*. You need to know about these plans as you might need to manage one, either directly or with help, sooner rather than later. I will discuss RRSPs to show you some issues you must consider as you set aside retirement funds.

An RRSP is a savings plan registered with *Canada Customs and Revenue Agency* (CCRA) to produce retirement income. It's tax-deferred savings for retirement income—not savings for a down payment on a home, education or for emergencies. But more important, you must manage it as a part of a retirement plan.

Table XIV shows the effects of your RRSP contribution. Rules change, allowable deduction changes, but the tax deferral principle, and other tax effects remain.

Table XIV

RRSP Computation

	Year 1	Year 2	Year 3
Salary	$50,000		
Contribution to company pension plan (5%)	$2,500		
Top tax rate [4]	45%		
RRSP Contribution:			
(50,000x18%) = $9000 minus $2500	$6,500		
Tax Refund in Year 2 ($6500 x 45%)		$2,925	
Net cost to you ($6500-$2925)		$3,575	
After one year – income (10% of 6500)		$650	
Tax saved (sheltered) - (45% of $650)		$293	
After two years – Investment (Contribution and interest - $6500+$650)		$7,150	
After two years – income (10% of $7150)			$715
Tax saved (45% of $715)			$322

Observations on Table XIV

1. CCRA will not tax earnings of $6,500 in your RRSP account; those earnings will benefit from compounding.[5] When withdrawn, CCRA will tax funds you withdraw from your RRSP as ordinary income, even if investments produced capital gains that today they tax at a lower rate.

2. Although your net cost is $3,575, your investment in the RRSP is $6,500. You will get $2,925 tax refund in

year two for your $6,500 RRSP contribution in year one.

3. You save taxes of $293[6] in year two based on income of $650 in year two.
4. You save $322 taxes in year three based on income of $715 in year three.
5. Taxes saved produce an instant return that poor investment performance could erase. Some folks choose to invest RRSP funds in safe fixed income instruments to protect this tax benefit.
6. Don't borrow to contribute. In year one, your RRSP contribution was $6500 and your refund in year two was $2925, $3575 short of the amount you would have had to borrow to contribute to your RRSP. Be patient.

RRSP Benefits

Benefits are huge if you are patient, knowledgeable, and you manage the RRSP as part of a basic strategy.

Note, if you deposited your RRSP contribution of $6500 outside an RRSP account, you would not get a tax deduction for that amount. And non-registered plans do not *shelter* income. Here is a summary of key RRSP benefits:

1. If you contribute less than your maximum allowed by CCRA in one year, you can carry the shortfall into later years, subject only to your annual limit.
2. Subject to your annual limit, you can decide when to deduct allowable contributions from earned income for tax purposes. You can contribute in one year but not claim the tax deduction until later: maybe you have a low tax rate in year one and choose to take the deduction later in year three at a higher tax rate.
3. Investments grow tax-free in the RRSP account but are taxed when withdrawn, theoretically at a lower tax rate.

4. Income earned in your RRSP account grows tax-free on your gross deposit until withdrawn. Imagine your RRSP as containing two streams, each earning income: one with your net cost, the other *the re-invested tax refund.*
5. You can contribute to a *spousal RRSP* provided you have contribution room. The benefit here arises if your income is higher than your spouse's income, and you expect it to remain higher. The RRSP becomes your spouse's. In theory, later, your spouse will withdraw funds at a lower tax rate than you. Get to know the rules.

RRSP rules allow you two decisions that bother me. I don't consider the *Home Buyers' Plan* and the *Lifelong Learning Plan* as benefits. Your RRSP is for retirement and you should develop alternatives, such as *Capital Fund* savings, to save for education and for a down payment on your first home. If you don't have the down payment to buy a home or if you don't have education funds, review your budget—spending and savings— and then ask the Lord to show you His goals and plans for your education and housing.

As well, using your RRSP to pay down on your first home can become expensive. If you borrowed from your RRSP, and you missed or lowered an instalment to repay the loan, you must pay tax on the shortfall. So, if you needed to repay $2000 yearly and you paid $1500 only in one year, you have to pay tax on $500 ($2000-$1500).

Besides your RRSP, your spouse should contribute to her RRSP based on the same principles. If your spouse does not have earned income, you can contribute on her behalf to an RRSP provided your contribution and the amount you contribute to her RRSP does not exceed your maximum allowable deduction.

Where to Save Your RRSP Funds

Where do you deposit your contribution? This is another positive feature of an RRSP. You have flexibility. You can deposit funds in financial instruments ranging from conservative types such as Guaranteed Investment Certificates (GICs), to aggressive investment instruments such as equity funds that you "manage". Many people go the safe, GIC or fixed income route. This is wise for at least three reasons:

1. You get an immediate tax saving (deferral) when you contribute to your RRSP; why not secure it?
2. Your company's matching contributions, fully or partly, is free; why not protect it?
3. CCRA taxes capital gains lower than ordinary income; why not go for safe fixed income investments in your RRSP and more aggressive investments that could be subject to capital gains in your non-registered account? If your RRSP produced $10,000 capital gains and you withdrew it after age 71, CCRA would tax it at your marginal tax rate. But if your non registered account produced this gain, CCRA would tax half only ($5,000) at your marginal tax rate.

After considering those three points, still, if you are young you might want more equity investments in your RRSP. Get advice; calculate likely returns from secure investments, counting your company's matching contribution as part of the return on investment.

I do not recommend speculation with your RRSP investments. Find a trusted investment advisor and learn questions you need to ask to understand how to oversee your RRSP's performance. Most people do not want to manage their RRSPs directly. I agree with them. This needs specific knowledge and can be time-consuming. Still, you must get to know accounts that would be right for you.

I invest in a self-directed RRSP account, which means I invest the funds directly. I can place the funds in Government Treasury Bills, leave them in cash, and invest in shares of a company listed on Canadian or other stock exchanges, or a combination. Although most folks can't do as I do, give your advisor guidelines and oversee results to see he follows them. If he doesn't know your principles and values, he will use his, which could differ.

Although in chapter 6, money value and investing, I discussed investing and investment strategies, remember the following when you consider investing your RRSP funds directly or with an advisor's help:

- The GAS Principle; it is God's money, so He must guide you.
- You are investing for the long-term, so do not listen to those short-term focused Wall Street, Bay Street and other analysts who use the stock market more for gambling than for prudent investing.
- One or two quarter's poor earnings do not mean a company's doom! Understand investing principles, and stay with them. Don't speculate.
- You do not pay capital gains tax when you sell investments in your RRSP account and keep funds there.
- If your company matches 100% or a part of your contribution, remember this is a tax-free return (tax deferred). So with the tax benefit, you start with a major return on investment. For example, if you deposit $1000 for the year and your employer gives you $500, already, you have a 50% return. So, you might consider placing the funds in a secure interest bearing deposit.

The Statistic Canada Survey of Wealth of Canadians found 58% of all family units had RRSPs, more than half invested[7] in mutual funds and income trusts, and almost 25% in Canada Savings Bonds and Provisional Savings Bonds.

Closing out Your RRSP Account

What happens if you need funds urgently and your only source is your RRSP account? First, pray and seek to know God's will. Then review the PEACE, the PLANE, and the Affordability

Index. Next, re-examine your budget. Then go exploring in those areas about which we spoke in chapter 10. If you sense you must, withdraw the funds but understand you will pay taxes on the amount withdrawn. And you lose that contribution room forever!

Under present rules, in the year you turn 71 you must choose one of the following:

- Lump-sum withdrawal
  - CCRA will tax the cash you withdraw in the year you withdraw it.
- Convert your RRSP balance to an annuity
  - Convert your lump sum into monthly payments for life or a fixed term. CCRA will tax monthly payments when you get them.
- Convert to a Registered Retirement Income Fund (RRIF)
  - Probably this will be the best. It's like your RRSP except for compulsory withdrawals each year but the year you set it up. You can keep the same investments that you had in your RRSP.

This RRSP closure decision is important; consult an independent financial advisor to help you.

Summary

Companies are moving to defined contribution pension plans. As well, self-employment is rising. So you need to know enough to either invest your pension on your own or to ask questions of an investment advisor. Because of the benefits mentioned above, you might think you should maximize your RRSP contribution yearly. But, as we saw earlier, an RRSP is one part of retirement planning which must fit your retirement goals and plans.

Remember, the final decision is yours, not your advisors. Pray and ask the Lord to guide you in this matter. Couples, ensure you get on the same page. Think about and discuss these matters with your independent advisor before investing in an RRSP:

1. Goals and Plans
   a. Have you prepared a retirement plan in writing?
      i. If you don't have a plan, start planning your retirement, including a plan to *become debt free before starting RRSP* contributions—you are never too young.
      ii. If you have a plan, are you following it? If it includes RRSP contributions, when will you start, and how do you stay invested.
   b. Yearly, review retirement goals and plans, specifically for proposed timing of retirement, estimated value of other pension plans, projected material worth, and size of retirement budget gap. Identifying this gap is essential because it's what you want to "fill" with your RRSP and other investments.
2. Investments
   a. Despite pressure from media and salespeople, don't consider your RRSP decision alone. Especially, don't decide based solely on the tax benefit.
   b. How much of your portfolio should be inside an RRSP compared with outside? Get advice. When withdrawn from an RRSP account, all income, including capital gains, are taxed as ordinary income.
   c. Are you comfortable with the investing procedure? Get to know about investing and investment choices before you choose the *self directed* alternative. You don't have to be an expert but you need to know a few questions to ask, such as those I mention in chapter 6.
   d. Are your expectations realistic? Your age, risk tolerance, personal and family values will decide where you invest, including investing abroad. Also, many investments rise and fall—some keep falling!

3. Loans
   a. Don't borrow to contribute, if you need to borrow, you probably will not have funds to repay the loan amount above your tax refund. In Table XIV, a $6,500 deposit produced a tax refund of only $2,925; so, if you borrowed $6,500, how would you repay $3,575 not covered by the refund?
   b. Interest on an RRSP loan is not tax deductible.
   c. If you are in debt, you need to understand the pre-tax cost of each debt and potential income from investments.
      i. Erasing debt produces a guaranteed interest saving, usually from after-tax earnings. If you repaid a $10,000 debt with a pre-tax interest cost of 30%, the after tax cost of a department store credit card, you would save $3,000 in ONE YEAR—guaranteed! Even at a lower interest cost, consider debt repayment because of the sure interest saving, compared with an RRSP investment. Remember also the emotional and family cost of carrying debt.
   d. Should you repay your mortgage before starting an RRSP? As a reminder, let me show a few mortgage-related numbers. If you have a mortgage of $100,000 at 6% repayable over 25 years, you will pay around $500 monthly in interest in the early years. The table below shows the assured investment return by putting annual lump sums toward your mortgage:

Mortgage	No Prepayments $100,000	Prepay $1000 yearly	Prepay $3000 yearly
Interest paid	$92,000	$69,600	$48,000
Interest saved	0	$22,400	$44,000
Repayment period	25 years	19.7 years	14 years

Consider debt repayment as an investment with a guaranteed return, and so except your employer matches your contributions fully or partly, repay your mortgage before you start your RRSP contribution. If you don't contribute, you will loose the matching contribution, but you do not loose your RRSP contributions you defer.

After repaying your loans, your age and timing of retirement should influence how you invest retirement funds; the closer to retirement, the more secure should be your investments.

I could display mathematically that if all went well, you'd be "better off" borrowing to contribute to an RRSP. Equally, I could show the dangers if investments didn't perform. But, I won't go there! I prefer the debt elimination route that produces a certain return.

Think About This

Half our life is spent trying to find something to do with the time we have rushed through life trying to save.[8]

Chapter Notes:

1. Statistics Canada, Research Paper, *The Wealth of Canadians: An Overview of the Results of the Survey of Financial Security*, 2005
2. A retirement budget gap shows the difference between our estimated retirement income and estimated retirement expenses. One key part of retirement planning is to decide how to fill this gap. Additional RRSP contribution is only one way to fill it.
3. The *median* is the value at which half of the units in a series have lower values and half have higher values. So the median of 1, 3, 5, 99, 2500 is 5, the middle value.
4. Marginal Tax rate is the tax rate that applies to the last dollar of income you earn.
5. If you deposit $100 at 10 percent, at the end of one year it will grow to $110. At the end of the second year, both your original $100 and the $10 earned will attract interest: the value at the end of the second year will be $121, of which, $10 earned from your original deposit and $1 from income earned in year 1.
6. CCRA does not tax income earned in the RRSP account until you withdraw it. Notice that compound interest is at work here!
7. This investment number included Registered Education Savings Plans (RESP's).
8. Will Rogers, *Autobiography*, 1949.

17

Executors
Beneficiaries
Trustees
Wills
Powers of Attorney

Estate Planning

E state planning is arranging to dispose of your assets—valuable items—when you die. It includes assessing your dependents' likely future needs when you die, and planning to meet at least some of those needs. It entails preparing a *material worth statement,* assessing future tax effects, and writing a will. And I suggest, it should take in preparing *powers of attorney* and writing or updating your *financial plan.* In this chapter, I will look at putting in place a will and powers of attorney.

What is a will? A will is a written, signed document that you write, alone or with professional help, showing how you would like your belongings shared when you die. It can include other information such as funeral details. Among other matters, a Canadian English Law will, needs the following:

1. You must be at least the *age of majority* (18 or 19 in Canada depending on the province in which you live)

2. It must be in writing and signed at the end
3. At least two people must witness it
4. Anyone who will benefit under the will, can't witness it

Before I accepted Christ as my Lord and my Saviour, I had great difficulty discussing this subject; I refused to think about it. Looking back, I realise why I would not talk about death. The thought of dying and not knowing what would happened after, bothered me. But not today, I know I have *eternal life* and I am sure one day I will see Jesus face-to-face. So, I know I do not need to fear death; it is certain, so I should plan for it under Jesus' direction.

Why You Should Prepare a Will

Since you cannot take your belongings with you when you die, hold them loosely, ready to let them go. Pray; ask God how to share them today, and when you die. If you don't leave instructions to get rid of your belongings, *Governments' rules will apply.* I am sure you don't like this alternative. Besides, lack of a will, likely, might cause anxiety for your remaining loved ones.

Who Should Prepare a Will
and What it Should Contain

Everyone over the *age of majority* (18 or 19 years old) should prepare a will that should include some of the following:

- How to divide your assets, net of liabilities
  - Specific asset[1] list with names of people and, or organisations to get them, and names of people to share the rest of the estate—*beneficiaries* is the name for people who get stuff from a will.

- Names of *alternative beneficiaries*
  - You need alternatives if present beneficiaries die before you, or if your chosen organisations don't exist at your death. As well, if relevant, you need beneficiaries under a *disastrous circumstance* where the family dies together, and family members were beneficiaries.
- If you have minor children, *a guardian* to care for them when you die
  - Though difficult, discuss this with your children at suitable ages.
- Name of someone and an alternate (the executor) to carry out instructions in your will:
  - Paying funeral and related expenses
  - Collecting money owing at death
  - Paying bills outstanding at death
  - After paying bills, dealing out your assets to beneficiaries
  - Other details such as funeral arrangements

My first will in my late 20s was simple. I left everything to wife, who did the same to me. A lawyer prepared the two wills. Although you can prepare your will, I recommend you use professional help, even if your financial affairs appear simple. Laws change; you might not know some subtleties in your province that could benefit your beneficiary. Ask the Lord to guide you.

Sometimes you do not want to give out all assets at death so you set up a trust or trusts[2] in your will. Each trust will have a beneficiary or beneficiaries, who will get income from assets in the trust. The beneficiary might get some capital (the value of assets owned less amounts owed at death) at fix periods, or later when the trustee or trustees dissolve the trust.

My will and my wife's include trusts for some assets. Here are three reasons to create a trust:

- You want to leave a stream of annual income to young children and, or grandchildren. The trustee would manage the assets and as you directed, pay income to the children or grandchildren periodically.
- You wish to give out income regularly or sporadically to charities.
- You wish to deal out capital periodically; you might want the trustee to pay out assets over a fixed period.

Review your wills occasionally and change them as needed.

Who Should Benefit From Your Will

Often, as individuals and families discuss their wills, I see them wrestle with dividing possessions among their children and grandchildren. Should they leave an amount to each child and grandchild? How much should they leave? What is the best approach? Always the focus during these discussions is on material stuff for a *secure future*; seldom is it about their descendant's *spiritual inheritance*.

Already Jesus has secured for His followers, eternal life in heaven. So each believer's future is secured in Jesus. Listen to Apostle Peter in 1 Peter 1:3-5 as he points us to the true and lasting inheritance that each born-again believer gets when he accepts Christ as his Lord and Saviour:

Blessed be the God and Father of our Lord Jesus Christ, who according to His great mercy has caused us to be born again to a living hope through the resurrection of Jesus Christ from the dead, to *obtain* an inheritance *which is* imperishable and undefiled and will not fade away, reserved in heaven for you, who are protected by the power of God through faith for a salvation ready to be revealed in the last time.

Did you get that: "to *obtain* an inheritance *which is* imperishable and undefiled and will not fade away?" Here is one of many definitive assurances in the Bible about our *spiritual inheritance* that we ought to teach our children. Our lifestyles should show our children and grand children this wonderful inheritance.

In Luke 12:13-15,[3] Jesus reminds us of the folly to store material possessions as our security for our later years. Belongings will burn, evaporate, wear out, and decay. Sure, you need to prepare for your later years on earth, but you must work with God's plans, not yours. And know you can't secure the future with stuff.

The essence of Jesus' message in Luke 12:13-15 is this: Look at your heart and your motives as you pile up wealth; it is temporary. In Matthew 22:37-39 Jesus told an *expert in the law*, the first and greatest commandment is to:

> "'...love the Lord your God with all your heart, and with all your soul, and with all your mind.' "This is the great and foremost commandment. "The second is like it, 'You shall love your neighbor as yourself.' "On these two commandments depend the whole Law and the Prophets."

So, in all we do, a prime responsibility is to show this attitude of love, to family, siblings, and others. Moses gave a specific example of how to leave this legacy of love of God in Deuteronomy 6:4-9. He told the children of Israel:

> "Hear, O Israel! The LORD is our God, the LORD is one! "You shall love the LORD your God with all your heart and with all your soul and with all your might. "These words, which I am commanding you today, shall be on your heart. You shall teach them diligently to your sons and shall talk of them when you sit in your house and when you walk by the way and when you lie down and when you rise up. "You shall

bind them as a sign on your hand and they shall be as frontals on your forehead. "You shall write them on the doorposts of your house and on your gates.

As I mentioned in chapter 12, *Family Finances,* the *Family Council* is one place you can teach and model to your children this *spiritual inheritance.* Choose to put in effect with your children and grand children, Moses' urging to the children of Israel. By the grace of God, you will stop concentrating your efforts on storing up wealth, and stop worrying about your children's *material future.* Daily, pray for your children, and let them see Christ in you; Jesus will take care of the rest.

What's wrong with leaving financial and other material assets to your children when you die? Nothing; if God directs it. If you decide to leave material possessions to your descendants, try to understand your motive. Is it to *secure their future?* That won't work. You don't know the future and you can't secure it! Only through a personal relationship with Jesus can you secure your future in eternity.

Model and teach your children to depend on Jesus for everything, not on material objects that are here today and gone tomorrow. Apostle Paul puts the material and eternal in perspective in 1 Corinthians 15, verse 50 which says: "Now I say this, brethren, that flesh and blood cannot inherit the kingdom of God; nor does the perishable inherit the imperishable."

In earlier verses, Paul speaks about Christ's resurrection and believers' resurrection. In verse 50, he starts to speak about the mystery of resurrection and ends with this positive message in verse 58:

Therefore, my beloved brethren, be steadfast, immovable, always abounding in the work of the Lord, knowing that your toil is not in vain in the Lord.

Jesus' resurrection and the promise of yours is the basis for your secure future in heaven. You do not need to worry about your future or your children's future because Jesus has secured a place in heaven for each believer. Leave *a spiritual inheritance* for your children by obeying Christ and teaching your children as Moses commanded in Deuteronomy 6:4-9.

Financial and material wealth left to your children who do not know Jesus as Lord and Saviour will become curses and entrench them in the *world:* your children will be unable to subject these belongings to His direction. For your children who know Christ, don't remove their dependency on Him by providing for all their foreseeable material needs. Teach your descendants how to view and share money, wealth, and belongings. Most of all, ask Jesus to show you how to divide material belongings you hold on His behalf.

Since God owns everything, He should decide who should benefit from your will. Ask Him to show you how your will should fund the Great Commission. A believer's will, should include funds for God, unless He directs to the contrary.

If You Don't Have a Will

If you don't have a will, ask Jesus to give you the wisdom to prepare one or to lead you to someone to guide you through the procedures to write one. As well, before you write your will, *write your epitaph;* when you finish, answer these questions:

1. Have I accepted Christ as Lord and Saviour? If yes, do I believe I have received "an inheritance *which is* imperishable and undefiled and will not fade away?"
   a. Have I surrendered every area of my life to Jesus or am I withholding parts? He wants all.
2. What's the legacy I am leaving my children and grandchildren?
   a. Does my behaviour conform to my words?[4]

b. Do I accept when I am wrong, and seek forgiveness, or do I rationalize my actions?

c. Am I defensive, not teachable, seldom accepting correction?

3. Have I taught my children to handle money according to Jesus' principles?

   a. Am I teaching them by words and deeds, biblical attitudes toward money?

   b. How am I dealing with negative messages from schools, banks, and the media about money, wealth, and possessions?

2. Am I living in silos—Am I applying different principles to similar events based on where I am and what I do: such as at church, work, school, and other places?

   a. What lifestyle changes do I need to carry out to start showing Jesus' unconditional love in my daily walk?

How to Prepare a Will

To prepare your will, the key document you need is your material worth statement, with the supporting details of individual assets and liabilities. Recall, your material worth statement shows details of what you *own* and what you owe. I repeat my recommendation that you seek professional advice to prepare your will. Decide if you will work with an independent financial advisor and a lawyer or a lawyer alone.

If you worked with an independent financial advisor before you met a lawyer, he would prepare or help you to prepare a financial plan, including your material worth statement, and would tell you about taxation and other related financial matters.

It is important you understand precisely your financial affairs before thinking about the complexities of the will. After sorting out your financial affairs, your lawyer can tell you about preparing the will. You know your circumstance and you must decide whom you want to prepare your will; it's your call.

When you prepare your will, think of the *before* and *after* goals:

- *Before* you die, leave your will where your executor or executors can get at it easily, and leave *clear instructions* to your executor or executors to deal out your assets and carry out your wishes precisely.
- Follow all legal procedures to prepare your will to ensure that *after* you die, your executor will settle the estate quickly and smoothly, according to your instructions.

You control the first item. For the second, discuss with your lawyer the legal nuances that apply in your province; follow them closely. A Notary[5] prepared our wills in Quebec; lawyers prepared them in Ontario and British Columbia. In Quebec, we *registered* them for quick processing when needed. If we did not *notarize* them in Quebec, they might need more processing time at death.

Selecting an Executor

Who should be your executor? Should you use a professional firm? I mentioned the role of the executor already. The person you choose should be able to carry out your requests. Besides, he should have unblemished integrity, share your values or at least be ready to follow them, and be reliable. If you chose a professional, realise the firm will charge a fee, probably a percent of your assets less your liabilities. Interview the firm and be comfortable with their skills to do the job you defined.

Keep your will in a safe place, such as with your lawyer or in your fireproof, secure safe. Tell your family and executor the location. Keep your current will only; destroy all previous wills. Update your will as needed.

With the will, keep an updated file with key information for your spouse, siblings, or other dependents or interested survivors. I call my file, my *when I die* file. In it, I mention:

1. Funeral details
   - Casket (cheapest possible), songs at the service, what happens if I die abroad, and so on
2. Household affairs
   - Where I file important papers such as, name of tax preparer, and investment details
3. Ministry details
   - Website details, and so on

This file's purpose is to ease the transition for people who will takeover stuff I do today. Still, I talk about most of this information at some weekly *Family Council* meetings with my wife and at periodic meetings with my wife and children.

I believe each of us with dependents should seek God continually about his asset's division. We need to know if we should give out assets (how much, when) while we are alive, to our children and, or our bible teaching church, Christ centered Ministries, and others the Lord brings our way.

Powers Of Attorney

A power of attorney is a legal document in which one party gives another the right to act on his behalf. In Ontario, there are these Powers of Attorney:

1. A *Continuing Power of Attorney for Property* for your financial affairs, which allows someone you identify to act for you *even if* you become mentally incapable
2. A *Power of Attorney for Personal Care* for your personal decisions, such as health care

3. *A non-continuing Power of Attorney for Property* for your financial affairs
   a. It is temporary. Your attorney can't use it if you become mentally incapable.
   b. You might give it to someone to look after your financial affairs while you are away from home for a while.

My wife and I give each other powers of attorney for bullets one and two above so, as needed, she and I can decide for each other. We think we need to do this for three reasons.

1. If one of us becomes incapable, the other can decide.
2. If one of us is out of town, the other can decide formal legal matters that need agreement by two of us.
3. If two of us became incapable, our stated attorney can decide as we have pointed out, or as she sees fit.

We found indispensable the power of attorney in bullet one when I travelled overseas on business often. Writing powers of attorney is a personal matter each couple must address as it see fit. Understand, like a will, if you do not give someone power of attorney and you became incapable, your Government will decide.

If you get a power of attorney from your spouse, do not abuse it to decide outside boundaries you and your spouse set. Except for incapacity, a power of attorney is a convenient method to decide jointly when either husband or wife is unavailable. Actions that I do on my own using my wife's power of attorney to me have her earlier blessing, and conversely.

Probably you have heard about a "living will." It is like a power of attorney for personal care except, usually it is specific about what you want to happen if you become ill and can't communicate your wishes about treatment. For example, if doctors say you have no hope of recovery, in your "living will" you might specify if you want artificial life supports to keep you alive.

Summary

The best legacy you can leave your children and grand-children is a spiritual legacy as they see Christ in all you do. Focus there and let Jesus guide your stewardship of His funds including your assets' division while you live, and in your will. Today, set aside time to seek God's direction about your will and powers of attorney. Don't let Governments decide future care of your dependent children; how to share God's belongings you manage, or your critical health alternatives.

Tell your executor where he will find your will and other relevant files when you die. Keep your will and powers of attorney up-to-date. Write or review your powers of attorney when you write or review your will. As with the will, you do not need a lawyer because many templates exist; but I recommend you use a professional to guide you. The small cost of the will and powers of attorney is worth it. Not writing a will or powers of attorney is a decision by default and is final until changed; ask the Lord to guide you to His path.

Think About This

The Bible is the instruction manual for life; live by it, die by it!

Chapter Notes:

1. Normally you would not identify every asset you own in your will because you discard or replace assets periodically. If you intend to divide your estate, it is better to identify and allocate directly, few specific assets, and then allocate the rest in total. So rather than identify the car, stereo, TV you own today, identify separately your sentimental and special items such as, wedding ring and antique dining table, and divide the rest of the estate in the proportion you chose. That way you won't need to change the will when you replace your car.
2. A Trust is property held by one party (the trustee) for the benefit of another (the beneficiary).
3. Luke 12:13-15: Someone in the crowd said to Him, "Teacher, tell my brother to divide the *family* inheritance with me." But He said to him, "Man, who appointed Me a judge or arbitrator over you?" Then He said to them, "Beware, and be on your guard against every form of greed; for not *even* when one has an abundance does his life consist of his possessions."
4. I mentioned earlier about the card my daughter gave me. At age 12, she gave me a card she designed, which said my words didn't match my actions. I was devastated! As I write this, I glimpsed at this card, which has hung in my home office since I got it over 20 years ago.
5. A Notary is a member of the legal profession who specialises in non-litigious matters such as property issues and wills. A notarial will is prepared only in Quebec. Notarial wills prepared in Quebec do not have to go through the verification and probate process when you die.

18

Choosing
A
Financial Advisor

Would you do dental surgery on yourself? Would you try to remove your tonsils? No, you wouldn't! So if you don't know how to handle finances, why would you try to tackle technical financial matters without consulting a financial professional? Once you have the right attitude to money, seek competent, expert advice to help you handle your financial affairs well. Without the right attitude we discussed in earlier chapters, you will look for solutions in the wrong places—you will look to money to solve behaviour issues (you might benefit from reviewing chapter 1).

Many companies moved to self-directed pension plans. They extend share option[1] plans to large employee groups, they offer savings, life insurance, and several benefit plans. So you can access directly, savings, life insurance, retirement, education savings, and many other benefit plans. How do you cope with financial decisions about these matters? How do you maximize investment value? Then again, how do you decide when to start investing, where to invest, and how to develop a retirement portfolio? Unless you are a trained financial professional, you will find your financial affairs and choices complex, and you might need help.

What Can a Financial Advisor Do For You

Often, to help sort out their financial affairs, folks ask me to recommend a *financial planner* or *advisor*—they use these titles interchangeably. But they don't know who is an advisor, who is a planner, or what to expect from him or her. And today's job titles don't help! Have you noticed titles don't tell you what people do? Some car companies call their salespeople *product advisors!* In previous chapters, I encouraged you to consult an *independent financial advisor* to help with sections of this money management trip. I stressed the need for independence to avoid possible *conflicts of interest.*

Before looking at why *conflicts of interest* exist and how to manage them, let's understand what a financial advisor can do for you. In this chapter, I look at these matters to help you choose someone to give you *objective, unbiased* personal financial advice:

- What Type of Financial Advice You Can Expect to Get
- Conflict of Interest
- Who is a Financial Advisor
- How to Choose a Financial Advisor
- For Whom Does She Work

What Type of Financial Advice You Can Expect to Get

What can you expect from your *financial advisor?* First, don't confuse your need for counseling to fix bad *attitudes*, with a need for financial planning advice. Riddled with debt, first you need counseling that addresses your *attitude* and *behaviour!* Expect to pay for this counsel.

Many folks think of financial advisors mostly for investment advice. To be sure, they can help with this advice, but you need solid financial advice before you start to invest. We saw earlier, repaying expensive debt is a guaranteed, high *return on investment.* So, earmarking more funds to one debt rather than another could be a key financial advice you get from an *independent financial advisor.*

If you follow the three-step debt free procedure I outline in this book, after step three, setting up your *life and material goals,* consult an independent financial advisor to help you do your material worth statement—the *still photograph* of your financial affairs at a specific date—and your financial plan.

But before you see a financial advisor, write clear goals you expect to get by working with him. When you set your goals, do not try to define solutions, which you would not know, but stick to issues you want dealt with. You might not know about a cash flow statement, and that's fine. You might define an issue like this: given specific assumptions, what are likely cash balances at each month-end. Your advisor will know questions to ask you to do your cash flow statement.

A financial advisor can assist you to interpret and understand your financial affairs. As well, he can *aid you*[2] to do specific plans, financial statements and analyses. Here is a non-comprehensive list of help you can expect from your financial advisor:

1. Financial plans:
   a. Write and explain financial and spending plans, and coach you to use them regularly and effectively.
   b. Arrange education savings plans.
   c. Put together debt repayment alternatives and a debt repayment plan.
2. Financial Statements:
   a. Figure out cash flow and material worth statements, and show you how to use them.
3. Taxation: Write estimates, prepare, and review tax returns.
4. Investment plans: Help set goals, set up a portfolio, watch, and review them regularly against your goals.
5. Retirement plans: Write, review, and oversee these plans.
6. Insurance: Identify the need, different types, and in some areas, possible self-insurance.
7. Estate Planning: Look at financial parts of a will—tax effects, setting up trusts and so on.
8. General: Advice to help you handle your financial affairs.

Your knowledge, circumstance, and time available to spend handling your financial affairs, will decide the type and frequency of help you need from a financial advisor.

Chapter 19 shows an example of someone working with a financial advisor to prepare her financial plan. Each person's needs and approach will differ, but that example shows some needed decisions as you work with a financial advisor.

Conflict of Interest

Previously, we had no difficulty identifying salespeople with their products. We knew a *stockbroker* bought and sold stocks and bonds, an *insurance agent* sold insurance, a *real estate agent* bought and sold properties, and a *mutual fund representative* sold mutual funds.

That's changed and many salespersons' titles suggest they are your *advisors*. This practice discounts an important reality. These advisors need to sell products to earn their income. So unconsciously, sometimes they sell you products you don't need and can't afford—especially when they offer good quality products! As one financial advisor told me, "at the end of the day, I must sell products to earn a decent living; I cannot live on fees alone!"

Too often, I see folks get advice and then buy financial products they didn't need and couldn't afford. In Canada, in February, I see people deep in debt get deeper in debt as they acted on advice to invest in their retirement savings. What enticed them? A *tax write-off!* Folks, a tax benefit should be a by-product, not a deciding feature!

This excerpt from a piece in the 13 May 2003 *Wall Street Journal* shows clearly what happened to some titles over the years. Called, "How to Pick a Financial Planner," the article comments on the transition in financial salespersons titles' from salespeople to advisors or planners:

> "Nobody agrees on which way the stock market is headed these days, but everyone wants to tell you how to invest.
>
> Stockbrokers, insurance agents, bankers, certified public accountants and even some lawyers are vying to make money by advising where to put yours. The down-turn has been as brutal for investment pros as it has been for individuals. Providing financial planning is a way for them to generate income and at the same time encourage skittish investors to wade back in.
>
> Merrill Lynch & Co.'s 14000 stockbrokers are now called "financial advisors." J. P. Morgan Chase & Co. is trying to convince affluent people who bank there to use its financial planners. And a host of others are offering everything from software services to one-on-ones..."

These comments apply to professionals who sell financial products and *try* to give *independent* advice about those products. Happily, most professional associations to which these folks belong have *codes of conduct* regulating objectivity, integrity, and more.

Still, many of these planners and advisors, who advise and sell products, believe they act objectively when they give advice. Many do, but to folks they advise, they don't admit the *potential conflict of interest*. That's the problem—before starting the advisory relationship, they need to highlight the conflict or potential conflict of interest to clients!

What is a conflict of interest? The definition that follows captures the essence of the conflict of interest policy with which I worked during my business career and other conflict of interest policies I reviewed:

> A conflict of interest exists, or a perceived conflict of interest can exist, if a person *(a financial advisor)* has a direct or indirect personal interest in a decision being made where that decision should, or needs to be made objectively, free from bias and in the best interests of another person (a client).
>
> Operating under a conflict of interest compromises independent judgment. Even if there is no evidence of improper actions, each person should avoid the appearance of a conflict of interest because it can undermine confidence in his ability to act objectively, free from bias.
>
> So, each person in this position must disclose the conflict or potential conflict of interest and discuss it with the affected party or parties.

Let's breakdown this definition to see how it applies to financial salespeople who advise:

1. *A conflict of interest exists, or a perceived conflict of interest can exist, if a person (a financial advisor) has a direct or indirect personal interest in a decision*

being made where that decision should, or needs to be made objectively, free from bias and in the best interests of another person (a client).

a. A non-independent *financial advisor* is *in a position of trust* and has a direct personal interest in products discussed with his client. The client sees the advisor as someone *he can trust* for solid, objective, unbiased advice. As well, a salesperson acting as *financial advisor* has a *competing personal interest:* to earn a living, he depends on product sales for fees and commissions, and might not give advice that's *objective, free from bias and in the best interests* of the client.

2. *Operating under a conflict of interest compromises independent judgment.*

a. The non-independent financial advisor's competing interest could make it difficult to give solid *independent advice.* The financial advisor might believe sincerely, the products he sells are the best, but competing products he doesn't offer, could be better for you. I have seen this happen. Still, I do not know anyone who knowingly gave bad advice. But unwittingly, the need to earn an income can affect objectivity!

3. *Even if there is no evidence of improper actions, each person should avoid the appearance of a conflict of interest because it can undermine confidence in his ability to act objectively, free from bias. So, each person in this position must disclose the conflict or potential conflict of interest and discuss it with the affected party.*

a. This is the crux—the appearance! How does someone become confident in a financial advisor who does not admit the potential conflict of interest?

b. The financial advisor must disclose the conflict or potential conflict of interest and tell the client how he plans to deal with it.

Please understand my concern; these folks' integrity or personalities—*who they are*—do not bother me. Rather, *what they do* bothers me. Do you see the difference? Even if your financial advisor denies his conflict of interest, look for these two conditions to confirm a conflict of interest exists:

1. A *financial advisor* (or other advisor) is in a position of trust, and depends on income from product sales (from advice given).
2. A *client* depends on him for independent, unbiased advice in the client's best interest.

Folks looking for independent financial advice face two challenges:

1. Learning to spot conflicts of interest.
2. Learning to manage this conflict when they have no alternatives, or when they choose to work with someone in a conflict of interest.

Who is a Financial Advisor

So, who should give you the independent financial advice you need and deserve? I want to stress again that a person's title is irrelevant. Do not rely on it! No matter his title, you and your advisor must understand and safeguard *you* against potential effects of the advisor's conflict of interest. Besides, for *independent* financial advice, do not rely *solely* on people or companies, if *what they do* fits one of these descriptions:

- Trade in securities, stocks and bonds, for a living (*Stockbrokers*).
- Earn a living from selling insurance *(Insurance Agents)*.
- Buy and sell mutual funds for a living *(Mutual Fund Representatives)*.
- Sell banks' products *(Bankers)*.
- Advise about financial products they sell, and they can benefit from their advice *(Financial Advisors or Planners)*.

For independent advice, consult a professional *independent* financial advisor—a *fee only* advisor. For a consultation or consultations, he charges either a fixed fee, or a fixed hourly rate. He is not in a *conflict of interest*, he sells no products—apart from consultation fees, he gets no benefit from advice he gives.

He will give advice according to his ability. He might target different markets—perhaps setting minimum net worth values for his clientele.

If you work with a fee only advisor, don't complain about his fees. You can't have it both ways: he depends on *fees only* to cover his costs and to earn an income. You must decide the value you put on independent advice!

Am I suggesting you must use an independent, fee only financial advisor? No, I suggest you need to identify conflicts of interest and learn to manage them. As well, please note *I am not saying independent financial advisors give better quality advice. An independent financial advisor can give lousy advice, even though he is not in a conflict of interest. Conversely, someone in a conflict of interest can give excellent advice.*

Here are three cautions:

1. Know when a conflict of interest exists and learn to either walk away, or work with it in your best interest.
2. Watch out; independence doesn't mean competence.

3. Beware; advice from a *fee only or other advisor* though technically sound might not be in your best interest. On page 182 of the second edition of my book, *Managing God's Money-The Basics,* I said, "some technically acceptable and feasible financial decisions I reject because of my Christian beliefs. ... I have many problems with leverage,[3] but one is relevant! It violates the *GAS Principle:*[4] It's God's money. Thou shalt not speculate! Period!"

Choosing the Financial Advisor

What if you can't find or don't wish to use an independent advisor? It doesn't matter! Follow these three preconditions to select a financial advisor, independent or other:

- *Define* clearly why you want to see a financial advisor—your goal.
  - Define your goal without looking at likely solutions. You might think you need a financial plan, but you don't know what that might entail. Tell your advisor your need, he will tell you how to fill it.
- *Accept* you are in charge, not the financial advisor—you get choices from your advisor to pray about and then decide.
- *Know* you can do preconditions one and two with your knowledge; you do not need special financial knowledge.

After accepting these three points, before you work with a financial advisor, interview him to ensure he has the qualities to perform as you expect. Follow the same procedure to choose an independent or other advisor. If the advisor is not independent, ensure you understand and can become comfortable working with conflicts of interest.

As a Christian, do you need a Christian advisor? No, provided you accept the earlier three preconditions.

Here are questions to ask as you interview a financial advisor:

- Conflict of Interest:
  - Independence
    - Is she independent?
    - Does she represent mutual funds, insurance or other companies? Which companies?
    - Is she in a conflict of interest, *or* potential conflict of interest? How does she plan to handle it?
- Fees:[5]
    - How will she charge you for advice you seek?
    - What's the deal with payment for product sales?
- Terms:
    - Will she set out in writing:
      - Engagement terms?
      - Answers to questions about her relationship with and payment by organizations she represents?
      - Your goals, as *she understands* them?
- Qualifications:
    - Qualification and experience?
    - Does she have references you can check?
- Clientele:
    - Tell her about you, your goals, present need, and ask:
      - Is she interested in taking you as a client?
      - Will she set aside time for you, or will she pass you to an assistant?

If you are looking for investment advice, you might add these questions:

- Specialization:
  - Does she or her company specialize: do they deal in specific products or specific clients?
- Education and Training:

- Does she or the company offer educational seminars that you could attend? Frequency? Location?
- Company:
  - How long in business?
  - Does the company work in other Provinces?
  - Size: Employees? Clients?
  - Does the company provide internal research reports to clients?
  - Has the company been subject to disciplinary proceedings in the past few years? What about her and others in the company, have they been subject to these proceedings?
- Commissions:
  - What commission rates should a client like you expect to pay?
- Servicing Account:
  - If you opened an account, will her other colleagues be available to you?
  - What are their experiences and qualifications?

Don't rush to decide; it's God's money, you are His steward, and you will account to Him not only for using His funds, but also for whom you choose as advisor. Check references, pray, seek God's direction. If you don't feel comfortable that an advisor will listen to you and do as you ask, don't work with him.

I know an instance when a client told an advisor that she wanted her six figure funds in Guaranteed Investment Certificates only. The advisor scoffed at her and said that wasn't a smart choice! It might not be *smart*, but if that's what you choose to do, the advisor's role is to explain the effects of that decision, compared with other alternatives. I repeat, let Jesus guide your decisions!

Shop around before your final choice. After your interview, if you decide to work with an advisor in a conflict of interest, do the following:

1. Ask him to give an example of a potential conflict and tell you how he would manage it. If you see a potential conflict and he doesn't, don't work with him, interview another person.
2. Get a list of represented products.
3. Get in writing his payment arrangements with you and financial companies.
4. Agree to separate his *advice* to you from his *product sales* to you. This can be easy if you understand that his advice is the *planning* stage—what to do. Product sales follow; it's the *doing* phase.
   a. If you need insurance advice, agree to separate *planning*—the nature, type and amount of insurance, from *doing*—buying insurance. Receive advice, such as *term insurance, 30 years, $250,000;* understand it, pray about it, and ask the Lord to show you how to do it. Ask your advisor for a quotation, and then check its competitiveness. Price is not the only feature.
   b. The same principle applies to investment advice. Separate *planning* from *doing:* separate nature, portfolio type, from individual investment instruments. So, understand why you need that portfolio, that mix; likely risks and returns and so on. Then pray; seek God's direction before looking at alternatives and agreeing to buy stocks, bonds, or mutual fund. If after getting advice[6] you choose not to buy from this advisor, you need to pay for the advice! Be transparent, honest and fair.

For Whom Does She Work

After you get advice, carry out my three-step plan:

1. First, ask clarifying questions; be open, direct and honest!

2. Second, ask further clarifying questions!
3. Third, ask further clarifying questions until *you understand* the proposals!

Communicate your goals and values clearly and directly to your *advisor*. She should know you are a Christian, and the specific values that guide you. She should know you do not tolerate anything but transparency on your tax returns—you will pay taxes due while taking advantage of available benefits.

Many folks complain about *bad decisions* from their financial advisors. They don't realize their advisor advises, does not know the future, and might give them what turns out to be *bad advice*.

Your advisor presents choices, you decide. So you need to ask questions until you understand issues she presents to you. If you are uncomfortable with advice you get, seek a second opinion. The buck stops with you!

Summary

As you choose an advisor for independent financial advice, keep in mind three key points. *First*, ignore titles; look at what he does. *Second*, identify and discuss potential conflicts of interest. If he is in a conflict or potential conflict of interest and won't accept it, go to another person. *Third*, let Jesus guide your choice; you will account to Him for it. In your dealings, show integrity, respect, and grace—let Jesus' light shine through you.

Think About This

The way of a fool is right in his own eyes, But a wise man is he who listens to counsel.[7]

Chapter Notes:

1. A share option is the time-limited right to buy shares in a company at a predetermined price. Company X may grant an Option to you to buy 100 shares at $5 per share. Usually there is a waiting period before you may "exercise" the options. If in one year the shares were traded at $10 per share you could exercise the option by purchasing those shares at $5 then selling them. Alternatively, you could purchase shares and retain them.
2. Even if your *advisor* computes and analyses statements and summaries, you are responsible for decisions they might lead to; *he advises only!*
3. Simply, financial leveraging is borrowing to invest. I borrow and invest $1000; it doubles, and *voila! The opposite can happen; then what!*
4. Michel A. Bell, *Managing God's Money-The Basics,* pages 25-27.
5. Be fair; don't go around collecting free advice on the pretext you are screening advisors! That happens! That's not right! That's not fair!
6. Pay for *advice* not *sales presentations.* Expect a salesperson to explain product features and to present alternatives.
7. Proverbs 12:15.

19

Writing Your Personal Financial Plan

We are almost at the end of this ride. In this chapter, we pull together knowledge we picked up along the way and prepare a personal financial plan. Normally folks don't see the link between a personal financial plan and daily lifestyle choices. They don't realize that with the right *attitude,* a financial plan could help them lower debt, save regularly for children's education, and save to pay cash for a car and other stuff.

A financial plan shows in different forms, your likely financial picture from doing goals and plans during a specific period—it captures expected financial results from goal setting. With the Holy Spirit's help, I am confident you can do or you can guide your financial plan make up. If you choose to use a financial advisor to compile a financial plan, information in this chapter will help you ask right questions.

Most folks don't write financial plans because they don't know about it, think about it, or because they need help, but don't know where to go. You know who an advisor is and who he isn't, so if you sense the Lord telling you to write a financial plan, ask Him to tell you who should prepare it, when to do it, and to guide you through the exercise.

Deciding who should do it—you or an independent financial advisor—is your first important decision. Chapter 18 will help you decide whom to choose, an independent advisor, or a financial salesperson that you manage. Still, whomever you select, separate putting the plan together from doing it. So, if you work with a non-independent[1] advisor, don't buy products from her as part of the financial planning procedure. Finish the plan, understand it, look at alternatives, *count the cost,* and then decide how to start doing it—buying financial products, if needed.

Invest time with Jesus to hear what He arranged for you. Otherwise, you and your advisor will develop goals and plans based on financial feasibility only. Review chapter 4, especially goals you wrote as you read it.

Fiona, and Betsy, her nine-year-old daughter, a one-parent family, will provide their information to help us discuss essential questions you need to answer to write your financial plan:

- Where am I spiritually?
- Where am I materially?
- What goals should I work on and over what period?
- What main inputs and outputs will I need?
- How do I stay on track?

Where Am I Spiritually

This will set the principles to apply. If you are starting this journey and don't have a personal relationship with Christ, I encourage you to reread chapter 4. As I said consistently, without Christ, this and other financial matters will be stressful, mechanical and highlight money, which you know is just a bridge between your wants and needs, and products and services. In your financial plan, money measures results of your goals. If money becomes the focus, you will work on wrong topics and monitor wrong results. As you work on the plan, keep in mind University of Missouri's Kennon Sheldon's findings: "People who say money is most important to them are the unhappiest."

Fiona surrendered her life to Christ 10 years ago; she accepts Jesus' ownership, her stewardship of possessions, and wants to honour Him with her finances. She is working with a non-independent financial advisor, Conrad, who doesn't know the Lord as personal Saviour, and who sells financial products, still, she is comfortable.

She turned over the procedure to God, accepts her role to lead it under God's guidance, and will not buy products until she finishes the plan and knows it fits God's plan. As well, Conrad accepts his role: To give advice to help her decide under God's guidance. Fiona agrees to work with Conrad in two phases. She will pay him *a flat fee* for advice. If after she understands and feels comfortable with what she needs to carry out the plan, she will work with Conrad as a salesperson.

Where Am I Materially

At 30 September what does Fiona *own* as manager, and how much does she owe? Her material worth statement shows this information.

Material Worth $000 At 30 September	
House	110
Car	15
Betsy's Education Savings	2
Other Stuff	0
Assets	**127**
Financed by:	
Mortgage	105
Car Loan	10
Family Loan	2
Equity	10
Loans and Equity	**127**

Fiona's yearly income and expenses, shown next page, completes the base to build on. She knows she cannot assume today's income and expenses will continue. So she and Conrad will look at each income and expense category and decide its estimated yearly value.

Present Yearly Income $000	
Gross Salary	50
Less: "Giving"	(7)
Less: Taxes	(17)
Less: Capital Fund	0
Less: Savings	0
Net	**26**
Net Allocation	
Food	5
Shelter (including mortgage)	11
Clothing	1
Transport (including loan)	6
Family loan payment	0
Betsy's Education	0
Entertainment	1
Other	2
Total Spending	**26**

Fiona and Conrad will use this as the base to project Fiona's income and expenses for the twelve-year plan period. They will review existing categories and based on Fiona's goals and plans, decide if they should add new categories.

What Goals Should I Work On

Answering this question is personal and often difficult because you might not like where you are and what you have. So, you might become preoccupied with your condition, blaming others for it. Don't! Move on! You are where you are. Understand, accept, learn from, and work with what you have.

For over one year, Fiona has been seeking God's direction for her finances. She accepts her condition, and developing this plan excites her. But before she can think or pray about goals to work on, she has questions on these topics:

- Loan repayments
- Postsecondary education
- Car replacement
- Insurance needs
- Pension and investments

Loan repayment

How should I go about repaying my debts? Should I repay the family loan before the car loan? Should I pay more than needed against my mortgage?

At first, the answer, "it depends," confused Fiona, but later she understood and developed a debt repayment schedule similar to Appendix 5. She and Conrad agreed she must repay each loan based on her agreement with the lender. If she has extra funds, she should apply them first to the highest annual interest rate loan. So, she should repay her car loan, 8.5% interest after-tax, and then the family loan. Though the family loan is interest free, Fiona felt a moral duty to repay it after the car loan, and before putting extra funds against mortgage principal that costs 5.5% interest after-tax.

Post Secondary Education

"But how do I repay debt and save for Betsy's post secondary education?" Fiona asked Conrad.

Conrad told her the best savings is debt repayment. After repaying the car and family loans, Fiona will need to start saving for Betsy's education. She and Conrad worked out the amount she needed to save monthly for Betsy's university education: estimated cost minus Government benefits available over the nine-year saving period. Fiona agreed to save at least this amount yearly.

As well, Fiona decided she and Betsy would be alert to scholarship availability, especially three to five years before Betsy was ready for university. Fiona's friend Mildred's daughter took off last summer and sent 100 essays and letters to universities, corporations, foundations, and Government agencies telling them about her academic qualifications (she graduated from high school) and her goal to study medicine. She got two scholarship offers and took one. Fiona's message: she knows she can get funds for Betsy's education as long as she listens for and does God's goal like her friend. Fiona knows and wants to honour, Apostle Paul's teachings in 2 Corinthians 12:14 that parents are responsible to save for their children.

Replacing the Car

Conrad told Fiona most folks he sees fall in debt because of major unplanned car repairs, or because they didn't save to replace their cars. The issue here is how to get out of the debt cycle. How could Fiona buy the next car for cash? She and Conrad agreed she would review her transport needs. Did she need a car? Long-term, is it feasible to get to work using public transport and renting a car when needed? In the next year, Fiona would look at this.

Meanwhile, Fiona would start a *Capital Fund* after repaying car and family loans, and while saving to get the yearly maximum Government benefits for Betsy's education. She decided she would not buy another car unless she paid cash, a big challenge. But with God's help, she knew she could do it.

Insurance

This was Fiona's greatest concern: Do I need insurance? What type of insurance, and how much do I need? Fiona learned insurance was about identifying, quantifying, and covering risks. She and Conrad identified and quantified life and disability insurance needs.

She would look at taking out a term life policy to provide income for Betsy if she died. Her estate would get funds to pay Betsy's guardian whom Fiona identified in her recent will. The policy would provide enough funds to care for Betsy through university.

Fiona agreed to arrange disability insurance through her employer. As well, to lower premiums on the car and on her house, she agreed to raise *insurance deductibles*. But she would do this only after saving the deductible amounts in her Capital Fund.

Still, Fiona and Conrad decided she would not buy or change her insurance until she finished working on the financial plan and prayed about it.

Pension and investments

Fiona wants to start putting funds in a pension plan, and investing funds like "other people." She learned that debt repayment is her best investment because it is risk free and improves her financial position immediately. Still, she would like to invest. Conrad stressed that she should finish the plan before thinking about this matter.

Her employer did not offer a matching pension or savings plan so by not saving in a pension plan she was not losing this potential benefit. At 31 years old, two of Fiona's wishes were to be debt free except for her mortgage, and to save for Betsy's education.

Fiona decided she would not borrow to invest because borrowing to invest guaranteed more debt without a guaranteed investment return. Besides, that was putting God's money at unneeded risks.

Fiona was ready to look at goals, understanding some goals would differ at different life stages. She wanted this financial plan to cover at least 12 years, estimated time for Betsy to finish her under graduate university education. After prayer, she came up with these goals:

- **Attitude, Behaviour, Choices (ABCs)**
  - **Attitude:** Her relationship with Christ will shine through her finances.
  - **Behaviour:** Her spending would not dishonour Jesus.
  - **Choices:** Jesus would direct all spending. She would develop a formal procedure to follow before committing or spending $25 or over.
- **Financial**
  - **Betsy's Education:** Her savings, Government incentives, and interest income would cover the estimated cost. She would review estimates six-monthly, and be alert to available grants and scholarships.
  - **Debt Free Lifestyle:** She will live a lifestyle so that in five years, she would be debt free except for the mortgage. Under God's guidance, she will follow the spending schedule worked out, reviewing it six monthly. She will listen and respond to the Lord.
  - **Pay Cash:** She will pay cash for stuff she buys, using the Capital Fund as the savings medium. She knows she will need Jesus' help to ignore seductive advertising.

- **Budget:** She will work with a budget and money map under God's guidance, ensuring she does not lower giving to God to get her goals.
- **Saving and Investments:** Her only savings will be for Betsy's education and in a Capital Fund for emergency funds (3-6 months wages), to raise insurance deductible, and to be able to pay cash for major buys and major equipment and appliances' repairs and maintenance.

Key Inputs and Outputs

Before answering this question, to help Fiona understand amounts to set aside for Betsy's education, Conrad described briefly two important terms discussed in chapter 6: inflation and time value of money. For completeness, I mention them briefly.

Inflation

Inflation is a general and continued rise in price levels. We need to estimate inflation for each of the twelve plan years. It's a key assumption that could affect the plan significantly. If the plan estimates differed from reality that would affect savings and spending decisions, such as amount to save for Betsy's education.

Conrad told Fiona she needed to get a *real* return on savings—the savings return should be greater than inflation. He suggested inflation would average 2% each year and her savings would earn 5%, so she would get a yearly 3% real return. If the reverse happened, she would lose savings each year.

Inflation and interest rates estimates can affect plan results significantly, so Fiona must review them at least six-monthly. If they change notably, to stay on course to get to the plan, she might need to change her behaviour.

Time Value of Money

This term includes these matters discussed also in chapter six:

- Multiplication Principle and compound interest
- Present value
- Future value

I coined the term *multiplication principle* meaning interest on debt grows faster than interest on savings. So your best savings is to repay debt.

Chapter 6 shows what happens when you set aside one dollar and you reinvest interest received. Interest compounds—you get interest on interest. As well, it shows, the sooner you save, the more interest compounds. Sadly, when you owe funds, sometimes interest compounds at a much faster rate!

The other side of compound interest is present value. The present value or today's value of $155 you will get in nine years at 5% is $100. One fifty five dollars is the future value.

This knowledge helped Fiona understand and calculate amounts she needed to set aside for Betsy's education.

Fiona was ready to go over needed inputs and outputs. She had great difficult working with so many unknowns but realized only God knows the future so every plan will be somebody's estimates and likely to change.

Inputs

- Fiona's beliefs and values
- Fiona's goals and plans
- Betsy's involvement
- State of the economy
- Interest and inflation rates
- Timing of Fiona's income and expenses
- Timing of major buys

Fiona and Conrad did their best working with information they knew, such as present salary and spending pattern. For each input, they applied a realistic inflation factor: they applied a higher inflation to gas prices than to salaries.

When the information was fuzzy, they asked three questions: What's the worse it could be? What's the best? What's the most likely? They chose the most likely and noted it for regular reviews.

Fiona believed the two most crucial inputs were her time with the Lord and her discussions with Betsy. She told Betsy what she did, why, and how they could work together. They agreed they would need patience. As well, they would listen to God and depend on Him.

After Fiona and Conrad agreed inputs for each of the plan years, they produced output statements that Fiona decided to reflect on and pray about before acting.

Outputs
- Material Worth Statement
- Cash Flow Statement and Budget
- Capital Fund Worksheet
- Debt Repayment Schedule
- Stewardship Covenant
- Will and Powers of Attorney
- Explanation to Betsy about main goals and the education savings plan

Financial Plan Schedules

One month after their first meeting, Fiona and Conrad finished the plan. Financial statements in Table XV show the results. Conrad put the statements together, but Fiona gave him her goals, plans and other inputs. Conrad gave Fiona the *spreadsheets*. The statements intimidated Fiona a bit, but

Conrad was a good teacher, and after the sessions with him, she felt she understood the results. As well, she planned to sit with him six-monthly so he could update it and clarify sections, as needed.

She knew some key figures. Still, she knew this was a plan, and to turn out the same or better, her behaviour, and the assumptions such as inflation rate and interest rates, need to be the *same or better* than planned. So, if she planned to save and she didn't, *her behaviour* would cause her not to meet that part of the plan. In the same way, if she got 3% on savings instead of 5%, she might need to adjust *her behaviour* and spend less to get the planned cash flow—Fiona understood this message that Conrad stressed. As well, for the first time, she appreciated the emphasis on ABCs—attitude, behaviour, and choices.

Here are some important messages Fiona took from her plan:

1. She would be debt free by the end of year 3 – see arrow on the material worth statement.
2. She would be able to save almost $50,000 for Betsy's education and capital items' replacement in 10 years—see numbers in the rectangle. As well, she knew she would be able to replace her car in around six years. Still, she did not include replacement in this plan because she will look at going without a car, relying on public transport, and occasionally renting a car. When she meets Conrad in six months, she will tell him the results of her study and then they will adjust the plan. This pleased Fiona; she didn't need to get all answers now, rather she would develop the plan further as she looked in more detail at different matters.
3. She saw clearly how slowly her mortgage loan reduced ($30,000 in 12 years). She appreciated Conrad's advice to prepay mortgage principal, if feasible. Still, they did not provide for prepayments in this plan.

4. She understood her house value rose, but she did not want to consider it in the plan because she did not view her home as an investment against which she should take on more loans.
5. She was not happy with the amount assigned to giving, and she planned to keep praying, asking God to show her how much she should be giving.

Excited, Fiona thanked God for showing her how to write this plan and *covenanted* not to let it become her god. She would continue to listen and respond to God no matter what the plan said. She knew she had to lean on Him.

Sensitivity Analysis

Conrad and Fiona looked at the effects of assumptions turning out different from plan. They changed inflation, savings, taxes, and other assumptions separately and in different combinations. Fiona learned much from this exercise, including the effects of a 1% change in these items:

- **Salary increase:** A one-percent drop from 2.5 to 1.5% yearly lowers the 12th year's salary by $7000 and lower accumulated savings over 12 years by $26,000.
- **Savings Decrease:** A one-percent decrease in savings rate from 5 to 4% yearly lowers Betsy's education savings by $5,000 over the period.

How Do I Stay On Track

Fiona realized the plan would not turn out as expected because the future will not turn out as planned. God alone knows the future. She knows she needs to review her plan often, and as needed, change assumptions, behaviour, or goals under God's direction.

By God's grace and staying focused on Jesus, Fiona hoped to stay on track. She realized she would need patience and discipline. But she knew she would get them from the Lord because that was her heart's wish.

She asked her best friend and prayer partner Elizabeth to hold her accountable to stay close to God. With Betsy, Fiona planned to hold twice-monthly *Family Council* meetings to review progress against plan and budget.

She did not buy products from Conrad, but agreed to review the plan yearly with him. Six monthly she would update her Cash Flow, Material Worth and Debt Repayment schedules based on guidance Conrad gave her. Most of all, she knew that to stay on course she would need to *change her behaviour* when assumptions turned out different from plan.

Her final acts were signing the Stewardship Covenant[2] and committing to work with a budget, and a money map for regular spending trips.

Table XV-1
Fiona's and Betsy's Financial Plan
Goals Plans and Assumptions

Goals	Live debt free lifestyle Repay debt in next five years Save for Betsy's education
Plans	Live in income Follow debt repayment schedule Lean on Jesus
Assumptions	Inflation 2% , Salary 2.5%, Savings 5%, Transport 2% Other items 2%, Tax rate 35%

Table XV-2
Fiona and Betsy's Financial Plan
Material Worth Statement – $ 000
Periods 1-12

Stuff @ Market, except house $ 000	1	2	3	4	5	6	7	8	9	10	11	12
House	110	110	110	110	110	110	110	110	110	110	110	110
Car	15	10	7	3	1	1	1	1	0	0	0	0
Betsy's Education	0	0	0	2	6	10	15	20	25	30	35	41
Capital Fund	0	0	0	2	4	6	9	13	15	18	21	24
Other	2	3	2	2	2	2	2	2	2	3	4	5
Assets	127	123	119	119	123	129	137	146	152	161	170	180
financed by:												
Mortgage	105	103	101	98	96	94	91	88	85	82	79	75
Car Loan	10	5	0	0	0	0	0	0	0	0	0	0
Family Loan	2	2	0	0	0	0	0	0	0	0	0	0
Fiona's Funds	10	13	21	26	27	35	46	58	67	79	91	105
Loans & Equity	127	123	122	124	123	129	137	146	152	161	170	180

Table XV-3
Fiona's And Betsy's Financial Plan
Income and Expenses $'000
Periods 1-12

	1	2	3	4	5	6	7	8	9	10	11	12
Gross Salary	50	51	52	54	55	57	58	59	61	63	64	66
Less: "Giving"	(7)	(7)	(7)	(8)	(8)	(9)	(10)	(9)	(9)	(9)	(9)	(9)
Less: Taxes	(17)	(18)	(18)	(19)	(19)	(20)	(20)	(21)	(21)	(22)	(22)	(23)
Available to Spend	**26**	**26**	**27**	**27**	**28**	**28**	**28**	**29**	**31**	**32**	**33**	**34**
Food	5	5	5	5	5	5	5	5	5	5	5	5
Mortgage	8	8	8	8	8	8	8	8	9	10	11	12
Shelter excluding mortgage	2	2	2	2	2	2	2	2	3	3	3	3
Clothing	1	1	1	2	2	2	2	2	2	2	2	2
Car Loan	5	5	5	0	0	0	0	0	0	0	0	0
Transport excluding loan	2	2	2	2	2	2	2	2	2	2	2	2
Family loan payment	0	0	2	0	0	0	0	0	0	0	0	0
Betsy's Education	0	0	0	2	4	4	4	4	4	4	4	4
Capital Fund	0	0	0	2	2	2	2	3	2	2	2	2
Entertainment	1	1	1	1	2	2	2	2	2	2	2	2
Other	2	2	1	1	1	1	1	1	2	2	2	2
Total Spending	**26**	**26**	**27**	**25**	**28**	**28**	**28**	**29**	**31**	**32**	**33**	**34**

Table XV-4
Fiona's And Betsy's Financial Plan
Cash Flow Statement $ '000
Periods 1-12

	1	2	3	4	5	6	7	8	9	10	11	12
Gross Salary	50	51	52	54	55	57	58	59	61	62	64	66
Less: "Giving"	(7)	(7)	(7)	(8)	(8)	(9)	(10)	(10)	(10)	(9)	(9)	(9)
Less: Taxes	(17)	(18)	(18)	(19)	(19)	(20)	(20)	(21)	(21)	(22)	(22)	(23)
Available to Spend	26	26	27	27	28	28	28	28	30	31	33	34
Food	5	5	5	5	5	5	5	5	5	5	5	5
Mortgage	8	8	8	8	8	8	8	8	9	10	11	12
Shelter - excl mortgage	2	2	2	2	2	2	2	2	3	3	3	3
Clothing	1	1	1	2	2	2	2	2	2	2	2	2
Car Loan	5	5	5	0	0	0	0	0	0	0	0	0
Family loan payment	0	0	2	0	0	0	0	0	0	0	0	0
Transport excluding loan	2	2	2	2	2	2	2	2	2	2	2	2
Entertainment	1	1	1	1	1	1	1	1	1	1	1	1
Other	2	2	1	1	1	1	1	1	1	1	1	1
Total Spending	26	26	27	21	22	22	22	22	24	25	26	27
Balance before savings*	(0)	(0)	(0)	6	6	6	6	6	6	6	7	7
Cumulative	(0)	(0)	(0)	6	12	18	24	30	36	42	49	56

* These amounts are available for Betsy's education and savings

Summary

What is a financial plan?

It shows financial results you expect in a future time from specific goals and plans.

Why Do it?

To show you what might happen if you follow specific choices. While developing it, you might see alternatives you would not see without going through the procedure. And you will be able to focus your prayers.

When should you do it?

After you get God's goals and plans, but with enough time before a specific future period to look at different choices seriously.

How should you do it?

Guided by the Lord in the *Family Council*, with family members' views and using available information on goals, plans, and spending plans.

How will you stay on track?

By the grace of God, accepting your manager's role, and setting up an accountability procedure that you follow.

Do you need a Financial Planner?

Not always, you need to listen to God!

Think About This

 It's wise to listen to God and follow His goal and plan, His way, in His time! I am glad Noah did!

Chapter Notes:

1. A non-independent advisor is a person with a financial planner or advisor's title who sells products and is in a conflict of interest.

2. Stewardship Covenant: Agreement with Jesus that He is Owner, you are His manager committed to manage all belongings according to His principles. As well, you accept you will account to Him for your stewardship of time, talents, money, and everything He gives you. Refer to my book, *Managing God's Money: 7 Branches Workbook*, page 26.

20

A Forever to Remember

As we approach our final stop on this trip, let's recap. The main message of the book is clear: God owns everything; we own nothing. The subsidiary point is obvious too: Manage God's money knowing we will account to Him for our actions. And when we refer to *managing money*, recall we mean controlling our wants, needs and greed; we understand money isn't manageable but a *bridge* between *merchants* and *me*. So we must know right *attitudes*, follow right *behaviours*, and stick rigorously to the Gas Principle—three key truths about God's ownership and our stewardship of time, talents and money.

A Brief Recap

The GAS Principle, Three Key Truths from the Bible, is the engine, and right *attitudes*, *behaviours*, and *choices* (ABCs) like gasoline for a car.

Key Truth #1: God Owns Everything
(Psalm 24:1-2, Colossians 1:16)

Key Truth #2: Accept What You Have (1 Timothy 6:7-8; Hebrews 13:5)

Key Truth #3: Seek First His Kingdom and Submit Your Requests to Him
(Matthew 6:33, Proverbs 19:21)

Once the GAS Principle becomes ingrained and instinctive we will know we can trust Jesus to supply our needs. We will work with spending plans we prepare with Jesus at our sides. As well, we will practise *keeping* by presenting 100% of all we earn to God and let Him decide how much to *keep* in His kingdom. Then we will be able to say with confidence:

The
Shepherd
gives
Gas
for
PEACE
on the
PLANE

We will turn to PEACE Budgetary Control as our primary tool to help carry out the GAS Principle. PEACE is the performance recording and tracking tool that allows us to reach goals systematically; we need to follow it, to manage God's money effectively.

When we work with PEACE rigorously as part of the Gas Principle, we will focus on Jesus, He will bless us, and we will not suffer money-related stress, even when we have no money to meet our wants! We know PEACE never stops.

Figure 1

PEACE Budgetary Control

Meanwhile, as we stay with PEACE, we will notice we need these seven *sequential* steps to keep us on the debt free path:

1. We need to *surrender every area of our lives to Jesus;* we can't live in silos; we must practice *keeping* as part of stewarding God's money.
2. We must show and teach our children a *biblical worldview* including a biblical worldview about money; God commands us to do so daily.
3. We know buying a house prematurely is a main cause of deep debt, and so we need to study renting or buying a home. Wherever we are today, we need a time-out to do this. If we don't, we will slide along the consumer debt path, listen to merchants, and then buy a home before we are ready.
4. Unless we change our attitudes today and decide to stop consumer debt increase, repay debt, and ask the Holy Spirit to help adjust our lifestyles, we will remain on the debt path.
5. We know areas that challenge us, so plug those leaks today to stop expenses from rising. As we free funds

used previously to repay debt, we need to ask God to show us where to redirect those funds.

6. We will get in and remain in debt unless we start saving systematically for assets' (stuff that lasts longer than one year) renewal, repairs and replacement. After we repay consumer debt, we must ask God to give us the discipline to start saving systematically in a Capital Fund.

7. Most of all, we must ensure we fund the Great Commission habitually; ensure we store treasures in heaven, and then under God's direction, start retirement savings, and investing.

Yearly, we should check how we are doing by carrying out a quick financial check-up to prevent bad attitudes from seeping in unnoticed. I liken financial health to physical health. In my annual medical, my doctor does internal and external examinations. Based on my age and other personal data, he knows the condition I ought to be in—the *benchmark*. He uses blood tests, urine tests, x-rays and other tools to understand my internal organs compared to the benchmark.

For the external examination, he looks in my eyes, mouth, and ears. When he finishes, sometimes he stresses life style changes such as, the need for regular exercise, and the need to change to a more healthy diet.

I insist always we don't treat *symptoms*, but ensure we understand each problem's cause, so we can work on it. If my stomach aches, I need to understand what's causing the pain even if it will take much time to get the answer. So I bear the pain. I don't want a pill to mask it, because that doesn't fix the problem. Indeed, it might even worsen it by giving me false hope when the pain goes!

In the same way, for the financial health check, I do internal and external examinations to answer this question: *How am I managing God's money?* After the assessment, as with the medical, I don't treat the *symptoms* but get to the *causes* to deal with them. If I don't, I could get comfortable in my current unacceptable financial state and I might blame others.

As believers in Christ, we know God owns everything, so our benchmark is clear: to spend His money to bring Him glory and further His Kingdom. If we are not spending like good stewards, we need to change our behaviour. We have no alternative. After all, God provides what we need, when we need it (Matthew 6:33; 2 Peter 1:3; 2 Kings 4:1-7).

Just as my blood pressure reading tells my doctor my blood pressure when he took it, so my expense analysis will tell me where I *stored* treasures during the review period, here on earth or in heaven. In essence, what's important to me, God or me?

My financial health at a specific time represents the state of the finances God entrusts to me. I measure it against the benchmark the Holy Spirit shows me. Though this approach is subjective, each believer knows what his or her spending ought to be if he or she lives a God-centered life.

The *annual financial health check is an analytical procedure to help us see where we spent funds compared with our benchmark—the video camera view. In addition, we get a still photograph* by computing our debts and assets at the review date. Usually the results confirm what we know already, though some details might surprise us.

The procedure entails analyzing spending over a defined period, and reviewing value items (assets) and loans, at a fixed date. Based on the outcome, we might need to change our *attitude and behavior* toward money so our financial affairs come in line with our life goal and material goals—specific purposes God identifies for us to bring Him glory.

Carry out your financial-health check in October by reviewing spending from January to September, and valuing assets roughly, and loans at 30 September, precisely. Be sincere; ask the Lord to help you answer each question not as you would like the results to be, but as they have been. Husbands and wives, do this exercise together during a *Family Council* session.

At a suitable age, encourage your children to enter the family review. As well, teach them to do their own review.

Use the questionnaire below. To develop suitable goals and plans after the review, try to identify:

1. Symptoms
2. Causes
3. Cures

Financial Health-Check Questionnaire

Goals, Plans, Budgets

1. Do you have a *life goal* that guides everything you do? Yes ___ No ___
2. Regularly, do you work with other goals? Yes ___ No ___
3. Regularly, do you work with plans supporting these goals? Yes ___ No ___
4. Regularly, do you work with a budget? Yes ___ No ___
5. If you don't work with a budget, do you think you would handle your finances better if regularly you worked with one? Yes ___ No ___

Money Matters

1. Do you accept your role as manager of God's possessions He entrusts to you? Yes ___ No ___
2. Are you happy with the following:
   a. The state of your finances? Yes ___ No ___
   b. Your attitude toward money? Yes ___ No ___
   c. The procedure you use to choose when, and how much to spend? Yes ___ No ___
3. Do you know how much you need to live on each month? Yes ___ No ___

a. Do you live on this amount or less? Yes ____ No ____
b. Can you live on this amount? Yes ____ No ____
4. Do you feel guilty when you spend? Yes ___ No ___
5. Did you get more money over the past 12 months than 12 months earlier? Yes ___ No ___
6. Did you spend more during the past 12 months than the previous 12? Yes ___ No ___
7. Did your spending show you what's important? Yes ___ No ___
8. Are you in debt except for your mortgage? Yes ___ No ___
   a. Is your debt except your mortgage greater at 30 September this year than at 30 September last year? Yes ___ No ___
   b. Is your mortgage greater at 30 September this year than at 30 September last year? Yes ___ No ___
9. Regularly, do you earmark money to God's work according to direction from the Holy Spirit? Yes ___ No ___
10. Usually (six of ten times), do you buy stuff based on: (Answer (i) or (ii), and each of the others that apply)
    i.   Need? Yes ___ No ___
    ii. Want? Yes ___ No ___
    iii. Advertising? Yes ___ No ___
    iv. Spending plan or budget that you follow and review monthly? Yes ___ No ___

Financial Learning and Modeling

1. Are you learning regularly about Christ-centered attitudes to improve your financial affairs? Yes ___ No ___
2. Dads,[1] are you teaching your spouse and children how to manage *spending drivers*,[2] such as their attitudes toward money?
   a. By your decisions? Yes ___ No ___
   b. By your actions? Yes ___ No ___
   c. By talking with them? Yes ___ No ___

3. Do you know the details and choices available under the following:
   a. Your company's benefits plans? Yes __ No __
   b. Your mortgage? Yes __ No __
   c. Your other loans? Yes __ No __
4. Do you know if you need insurance and the amount?
   a. Life? Yes __ No __
   b. Disability? Yes __ No __
   c. Other? Yes __ No __

Wills, Powers of Attorney and Document Retrieval

1. Do you have an up-to-date will? Yes __ No __
2. Do you have up-to-date Powers of Attorney:
   a. Property? Yes __ No __
   b. Personal Care? Yes __ No __
3. Do you follow a regular procedure to store and find quickly when you need them, documents such as warranties, pension information, wills? Yes __ No __

Longer term Matters: Children Education

1. Are you saving for your children's postsecondary education? Yes __ No __
2. Are you using to the maximum available, funding from Government and other sources for your children's postsecondary education? Yes __ No __
3. Do your children know your decisions about their postsecondary education? Yes __ No __

Longer term Matters: Retirement planning

1. Do you know choices available to you for retirement from your employer and Government? Yes __ No __
2. Have you started planning for retirement, specifically, changing your career, by seeking God's direction?

Yes __ No __

3. Have you started to identify and save for your "retirement income gap"?[3] Yes __ No __

Longer term Matters: Major Buys and Repairs

1. Do you believe you should pay cash *always* for all items except a home (this includes using a credit card but *always* paying monthly balances in full)? Yes __ No __
   a. Did you practise this during the review period?
      Yes __ No __
   b. Will you start to follow this practice after this review?
      Yes __ No __

Before answering the questionnaire, you knew your specific symptoms. Either your finances concerned you to some degree, or they didn't. After this exercise what should you expect; in other words, so what?

Notice this check-up goes beyond daily finances; it's more comprehensive than monthly spending. So the key question is this: Are you happy with your individual answers? I do not believe in assigning scores because it is more important you understand the *causes* for each answer than to get a score that doesn't help you. This review's real benefits are the trends you see by comparing current with previous questionnaire's answers, and current replies with *benchmarks*. With the Holy Spirit's help, let your first review guide you to set *benchmarks*.

You benefit from this exercise not only by seeing where you are on each item compared to the past, but by deciding to do something about answers that deviate from the *benchmark*. But don't try to fix these items before you identify the cause. For example, if you did not write a will, don't decide to prepare one until you understand why you hadn't. It could be neglect, indecision, ignorance, or fear of discussing the topic. Deal with the cause, and then ask the Lord how to move ahead.

When you finish assessing your answers, prepare a table similar to Table XVI to identify *symptoms, causes,* and *cures.* Be honest during this exercise. It's essential you distinguish symptoms from causes to identify suitable cures. Your circumstance is unique; no entry from the table below might apply, still, reflect on each.

Table XVI
Symptoms Causes and Cures

Probable Symptoms	Probably Causes	Likely Cures
Money Matters: - Not enough income (living pay cheque-to-pay cheque) - Can't sleep - Worried	1. Difficulty distinguishing needs from wants 2. Lack of faith that Jesus will supply needs 3. Greed 4. Inability to set and stick with priorities 5. Poor planning and execution Accepting and working with the income you have – 2 Kings 4:1-7	1. Accepting and working with the income you have - 2 Kings 4:1-7 2. Changing your attitude and behavior toward money 3. Patience 4. Becoming more generous
Wills and Powers of Attorney: - Can't "make the time"	1. Ignorance about Estate Planning 2. Can't prioritize work in available time 3. Fear – uncomfortable discussing the subject 4. Don't believe they are needed	1. Need to get to know about this subject 2. Consult a trusted, Independent Financial Advisor 3. Ask the Lord to guide you

Probable Symptoms	Probably Causes	Likely Cures
Longer Term Matters-Children's Education: - Concerned about education's high cost - Worried you won't have enough money when needed	1. Ignorance 2. Victim attitude – easy to blame high tuition fees on Governments and others 3. You didn't plan	1. Understand your alternatives 2. Decide who is responsible for your children's education (2 Corinthians 12:14). If you choose not to provide, tell your children *early*. 3. Start *early* to use Government and other funding programs.
Retirement Planning: - Concerned you might not be able to retire - Worried because you don't know what to do - Don't know if or when to start planning	1. Victim attitude: Willing to blame Government or employer for not providing 2. Greed: Ill-advised investments in the stock market 3. Ignorance of God's retirement provisions Seek reliable independent advice	1. Ask the Lord to guide you 2. Take responsibility for this activity

After you finish your table with the Holy Spirit's help, listen for God's goals and plans that will address the cures during the current year's remaining months, and the following year, and then start doing them. His goals always have the 3-C's stamp: clear, complete, and concise. You might not get the goals all at once but you will get them and the plan when you need them. Just remember the details he gave Noah to build the ark! He will give you what you need in His time. Be patient!

For each item, set a goal then develop a plan to carry out the cure you identify under the Holy Spirit's direction.

Review your answers again in six months to see how you are doing.

The key is to decide to do His will. Remember, your goal as a believer in Christ is for your finances to glorify Him and further His Kingdom.

As you prepare to end your trip you might find these 65 money-saving ideas helpful, take them with you; review them periodically; use them often. They might help you remember and use many matters discussed in this book.

65 Money-Saving Ideas to Go

Your Role

1. Accept your role as manager of God's money and possessions, and decide to live in your income.
2. Seek Jesus' direction before spending: Let Him show you how to handle 100% of funds you get. Don't give Him 10% and then try to handle 90%. One hundred percent is His!
3. Know the money triangle, the 3-Ms of money transactions—The Merchant, Money and Me: The *Merchant* produces goods and services then entices *Me* to exchange *Money* for them. I can manage only *Me*—my attitude, behaviour and choices ? not *Money* or the *Merchant*.
4. Honour Jesus with your giving, spending, and savings.
5. Invest time at His feet daily to listen, hear, and seek His will.
6. Manage your wants, needs, and greed nature under His direction.

Good Habits

7. *Be thankful;* set your expenses below today's income for at least two years. Ask God to show you how to deliver to His Kingdom excess income you get during that time.

8. *Be accountable* to someone you can trust.
9. *Be aware:* know your vulnerable areas; plug leaking expenses.
10. *Be patient;* don't spend impulsively. When the urge comes, wait at least 24 hours; seek God's direction.
11. *Be healthy:* get yearly physical and financial check ups, and yearly do a *spending fast.*
12. *Be informed* about alternative funding sources for your children's post secondary education: save from funds you get for them and from funds available from Government incentives.
13. *Be thrifty:* comparison shop for "big ticket" items. When salespeople pressure you, pray, wait up to one week and answer this question: Will this item satisfy a fleeting want, or a longer term need?
14. *Beware:* don't sign agreements unless you read and understand your duties — usually the *small print* lowers benefits the *large print* promotes.
15. *Be steady:* avoid erratic spending: save to buy all items. For a home, save a deposit that gives an *affordable* mortgage.
16. *Be focused* on Jesus: apply biblical teachings always; start a *Family Council* to learn and teach your children good attitudes toward money.

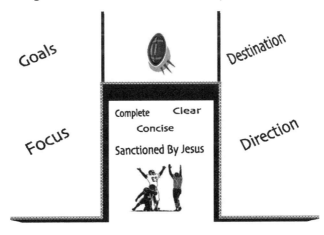

17. *Be cautious;* resist the temptation to buy junk food as you "shop", eat before you shop so you are "full", shop always with a *money map.*
18. *Be frugal;* borrow books and movies from public and church libraries; start a book club.
19. *Be creative;* write gift cards, give gifts using yours and your family's talents.
20. *Be vigilant,* don't give to TV evangelists, ministries, and others who manipulate you, focus on you, them, their ministries, rather than on Jesus. Give only after prayer.
21. *Be contrary;* don't buy brand name items only; shop wisely at *no-frills* and similar stores.
22. *Be discerning;* learn to recognize and deal with *conflicts of interest* that exist when a financial advisor will benefit financially from his or her advice to you.

Three Critical Spending Don'ts

23. *Don't act* solely on savings tips or financial incentives from *merchants;* they want you to spend. You benefit from a sale and incentive if you need the item, it is at or less than your budget price, and you can pay cash.
24. *Don't pay* to use funds in your bank account: stop paying ATM fees.
25. *Don't spend* coins you get in change — save them and at year-end ask God where to give amounts saved.

Useful Tools

26. Prepare, review, update, and follow a financial plan based on goals God gives you. Ask God to show you who should help you prepare and follow the plan.
27. Work with a budget to help select wants from needs, reduce financial stress, and direct you in line with the financial plan.

28. Prepare and stick with a *money map* for spending trips including vacation and trips to the mall.
29. Use the DNA pre-spending test to separate the need to spend, from the affordability. Ask three questions: (1) Will spending dishonour Jesus? (2) Do I need it? If yes, (3) Can I afford it?

Credit

30. Pay off credit card and loan balances.
31. Stop borrowing: Likely, a bad credit rating resulted from bad choices; don't try to fix the credit rating, understand the issues with you and deal with them.
32. Don't borrow against your home's equity; your house is not an *investment*.
33. Don't borrow from retirement savings.
34. Don't borrow to *upgrade*. Replace consumer items for cash when they wear out, not before.
35. Don't borrow to invest, go on vacation, or to "spend" to "save" taxes.
36. After you erase debts except your mortgage, start a *Capital Fund*.
37. Ask Jesus to show you where to put interest saved as you reduce debt: how to divide between giving to His work and saving in the *Capital Fund*.

Re-Financing

38. Don't change or re-negotiate your financial position—re-finance mortgage, withdraw pension—unless you understand the full effects.
39. Don't consolidate loans unless you change your attitude and behaviour to money and spending.

House

40. If you haven't saved a down payment that gives a mortgage you can afford in your monthly budget, you can't afford to own a home; wait.
41. Pay off your mortgage before you start investing—if feasible, regularly pay extra against the principal. But don't lower giving below amounts God shows.
42. Don't speculate on mortgage interest rates—pray; seek advice about locking-in interest rates. Try to get the ability to pay extra amounts against the mortgage principal.

Household

43. Get an energy audit of your home: use a programmable thermostat, lower the setting at specific times, especially at nights; plug leaks in the house.
44. If feasible, don't use a dryer in the summer.
45. Reduce eating out; pay cash always when you do.
46. If feasible, buy groceries in bulk; use coupons; focus on unit costs rather than total price—cost for each kg of flour.

Transport

47. Plan your vehicle trips: respect the speed limit and use cruise control where safe.
48. Maintain your vehicle at regular intervals to prevent expensive breakdown repairs.
49. If feasible, move where there is good public transport to get you to work so you can function without a car.

Insurance

50. Don't buy *extended warranties* for consumer items, save to repair and replace stuff.
51. Don't buy insurance unless you understand risks the insurance will cover.
52. Save to raise your car and house *deductibles* as high as affordable.

Taxes

53. Pay taxes when due. If self-employed, estimate tax liability, pay installments on time, and save to pay final liability on time.

54. You spend after-tax dollars so understand the effects; items cost more than you think.
55. Get receipts for charitable donations. Depending on your tax liability, you will get back a portion of your donations to registered charities so you can give more.

Children

56. Teach your children by example, to give, save and spend.
57. Give them allowances; hold them accountable to reach goals and plans.
58. Show them grace, mercy, and justice.

Investments

59. Learn investments preconditions; first, fund the Great Commission.
60. Understand that consumer debt repayment is your best and safest investment.
61. God alone knows the future, your investment advisors don't.
62. If an investment proposal is too good to be true it is not true.
63. Don't borrow to invest; when you invest your RRSP, remember, you start with a tax benefit, try to keep it by investing in low risk instruments.
64. Be patient; invest for the long-term.
65. Don't gamble or speculate under the investment guise.

A Memorable Encounter

I close this journey with a slightly changed version of a story I wrote in 1998 while waiting in the Qantas Lounge at Brisbane, Australia, airport:

One-day three individuals were walking along a deserted road. It was a gorgeous day! The sky was clear, the sun shone with an intensity that made a trip to the beach rather enticing. Several years later as the boy reflected on this day, he marvelled at the circumstances that brought them together.

He had left school earlier than usual on his bike. He planned to take a short cut through the park to hang out with his pals, but his bike got a flat tire.

The wealthy man was eccentric. He was going downtown using his usual route to avoid traffic when his car engine sputtered and stopped by the park. He forgot to fill-up at the gas station that morning!

The doctor was walking toward the bus station. As usual, he would take the bus to the hospital where he worked as the Chief Surgeon.

Each of these persons lived in a different section of town. Miraculously, today their paths crossed at the southern and violent section of Victoria Park. The wealthy man lived in the most expensive neighbourhood in the North. The doctor lived in a poor, Southern area near the park. The sixteen-year-old lad lived downtown with his dad, the caretaker, on the main campus of the Liberal Arts University.

As they walked together to the bus station, the boy said to the wealthy man,

'Sir, I go to school with your son. My friends say you and he live in a large home on that hill (the boy pointed north). They say it has every imaginable gadget! Yesterday, I overheard your son mention that you take long vacations on your yacht. Cool! I want to be like you when I grow up! Tell me, sir, how does it feel to be relaxing on a yacht? You must have a lot of fun! You have everything!'

The wealthy man rubbed his chin and stared straight ahead. The boy felt embarrassed because of the sad look on his face. After what seemed like one hour but really was just one minute, the man replied,

> 'Everything! Does anyone ever have everything? Try to understand this: When I am on the ocean under the beautiful sky, yes, I am peaceful. The sky is clear. The water is calm. The only sound I hear is the gentle tapping of water on the side of the yacht. Usually I enjoy this atmosphere . . . but for a short while only.
> After that, I feel empty. I have too much to drink. I watch the TV. I watch videos. I read. What else should a man do? I mean, there must be more to life than this? Yes, I get bored and tense after a few days. Today, I am thinking of getting a much larger vessel that will present a bigger challenge.'

This reply shocked the boy who thought, 'This man has everything and is bored, impossible!'

As he prepared to ask another question the doctor who did not seem interested in the discussions, spoke,

> 'Five years ago I had it all; at least, that's what I thought then. But, like this gentleman I felt empty. Life seemed futile. I considered seriously going to Thailand to become a Buddhist Monk. I wanted to get away from it all. Tell me lad, when you get a new bicycle or roller blades or basketball shoes you enjoy them, don't you? But do you enjoy them in the same way six months later?'

The doctor did not pause to allow the boy to reply, he continued,

'I delayed my trip to Thailand several times. I guess I became so confused I started to doubt the potential benefits of going. Later, I decided to stay home.

A colleague at the hospital introduced me to Transcendental Meditation. Something about it bothered me. When they initiated me, I felt uncomfortable with the religious ritual the instructor performed. I guess I knew what I did not like, but I didn't know what I liked. I was sure I did not want to be caught in religious rituals. I had paid my dues when I was your age and had to go to Church and watch people perform.

I am sorry, I am rambling, but I will make my point shortly. I became severely depressed and suicidal and one Saturday morning about 2:00 a.m., I was watching TV and met a man who changed my life.'

The wealthy man and the boy became confused. Nobody spoke for a few minutes as they walked, until the doctor resumed,

'The preacher on the TV said something simple that got my attention: He said, 'I invite all of you watching this morning to step forward and accept Jesus Christ as Lord and Saviour. I want you to know that when you do, you will start a personal relationship with Christ. I repeat, you will not be joining a religion, with a set of man-made rules, you will begin a personal relationship.'

The proverbial penny dropped that morning! I had problems with church folks who behave one way on Sunday mornings and differently during the week. Now I understood from this preacher that Christianity is not about man-made rules but a relationship with Christ based on the unchanging principles in the Bible.

This man I met is no ordinary Man! Yes, Jesus Christ came to earth as a man and was crucified, died, and rose again. Today He is the only living God. This is the Man I met. I accepted Him as my Lord and Saviour that morning. You too can know this Man.

In the Bible, Jesus said He is the good shepherd and we who believe in Him are His sheep. He said in the book of John (10:27-30) (RSV) 'My sheep hear my voice, and I know them, and they follow me; and I give them eternal life, and they shall never perish, and no one shall snatch them out of my hand. My Father, who has given them to me, is greater than all, and no one is able to snatch them out of the Father's hand. I and the Father are one."

Sombrely, the wealthy man said:

'May I collect you after work to learn more about your Man? Meanwhile, I must reflect on today's events.'

At 11:30 p.m. that night, two cars pulled up alongside the curb at St Mary's hospital, one with a wealthy man and his son, the other with a caretaker and his son. Patiently and silently, they waited to meet the doctor and His special Man.

Are you in one of those cars? [4]

Think About This

The God of Glory shines His mercy on you,
The God of Mercy shines His glory on you,
The god of this time is not the god, with whom
you must commune,
The god of this world is the evil, against which
you must become immune,
Know the One who has been revealed to you by
His gracious majesty.[5]

Chapter Notes:

1. In a single parent home, mom or dad needs to teach the children.
2. A *spending driver* represents factors that influence spending; it is what's behind the money. So, to control gas used in your car, you need to focus on factors like the efficiency of the car, distance driven, and your speed.
3. The *retirement income gap* is the difference between your estimated retirement income and retirement expenses from sources you can see today.
4. Michel A. Bell, *A Memorable Encounter*, Copyright © 1998, 2007.
5. Michel A. Bell, Excerpts from poem *The God Of Glory*, Copyright © 1998.

APPENDIX 1
Money Management Journey Outline

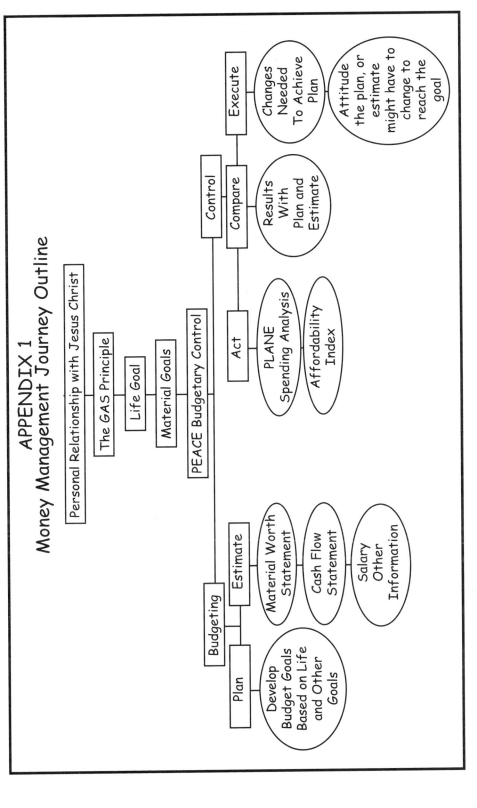

Personal Relationship with Jesus Christ

The GAS Principle

Life Goal

Material Goals

PEACE Budgetary Control

Budgeting

- Plan
  - Develop Budget Goals Based on Life and Other Goals
- Estimate
  - Material Worth Statement
  - Cash Flow Statement
  - Salary Other Information

Control

- Act
  - PLANE Spending Analysis
  - Affordability Index
- Compare
  - Results With Plan and Estimate
- Execute
  - Changes Needed To Achieve Plan
  - Attitude the plan, or estimate might have to change to reach the goal

APPENDIX 2
Personal Spending Analysis Form

Date	Description	Total	Books & Stationery	Clothing	Snacks & Fast Foods	Groceries	Transport	Other (Identify)
12 Jan	Wal-Mart: Shirt	$15		$15				
14 Jan	Booster Juice: Smoothie	$5			$5			
17 Jan	No Frills: Groceries					$75		

Notes: The purpose of this form is to help you learn about your spending habits. Use a similar form with headings that suit you. After about three to nine months, you will get to know where funds go and can *start planning to steer them where they ought to go!*
This form applies to *all spending:* cash, credit card and other, such as over the Internet.

Goal Statement Form (GSF)

Many are the plans in a man's heart,
but it is the LORD'S purpose that prevails – Proverbs 19:21

Name: _____ Period: _____

Goal Description (From God)	Goal Explanation (State clear, complete, concise statement including preconditions)
Early Retirement	Retire from present job no later than 55, after paying off mortgage, saving for children's education, and identifying second career.

Control Items (Sub Goals)

Description	Goals
Early Repayment of mortgage	Repay mortgage by age 50. At age 40 outstanding balance should not exceed $ 50,000. At age 45, it should not exceed $ 20,000
Children 's Education	By age 40, save total education cost of $20000.
Second Career	By age 45, identify second career

This is God's goal. Following the goal mustn't prevent me from listening to God.

APPENDIX 4
Goal Tracking Form (GSF)

Goal Tracking Form (GTF)

Trust in the LORD with all your heart and lean not on your own understanding; in all your ways acknowledge him, and he will make your paths straight – Proverbs 3:5-6

Name: _____ Review Period: _____

Goal Description (From God)	Goal Explanation (Clear, complete, concise statement including preconditions)
Early Retirement	Retire from present job no later than 55, after paying off mortgage, saving for children's education, and identifying second career.

Control Items(Sub Goals)

Description	Period: September to December	
	Goals for Period	Actual
Early Repayment of mortgage	No loans apart from mortgage Mortgage less than $ 55,000	Only mortgage Mortgage $55,000
Children's Education	Set aside $ 750	$ 750 set aside

COMMENTS

Mortgage payments are on track but interest rates are increasing. Might have to increase extra principal repayment. As well, need to review overall budget for lifestyle changes

This is God's goal. Doing the goal mustn't prevent me from listening to God.

APPENDIX 5
Debt Repayment Plan

Debt Repayment Plan				
(Review Six-Monthly)				

L O A N S	$ Owing		After tax Interest Rate %	Monthly Payment	Repayment Time
	Loan at Start	Interest			
Department Store	$6000	$500	28.5%	$170	8.5 years[1]
Bank Credit Card	$1900	$100	18.5%	$150	1.25 years

Savings	$ Amount	Pre-tax Interest Rate %	Annual Interest
Guaranteed Savings Certificate	$2000	3.75%	$75

---

1. Compute the date at which your monthly repayment will pay off the debt. Review this schedule at least every six months and increase repayments if feasible. But don't take away from amounts the Lord tells you to give.
   Because of interest costs, you will be surprised to know how long it takes to be debt free. Did you know, if you make no prepayments, you pay almost $ 100,000 interest on a $ 100,000 mortgage at 6% interest rate over 25 years?
   Normally, you hear about your loans' costs before tax, but savings after tax. Your best savings is to repay debt!

PEACE Budget Computation *Income* Form (PBCIF)

Life Goal:

"I want to know Christ and the power of his resurrection and the fellowship of sharing in his sufferings, becoming like him in his death" (Philippians 3:10 NIV).

Material Goals:

1. Accumulate Down Payment on Home in 3 years
2. Balanced Budget Every Year
3. Vacation Overseas Next Year

Budget Categories	Frequency of Income			Monthly Budget
	Weekly	Monthly	Yearly	
Salary Other income (show each separately)		3150		3150
Less: Giving ("keeping")		(415)		(415)
Less: Taxes		(600)		(600)
Less: Savings		(185)		(185)
Less: Capital Fund		(150)		(150)
Available to Spend		*1800*		*1800*

APPENDIX 6-2

PEACE Budget Computation *Expenses* Form

Available to Spend from Appendix 6-1: $1800

Budget Categories	Frequency of Expenses			Monthly Budget
	Weekly	Monthly	Yearly	
Rent		500		500
Car Expenses				
Loan Repayment		300		300
Gasoline	15	(15 ÷ 7 * 365/ 12)		65
Maintenance			360	30
Groceries	100	As for gasoline		434
Entertainment				
Meals	33	As for gasoline		145
Video Rental	20	As for gasoline		87
Movies	10	As for gasoline		43
Telephone		50		50
Clothing			480	40
Gifts				
Birthdays			60	5
Christmas			120	10
Contingency	21	As for gasoline		91
Total Expenses	199	850	1020	*1800*

Don't be surprised when you finish allocating budgeted amounts, that your total expenses represent twice your available income; a common first budget result. Now the fun begins as you start the inevitable "cutting" exercise! Before finalizing the budget, go exploring!

Review the following areas, and you may find available funds: Cable/Telephone/Internet charges; Entertainment/Eating out/Daily lunch expenses; Bank charges/Credit card interest; Insurance premiums; Car lease payments; Gifts/Vacation

PEACE Budget Worksheet

Date	Description	Total	Rent	Car Loan	Gas	Car Mtce	Groceries	Meals	Video	Movies	Telephone	Clothing	B'days	Christmas	Contingency
Sept 1	Allocation for September	1800	500	300	65	30	434	145	87	43	50	40	5	10	91
	Rent	500	500												
Sept 4	Lunch	35						35							
	Balance left	1265	0	300	65	30	434	110	87	43	50	40	5	10	91
Sept 7	Proviga	179					179								
	Balance left	1086	0	300	65	30	255	110	87	43	50	40	5	10	91
Sept 9	Cinema/Telephone	30								15	15				
	Balance left	1056	0	300	65	30	255	110	87	28	35	40	5	10	91
Sept 11	Shell	25			25										
	Balance left	1031	0	300	40	30	255	110	87	28	35	40	5	10	91
Sept 13	Royal Bank	300		300											
	Balance left	731	0	0	40	30	255	110	87	28	35	40	5	10	91
Sept 15	Dinner	75						75							
	Balance left	656	0	0	40	30	255	35	87	28	35	40	5	10	91
Sept 17	Proviga	150					150								
	Balance left	506	0	0	40	30	105	35	87	28	35	40	5	10	91
Sept 21	Shell	15			15										
	Balance left	491	0	0	25	30	105	35	87	28	35	40	5	10	91
Sept 23	Video	30							30						
	Balance left	461	0	0	25	30	105	35	57	28	35	40	5	10	91
Sept 23	Proviga	100					100								
	Balance left	361	0	0	25	30	5	35	57	28	35	40	5	10	91
Sept 27	Sears	76										76			
	Balance left	285	0	0	25	30	5	35	57	28	35	-36	5	10	91
Sept 29	Telephone	30									30				
	Balance left	255	0	0	25	30	5	35	57	28	5	-36	5	10	91
Sept 30	Budget for October	1800	500	300	65	30	434	145	87	43	50	40	5	10	91
	Total Allocation Oct	2055	500	300	90	60	439	180	144	71	55	4	10	20	182

APPENDIX 6-4
Weekly Budget Worksheet

Weekly Budget Worksheet

Appendix 6-4

Yearly Budget	Budget Item	Actual Expenses for Month				Actual for Month	Monthly Budget
		Week	Week	Week	Week		
	Income:						
	Bank Balance per Cheque book						
	Income - Regular						
	- Interest						
	- Other						
	Total Income						
	Expenses:						
	Giving						
	Savings						
	Capital Fund						
	Household expenses						
	Groceries						
	Toiletries						
	Telephone						
	Gifts						
	Clothing						
	Emergency						
	Total Expenses						
	Excess income over expenses						
	Notes:						

APPENDIX 6-5
PEACE Budget Worksheet

	December 1st to 15th		December 16th to 31st		Christmas Expenses	
	Budget	Actual	Budget	Actual	Budget	Act
Month of ____	1st to 15th	1st to 15th	16th to 31st	16th to 31st		
Income:					Income	
Salary						
Expenses					Expenses	
Giving						
Savings					Clothes	
Capital Fund					Gifts	
Mortgage						
Loan repayment						
Insurance						
Groceries						
Sub-Total						
Gas						
Sub-Total						
Phone						
Cable / Hydro						
Christmas						
Sub-Total						
Video / Vacation						
Snack						
Total Expenses	0		0		0	
Excess Income/(Expenses)	0		0		0	

APPENDIX 6-6
PEACE Budget Worksheet

PEACE Budget Worksheet — Appendix 6-6

"Ah Lord God behold you have made the heavens and the earth by your great power and by your outstretched arms, nothing is too difficult for you." Jeremiah 32:17

This "weekly summary section shows balance left each week for each category and for the total budget

SECTION 1

(A) Budget Category	(B) Date	(C) Description	(D) Spent $	(E) Budget Left	(F) Month of — Comments on "Spent" col "D"
ALLOCATION FOR MONTH * from Column "A"					
BUDGET LEFT * up to PRIOR Month $	/				
Budget for current Month $	/				
Allocation$	/				
Total SPENT for MONTH => $				Total budget left each week =>	
ALLOCATION FOR MONTH * from Column "A"					
BUDGET LEFT * up to PRIOR Month $	/				
Budget for current Month $	/				
Allocation $	/				
Total SPENT for MONTH => $				Total budget left each week =>	
ALLOCATION FOR MONTH * from Column "A"					
BUDGET LEFT * up to PRIOR Month $	/				
Budget for current Month $	/				
Allocation $	/				
Total SPENT for MONTH => $				Total budget left each week =>	
Total spent this page =>				Total this page => >	
				Total all pages => >	0

Weekly Summary - SECTION 2

(G)	(H)	(I)	(J)
Budget Allocation Left: Week Ending			
/	/	/	/

* "Allocation for month" includes the current month's budget plus or minus the "budget left" from the prior month from Section 2.

"I am the Lord the God of all mankind. Is anything too hard for me?" Jeremiah 32:27

(c) June 1996, Michel A. Bell

APPENDIX 7
House Purchase Guide

Goals				
Reason For Buying The House				
Key Criteria				
Location				
Size of house (sq.ft)				
Number of Bedrooms				
Other				
House Selection Guide	House #1	House #2	House #3	House #4
Address				
General External Appearance				
Roof				
Yard				
Other				
Entrance Hall				
Ceiling				
Floor				
Other				
Living Room				
Ceiling				
Floor				
Fixtures				
Drapes				
Other				
Kitchen				
Ceiling				
Floor				
Fixtures				
Drapes				
Other				
Den				
Ceiling				
Floor				
Fixtures				
Drapes				
Other				
Bedroom - Master				
Ceiling				
Floor				
Fixtures				
Drapes				
Other				
Bedroom - #2				
Ceiling				
Floor				
Fixtures				
Drapes				
Other				
Bedroom # 3				
Ceiling				
Floor				
Fixtures				
Drapes				
Other				
Fireplace/Basement				
Garage/Swimming pool				
Taxes				
Access to Amenities/Facilities				
Commuting Facilities				
Medical facilities				
Shopping facilities				
Other				
Possession date				
Estimated repairs necessary				
Rating:Scale of 1(Bad) to 10 (Best)				
General Comments				

Glossary

Affordability Index: Quantified answers to the five questions of the *PLANE Spending Analysis* that helps you decide to commit or not to a major expense.

Amortization Period: The period over which you repay your entire mortgage.

Asset: Items of value that you own, such as a car and a house.

Bankruptcy: It occurs when a borrower decides he can no longer pay what he owes and his lenders are unwilling to restructure his loans or provide more credit.

Bond: A loan (typically for longer than ten years) where the borrower promises to pay the lender a specified interest per year or when the loan is repaid in full.

Beneficiary: Someone who benefits from a will.

Budget Deficit: Expenses exceeding income during the budget period.

Budget: Your best estimate of time, talents, and other resources needed to get to your goal—a record of the results of the **planning and estimating** parts of PEACE.

Budgeting: Systematic planning, estimating, allocating, and recording of resources to attain your goal or set of goals; counting the cost as in Luke 14:28.

Capital Fund: An account maintained to finance major purchases and large maintenance expenses to eliminate crises from annual budgets. It allows systematic planning and scheduling of necessary major maintenance and major purchases.

Cash Flow: Cash inflows and cash outflows during a specific period.

Common Stock (Stock): A document that represents ownership in a company.

Compound Interest: Interest paid or received on accumulated interest earned during previous periods, in addition to the amount loaned or deposited.

Consumer Price Index (CPI): A CPI is a means to measure the total change in the prices of retail goods and services that we buy. The measurement is done over a specific period (one month), and for a precise basket of goods and services.

Conventional Mortgage: For a conventional mortgage, you need 25% of the purchase price (or appraised value) of the home as a down payment.

Debt Repayment Ratio: Total loan payments (including mortgage principal and interest) for the period (one-year) as a percentage of gross income for the period.

Discounting (Discounted): The process of finding the present value of a series of future cash flows.

Discretionary Expense: An expense you may decide not to incur such as for entertainment and for a vacation.

Disposable Income: The income you have available after taxes and payroll deductions have been taken from your salary.

Dividend: Voluntary payment by companies to their stockholders.

Equity: Assets minus liabilities (same as net worth).

Estimate: The likely cost of the **plan** - the cost of the steps in the **plans**.

Executor: Someone who carries out the instructions in a will of a deceased person.

Future Value: The value of money in the future; it is influenced by interest.

GAS Principle: Three Key Truths in the Bible concerning your stewardship:

- **Key Truth #1: God Owns Everything** (Psalm 24:1, Colossians 1:16)

- **Key Truth #2: Accept What You Have** (1 Timothy 6:7-8, Hebrews 13:5)
- **Key Truth #3: Seek First His Kingdom And Submit Your Requests To Him** (Matthew 6:33, Proverbs 19:21)

Goal: Your **destination** - where God wants you to go, or what He wants you to do.

Income Trust: An income trust holds income-producing assets. "Trust units" trade like stocks on securities exchanges (TSX). Income Trusts distribute income, usually higher than normal dividends on stocks, to its investors regularly.

Interest-Only Mortgage: An Interest-Only Mortgage gives *qualified homebuyers* the option to pay interest only for the first 5 or 10 years of their mortgage. Following the interest-only period, the lender will adjust payments to allow for principal and interest payments.

Inflation: A sustained and general rise in prices.

Lease: A rental agreement where someone (the lessee) agrees to use an asset and pays a fee to the owner, the lessor.

Lessee: Person receiving the asset from the lessor.

Lessor: Person granting the lease of an asset he owns to someone else, the lessee.

Leverage: Using borrowed funds usually to buy an asset.

Liabilities: Amounts you owe.

Line of Credit: A short term, revolving loan that banks extend to certain customers, sometimes based on a minimum net worth and "favourable" credit rating.

Marginal Tax Rate: The tax rate that applies to the last dollar of income you earn.

Maximum Debt Ratio: Total of all loans on the net worth statement as a percent of the total liabilities side of the net worth statement.

Mortgage Term: The life of the mortgage loan agreement with the financial institution.

Mortgage: A loan with a designated property (your home) as security.

Mortgage Open: With an **open** mortgage you can repay the principal fully or partially anytime without a penalty.

Mortgage Closed: For a **closed** mortgage you pay a penalty if you repay before the term expires.

Mortgage - Fixed Rate: A mortgage with fixed payments and the interest rate does not change during the mortgage term. Table IX shows the impact of a fixed rate mortgage.

Mortgage - Variable Rate: A mortgage with fixed payments, but which allows for fluctuation in interest rates due to changing market conditions. Changes in the interest rate will determine how much of each payment will go towards the principal. Thus if the mortgage interest rate increases, the allocation to principal as in Table IX will decrease and vice versa.

Mutual Fund: A Mutual Fund is an organisation that invests pooled funds of many depositors. Usually a professional manager manages it. Mutual Funds tend to specialise, each with a different investment objective.

Net Present Value: The present value of future cash flows discounted at a specific interest rate, minus an initial outlay.

Net Worth Statement: A statement showing assets, liabilities and equity.

Net Worth: Assets minus liabilities.

PEACE Budgetary Control: A planning and doing tool that allows you to reach **goals** systematically in the following manner:

Plan for a specific period to do precise **goals**.

Estimate and record the expenses needed to do those **goals**.

Act on the plan and record results as you do those **goals.**

Compare results **with plan** and with **estimated expenses** needed to do the **goals.**

EXECUTE needed changes to do the **goals.**

PLANE Spending Analysis: Five questions to answer before you commit to any major expenditure:

P Did I Plan and include this expense in my budget?

L Will the expense raise my Loans?

A Are there realistic Alternatives to fulfill the identified need?

N Is the expense Necessary to fulfill the identified need?

E Is this the most Effective use of funds compared with my life, budget and other goals?

Plan: Your **journey** - the steps to achieve your **goal.**

Power of Attorney: A document giving one person to act on behalf of another in specific areas.

Present Value: The value of money today.

Real Interest Rate: Actual interest rate less inflation rate.

Registered Education Savings Plan (RESP): A vehicle to help you to save toward your children's (or other identified beneficiary of the plan) post-secondary education. Unlike an RRSP you do not get a tax deduction for the amounts you contribute to the RESP, but the income on the amounts saved is compounded and not taxed until withdrawn.

Registered Retirement Savings Plan (RRSP): A savings plan to which your annual contribution is tax deductible. Since 1990, the maximum annual allowable tax deduction is 18% of your earned income for the prior year (to a maximum amount) less benefits accrued under your registered pension plans and deferred profit sharing plans for the previous year.

Tax Shield: The tax benefit you gain from certain expenses.

Trust: Property held by one party (the trustee) for the benefit of another (the beneficiary)

About the Author

In December 1985, after a two-year journey to show his twelve-year-old daughter Christianity was for uneducated, feeble-minded folks, Michel A. Bell surrendered his life to Jesus Christ. Married to Doreen in 1970, they have two children and four grand children. Michel and Doreen have lived in Jamaica, Japan, the United Kingdom, and the USA. Today they live in Ontario, Canada.

Michel held many senior finance, strategy, and planning positions in the Alcan Inc. group, including Regional Vice President Finance and Legal for Alcan's Pacific subsidiary and Chief Financial Officer for Alcan's worldwide bauxite and alumina group. In July 2002, after an exciting, enjoyable, and productive 32-year career, he left Alcan as Vice President Business Planning for this group to become full-time president of the private, Christian, non charity organization, Managing God's Money, which he started five years earlier.

Named an Alfred P. Sloan Fellow in 1975, he holds a Masters of Science degree in Management from the Sloan School of Management at Massachusetts Institute of Technology (M.I.T). He is a Fellow of the Chartered Certified Accountants of the UK and has authored four books:

1. Managing God's Money-The Basics
2. Managing God's Money-The Basics-WORKBOOK
3. Managing God's Time-Personal Effectiveness Improvement
4. Managing God's Money 7 Branches Workbook

Encouraged by his children, in the early 1990's Michel started presenting Bible-based money management principles at churches to individuals, couples, and groups. Since then He has presented seminars on Managing God's Money in Canada, England, Jamaica, and the USA. He also presented seminars on Managing God's Time: Personal Effectiveness Improvement in USA, Canada and England. In Canada, between 2001 and 2006, Michel partnered with *Focus on the Family* to present specific time and money seminars.

A frequent guest on radio and TV, he has appeared several times on *CTS* TV's *100 Huntley Street*, New Day Ministries, *It's a New Day*, *TCT* TV's *TCT Alive*. Weekly during 2005, Michel presented

"Money Matters" on 100 Huntley Street. As well, he has been on a *Focus on the Family* radio broadcast.

Contact Michel at michelbell@managinggodsmoney.com or P.O. Box 296, Campbellville, Ontario, L0P 1B0.

Index